ONE IN CHRIST

MARRIAGE RENEWAL

*A Spiritual Workout
to Strengthen Your Marriage*

Based on
Marriage: Love and Life in the Divine Plan

A Pastoral Letter of the
United States Conference of Catholic Bishops

Fr. Thomas Aschenbrener
and
Coleen Kelly Mast

Chicago
2011

ONE IN CHRIST

MARRIAGE RENEWAL

*A Spiritual Workout
to Strengthen Your Marriage*

About the Authors

Fr. Thomas Aschenbrener is a native of Wauwatosa, Wisconsin. He received a Bachelor's Degree in Communication Studies/Speech Communication and Rhetoric with a minor in Art History at the University of Wisconsin in Milwaukee. In 2002, he received a B.A. in Theology and, in 2003, a Master's in Divinity from Mundelein Seminary in Illinois. He is currently working on his Sacred Theological Licentiate. Fr. Aschenbrener was ordained to the priesthood by Francis Cardinal George of the Archdiocese of Chicago in May of 2003, and previously served at St. Luke's in River Forest and St. Alphonsus in Chicago. Currently, Fr. Aschenbrener serves as an Associate Pastor at Holy Name Cathedral in Chicago.

Coleen Kelly Mast is a wife and mother, author, speaker and radio talk show host. Mast is the author of both the "Love and Life" and "Sex Respect" Programs and has been an international leader in Catholic family life education for over twenty-five years. She holds a Master's Degree in Health Education with secondary teaching certificates in Science, Physical Education, Health and Theology, and was awarded an honorary doctorate degree in Humane Letters. Mast has worked with the USCCB and the Pontifical Council for the Family on the applications of *The Truth and Meaning of Human Sexuality*, and has debated Planned Parenthood, SEICUS and the ACLU on various media outlets. Her call-in radio show syndicated by Ave Maria Radio and EWTN Radio to more than 300 cities, offers advice for individuals and families from a Catholic perspective.

DEDICATION

"It takes three to make love in the Holy Family—
Mary, Joseph, and the consummation of their love, Jesus."

This book is dedicated to the Holy Family.

IT TAKES THREE TO GET MARRIED

It takes three to make love in Heaven—
Father, Son, and Holy Spirit.

It takes three for Heaven to make love on earth—
God, Man, and Mary, through whom God became Man.

It takes three to make love in the Holy Family—
Mary, Joseph, and the consummation of their love, Jesus.

It takes three to make love in hearts—
The Lover, the Beloved, and Love.

That nations, hearts, and homes may learn
that love does not so much mean to give oneself to another
as for both lovers to give themselves
to that Passionless Passion,
Which is God.

Fulton J. Sheen

From the Pastoral Letter

We rejoice that so many couples are living in fidelity to their marital commitment. We thank them for proclaiming in their daily lives the beauty, goodness, and truth of marriage. In countless ways, both ordinary and heroic, through good times and bad, they bear witness to the gift and blessing they have received from the hand of their Creator.[1]

While marriage is a special blessing for Christians because of the grace of Christ, marriage is also a natural blessing and gift for everyone in all times and cultures. It is a source of blessing to the couple, to their families, and to society and includes the wondrous gift of co-creating human life. Indeed, as Pope John Paul II never tired of reminding us, the future of humanity depends on marriage and the family.[2]

The family in the modern world, as much as and perhaps more than any other institution, has been beset by the many profound and rapid changes that have affected society and culture. Many families are living this situation in fidelity to those values that constitute the foundation of the institution of the family. Others have become uncertain and bewildered over their role or even doubtful and almost unaware of the ultimate meaning and truth of conjugal and family life. Finally, there are others who are hindered by various situations of injustice in the realization of their fundamental rights.[3]

Knowing that marriage and the family constitute one of the most precious of human values, the Church wishes to speak and offer her help to those who are already aware of the value of marriage and the family and seek to live it faithfully, to those who are uncertain and anxious and searching for the truth, and to those who are unjustly impeded from living freely their family lives. Supporting the first, illuminating the second, and assisting the others, the Church offers her services to every person who wonders about the destiny of marriage and the family.[4]

For all who seek to find *meaning in* their marriage will do so when they are open to accepting the transcendent *meaning of* marriage according to God's plan. Of this quest for meaning and truth, Pope Benedict XVI writes:

> All people feel the interior impulse to love authentically: love and truth never abandon them completely, because these are the vocation planted by God in the heart and mind of every human person. The search for love and truth is purified and liberated by Jesus Christ from the impoverishment that our humanity brings to it, and he reveals to us in all its fullness the initiative of love and the plan for true life that God has prepared for us.[5]

TABLE OF CONTENTS

Introductory Remarks

Workout Guide

One in Christ: A Spiritual Marriage Workout to Strengthen Your Marriage is a program based on *Marriage: Love and Life in the Divine Plan*, A Pastoral Letter of the United States Conference of Catholic Bishops, which is intended to strengthen marriages so that couples will come to a deeper understanding of their vocation in Christ. Moreover, this program is an "invitation to discover, or perhaps rediscover, the blessing given when God first established marriage as a natural institution and when Christ restored and elevated it as a sacramental sign of salvation." This "spiritual workout" is intended to instruct and engage couples in reflection, discussion, and prayer. Each of the sixteen couple sessions and four group sessions covers a different aspect of marriage and enables couples to delve deeper into the profound mystery of marriage by reflecting upon the Church's teaching in relation to marriage.

The purpose of *One in Christ: A Spiritual Workout to Strengthen Your Marriage* is to provide a series of opportunities for couples to learn, reflect on, and discuss principles that can help them live out the Sacrament of Matrimony and strengthen their bond of love.

This program is designed to be launched at the parish, implemented at home, and supported at each unit by the community of couples participating in the workout. In addition, any couple could work through the program on their own or with a group of friends in their home. Just as the repetition of physical exercises strengthens the body, the habits of reflection, discussion, and prayer will strengthen marital relationships.

The marriage workout is designed with a "Kick-off" meeting at the parish, time for the couples to complete four units with exercises, and outlines and activities for a follow up group meeting for each of the four units. There are four units of topics, each with four topical teachings followed by discussion exercises and prayers. Each home exercise can take from 30–60 minutes to complete. In general, there are 30–40 minutes of reading per topic. Then the couple engages in 20–30 minutes of discussion at home following the question guide. Couples conclude their discussion and reflection by joining their hearts and minds to God in prayer.

A formal, 90 minute, parish-based program with teachings for each of the four unit gatherings is included. This provides additional inspirational stories, a video, an interactive group activity, personal support, and discussion time for the couples "working out."

This spiritual marriage workout can be completed over various time frames, depending on the desires of the couples and needs or availability of the group.

Besides a kick-off session for the group, there are sixteen sessions for the couples, four unit wrap-up sessions, and nine readings in the appendix.

Some suggestions for possible time frames of implementation are:

- *Four Month Program*: Complete the program over a period of four months, having the couples attend the kick off, completing one unit per month, one exercise per week at home and meeting monthly between the units.

- *One Month Program*: A more "rigorous" marriage workout can be done in one month with weekly meetings at the parish, asking the couples to complete four exercises per week at home.

- *16 Month Program*: For those couples looking for an ongoing program, the workout can be done over the period of 16 months, with couples completing one session per month at home, and meeting quarterly for the group workouts. This program is highly recommended because marriage renewal happens over time, not overnight. Through learning, discussion and prayer, couples will discover the importance of ongoing support and encouragement within the family and from the Church community.

- *20 Month All-Group Program*: Couples who have so little time at home to complete the exercises, and only do the readings at the group meetings, might spread it over 20 months. They could meet together once a month going over the exercises together, either by having the couples read the exercise together or by having a couple or individual present the exercise. After the exercise has been completed, couples would have private time for couple discussion/prayer for each of the 16 unit sessions. The four group workouts for each unit would then be done following each set of four exercises.

- *Individualized Home Study*: This is another highly recommended program for renewing and strengthening your marriage. This program can be done with individual couples or with a group of friends. It follows the same format: Read the material, reflection/discussion and prayer. Couples doing the study at their own pace would be better off to set their calendar in advance so they make a commitment to completing the workout and making the most of the lessons.

How to do this Spiritual Workout ...

- Attend the Kick-off Meeting at the parish and receive your workout materials.

- Schedule four private home meetings with your spouse, once a day, once a week or once a month, depending on which program you choose, to complete the four readings and exercises for each unit.

- Attend the four group workouts that accompany the units between each set of exercises. The meetings may be held weekly, monthly or quarterly (every four months) depending on the spacing of the program schedule.

- Apply these principles to your daily life, and allow God to work in your marriage!

Group Workout:
The Kick-off

*T*o begin: Leaders introduce themselves and explain why we are here.

❧ What is this?

A Spiritual Workout for Strengthening Marriage in the context of the Catholic Faith.

❧ What's a spiritual workout?

A series of lessons and exercises, rooted in faith, that invite us to daily practice of the internal "core muscles" of our souls.

❧ Why are we doing this?

To strengthen our souls for a lifelong marriage in a world that seems to be concerned only with the externals of marriage and to disregard the internal, spiritual dimensions of this gift from God.

❧ What equipment will we need?
  * A willing and humble heart
  * US Bishops Pastoral Letter, *Marriage: Love and Life in the Divine Plan.* *http://foryourmarriage.org/bishops%E2%80%99-pastoral-letter-on-marriage/*
  * A copy of this workbook, *One in Christ: A Spiritual Workout to Strengthen Your Marriage.*

❧ Who is my personal trainer?

Jesus Christ. Meet with him for coaching each day.

❧ Do I need to make an appointment with him?

No. Jesus is there waiting for you all the time. Whenever you and your spouse get together for these exercises, he promises to be there with you.

❧ Who is going to support me in the workout?

God, your spouse, and the community of couples participating in the workout.

❧ Who is participating in this workout?

Each couple in the group states their names and something about themselves, i.e., when they were married, where they went on their honeymoon, how many children they have, what's their occupation, etc.

❧ How do we start and what should we expect from this program?

Leader to go over with group:

I. Purpose/Goals/Methodology as outlined in the introductory pages.

II. Overview of the Unit Themes and Assignments.

III. Our Calendar—according to the group's timing.
   A. Overview of the timetable and dates for this spiritual workout.
   B. Settings in which the sessions will take place.

IV. Warm-Up Game (Quiz Format)
   Read the article: "What Does it Mean to Love?" and answer the questions below for the Warm-Up Game

   1. What historical shift in thinking distanced man from God and the meaning of love?

   _____

   _____

   2. How does mankind's distance from God affect our human ideas regarding love?

   _____

   _____

   3. What are the new substitutes for love since it was distorted by Original Sin?

   _____

   _____

   4. How does an overbearing parent affect his or her child's perception of love?

   _____

   _____

   5. How does a marriage move from *phileo* to *agape* love?

   _____

   _____

   6. What does St. Gianna Beretta Molla say it means to "lay down my life for my spouse?"

   _____

   _____

   7. Give examples of "going out of your way" to love your spouse.

   _____

   _____

8. How does love enable us to overcome life's problems?

_____

_____

V. Warm-Up before Unit One: prepare our minds and hearts.
   A. Please review the Learning Goals for each of the four exercises in Unit One.
   B. Next week you should be able to answer the following questions:
      1. At what event did married love move from the natural to the supernatural?
      2. How do Catholics interpret the creation of Eve from the rib of Adam?
      3. What does it mean for a couple to live in a communion of self-giving love?
      4. What are three effects of Original Sin?
      5. What is the purpose of suffering?
      6. Name three reasons why Jesus came to save us.
      7. Who is the Bride of Christ?
      8. How do Catholics interpret the passage "Wives be submissive to your husbands" differently than some Protestant denominations?
      9. What is a vocation? Why is marriage called a vocation?
      10. What are the three properties of Christian marriage?
      11. What is the difference between a contract and a covenant?

What Does It Mean to Love?

Fr. Thomas Aschenbrener

Think about how often we use the word *love* and in what contexts we use it.

We often speak of love of country, love of one's profession, love between family and friends, love of property and possessions, animals, TV shows, etc. Deep down we know that there is an essential difference between the love of an animal, a TV sitcom, and another human being.

Using the word *love* indiscriminately can lead us to become numb or desensitized to the real meaning of true love and the consequences of saying, "*I love you*, or *this*, or *that*." One of the reasons love is so misunderstood and abused today is because we no longer see God as the quintessential source of love.

This is obviously the result of Original Sin. Looking back in history, we can see that beginning in the Renaissance and culminating in the Enlightenment, there was a fundamental shift of focus from God to the individual; it is what we like to call the *Copernican shift*: from God to man, or from the metaphysical to the existential.

Placing man at the center of the universe has led to a gradual breakdown of our relationship with God. For many people, God is a nice idea, an abstract concept, or a Creator who has no interaction with his creation. This is why we have seen a decrease in church attendance and religious conviction and an increase in atheism and agnosticism.

By distancing ourselves from God, we feel the need as a society to redefine or "dumb-down" the true meaning of love so as to satisfy our own selfish desires. If God is merely a transcendent being who has no interaction with his Creation, then love can become whatever we make of it. Thus, it is harder to discover what it truly means to love with a divine purpose. St. John wrote, "God is love, and whoever remains in love remains in God and God in him" (1 Jn 4:16).

By restricting God's presence in our lives and seeing the world through our eyes only, we not only lead ourselves away from the love of God, but we also subconsciously (maybe even consciously) project our understanding, our experience, and our limited knowledge of love onto God. St. John wrote, "God is love" (1 Jn 4:8, 16). If we think of God's love in the limited way we understand love, we will fall into a sentimental attitude by which God adopts our way of looking at things. We are attempting to lead God instead of God leading us. We are really indulging in self-love and self-will under a spiritual disguise.

So what is our experience or understanding of love? All of us have experienced love to a certain degree, and, for many of us, we probably have experienced a profound love that words cannot describe.

We have also experienced, because of Original Sin, a distorted or tainted understanding of love that seeks instantaneous gratification, indulgence, entitlement, power, greed, and pride—a deceptive love that leads to sadness, isolation, brokenness, and ultimately a destroyed sense of love.

Having experienced the consequences of "destroyed love" in our own relationships, we may begin to question. *Does God really love me? Does God love me less because of my sins?*

As a priest, I often hear penitents say, "I feel that God doesn't love me because of my sins. I feel that I can't be forgiven for this or that sin. I keep falling into this same sin, and I feel that God has had enough."

We all experience a deficiency in our capacity to love and a lack of forgiveness in our relationships. If we do not have a strong, loving relationship with God, we can project our imperfect experience of love (our experience of betrayal or infidelity) onto God and start to think that he treats us the same way as do our friends, spouses, neighbors, or co-workers.

This often happens with a person whose father or mother was overbearing or extremely harsh and critical. Eventually, this person's perception of God can become distorted as one who judges harshly and is not compassionate or merciful but rather domineering and ruthless. Another example could be if a person was abandoned as a child or teenager. This person's perception of God could lead him or her to think that God has abandoned him or her, especially when encountering difficulties and trials. Or if a person is constantly experiencing a lack of forgiveness from loved ones, he or she may never believe that God forgives. A healthy, loving, and Gospel-inspired perception of God is crucial to our relationships here on earth.

The first thing to realize is that God's ways are not our ways. The way we think, act, and love is not the way God thinks, acts, and loves. Only when we begin with God as a God who loves us unconditionally will we have a proper understanding of true love.

Chapter 21 of St. John's Gospel provides us a profound insight into what it truly means to love. Remember when Jesus asked St. Peter, "Do you love me?" (Jn 21:15–17). Many of us, if asked this question, would probably say, "Yes, Lord, I love you." But what does it truly mean to love the Lord? What does it truly mean to love your spouse? What was Jesus really asking St. Peter? In Greek, the words for love used in the narrative are *phileo* and *agape*. *Phileo* means *brotherly love* or *best-friend type of love*. *Agape* means *life-giving, sacrificial, and unconditional love.*

Jesus asked St. Peter, "Do you *agape* me more than these?" (more than your job and your friends), and St. Peter responded, "Yes, Lord, you know that I *phileo* you." Jesus asked him again, "Simon, Son of John, do you *agape* me?" and St. Peter responded, "Yes, Lord, you know that I *phileo* you." So Jesus asked a third time, "Simon, do you *phileo* me?" Jesus changed the third question to refer to *phileo-love*, and St. Peter wept, saying, "Lord, you know everything; you know that I *phileo* you." Why did St. Peter refuse to answer, "Yes, Lord, I *agape* you"?

St. Peter loved being with the Lord and hearing him preach and teach, but he was not yet at the point of total self-surrender. That is why our Lord said, "Truly, truly, I say to you, when you were young, you girded yourself and walked where you would; but when you are old, you will stretch out your hands, and another will gird you and carry you where you do not wish to go" (Jn 21:18).

After our Lord had ascended into Heaven, St. Peter preached, taught, and healed in the name of Jesus and probably started to understand what our Lord meant when he asked him, "Simon, do you *agape* me?" St. Peter finally understood what it meant to love unconditionally when he was being crucified upside down on a cross. Only then was he able to say, "Yes, Lord, I *agape* you."

Think of all the great saints who lived their lives with a *phileo* love for the Lord Jesus and eventually came to embrace an *agape* love that knows no limits or conditions, starting with God and then reaching out to their neighbors. Think about your relationship with your spouse and how our Lord Jesus is challenging you to move beyond a *phileo* love for him or her.

Many of us may never be called to give our lives to the point of death, but *agape* love requires a daily dying to self. This is truly *love in action*. St. John wrote, "Let us love one another, because love is of God … No one has greater love than this, to lay down one's life for one's friends" (1 Jn 4:7; Jn 15:13).

St. Gianna Beretta Molla gave her life so her newborn baby could live. She died shortly after giving birth to her fourth child. Through her ordinary daily acts of self-giving love, she was prepared to say, "Yes, Lord, I *agape* you." In a world that says, "I sacrifice the other for the good of myself," St. Gianna said, "I sacrifice myself for the good of another, my little girl." She said, "Save the child, whatever you do, save the child."

Bl. Teresa of Calcutta (Mother Teresa) once said, "Love, to be real, must cost, it must hurt, it must empty us of self." How can we change our love for Jesus from *phileo* love (real though imperfect love) to *agape* love (perfect love)? Jesus' answer to St. Peter was simple yet challenging: "Follow Me … If you keep my commandments you will remain in my love."

How can you develop your love for your present or future spouse from *phileo* love (real though imperfect love) to *agape* love (perfect love)? St. Gianna Beretta Molla said, "You cannot follow this path to heaven if you don't know how to love; love means to want to perfect yourself and your beloved; to overcome your selfishness and give yourself completely."

Think of the opportunities we have to grow in *agape* love: prayer, devotions, and the spiritual and corporal works of mercy. When you are willing to give up time, comfort, and resources for your spouse and children in a life-giving, sacrificial, and unconditional way, you are growing in *agape* love. *Agape* love consists of praying as a family and disciplining children out of love rather than out of anger or frustration. *Agape* love manifests itself when we listen or express sorrow not because we have to but because we want to. Selfless love means going out of the way to help your spouse and children, to seek their interests and needs before your own. Being resentful or holding onto grudges only obstructs your spouse and children from reaching Heaven. Forgiving and making amends is the road that leads to great holiness.

God put us in families for a specific purpose, and that purpose is to get each other to Heaven. This vocation requires a constant growing out of our selfishness and into a self-sacrificial love that no longer seeks our own interests and instead seeks to lay down our lives for the other, like our Lord. "God so loved the world that he gave his only begotten Son" (Jn 3:16) and the Son so loved the world that he gave himself for our salvation—"greater love has no man than this, that a man lay down his life for his friends" (Jn 15: 13). We know that by laying down our lives with an *agape* love bears much fruit. Never let a moment or an opportunity pass you by to show how much you truly love our Lord and your family. Love of God and neighbor are inseparable. Without true love of God, we will never truly be able to love our neighbor.

Our Lord gently and repeatedly reminds us that there will be problems and trials in life that might be very difficult. Genuine love, however, can make them easy, and perfect love can make them a joy. We are willing to give in proportion as we love. When love is perfect, the sacrifice is complete.

As Pope Benedict XVI said so well, "God's love is not something imposed from without or external, merely a 'religious duty', but rather a freely bestowed experience of love from within, a love which by its very nature must then be shared with others. Love grows through love. Love is 'divine' because it comes from God and unites us to God; through this unifying process it makes us a 'we' which transcends our divisions and worldly understandings of love and makes us one, until God is 'all in all.'"

The Spiritual
Workout Begins

Marriage Made in Heaven

Unit One: Week One Exercise

LEARNING GOALS

- ❧ To understand God's intention in establishing the marriage covenant between a man and a woman and that the human family is a reflection of God's rich, Trinitarian life.

- ❧ To explore the meaning of marital communion and relationship in relation to the Trinitarian communion of love.

WHAT DOES IT MEAN TO SAY THAT MAN AND WOMAN ARE CREATED IN THE IMAGE AND LIKENESS OF GOD?

What does the Pastoral Letter on Marriage have to say?

Among the many blessings that God has showered upon us in Christ is the blessing of marriage, a gift bestowed by the Creator from the creation of the human race. His hand has inscribed the vocation to marriage in the very nature of man and woman (see Gn 1:27–28, 2:21–24). (*Marriage: Love and Life*, 2)

Through the Sacrament of Matrimony, married love not only is modeled on Trinitarian love but also participates in it. Like all Sacraments, Matrimony draws believers more deeply into the Trinitarian life of God. It was not until the Father sent his Son into the world as man, and the subsequent outpouring of the Holy Spirit, that the full identity of God as a Trinity of Persons was revealed. This Revelation not only allowed humankind to come to a definitive knowledge of God—since the mystery of the Trinity is the source of all the other mysteries, the revelation of this mystery sheds light on all the rest. This includes both the mystery that human beings are created in the image and likeness of God and the mystery that is marriage and family life.

As we learn from the mystery of the Trinity, to be in the image and likeness of God is not simply to have intelligence and free will, but also to live in a communion of love. (*Marriage: Love and Life*, 35)

In the beginning God said, "Let us make man in our image, after our likeness … God created man in his image, in the divine image he created him; male and female he created them."[6]

Many theologians have considered the "our" and "us" in this passage to be the first reference to the Holy Trinity. God—Father, Son, and Holy Spirit—is a perfect communion of love, a relationship of Persons. God, who needs nothing, desires to create us in order to give us a share in his divine life. Here on earth, we strive to serve, know and love him so as to obtain eternal happiness with him in Heaven for all eternity.

> Marriage and the family are not in fact a chance sociological construction, the product of particular historical and financial situations. On the other hand, the question of the right relationship between the man and the woman is rooted in the essential core of the human being and it is only by starting from here that its response can be found.
>
> In other words, it cannot be separated from the ancient but ever new human question: Who am I? What is a human being? And this question, in turn, cannot be separated from the question about God: Does God exist? Who is God? What is his face truly like?
>
> The Bible gives one consequential answer to these two queries: the human being is created in the image of God, and God himself is love. It is therefore the vocation to love that makes the human person an authentic image of God: man and woman come to resemble God to the extent that they become loving people.[7]

Remember the day you exchanged your wedding vows and the depth of your love for each other? On your wedding day, the Lord Jesus transformed and elevated something ordinary and natural (your human love), and made it extraordinary and divine. God did this because you had responded wholeheartedly to his divine love and his call to love. Through your love for each other and God's grace, you manifested to your family, friends, the Church and society, the truth about God, yourselves, and marriage, in that, when we love as he loves, we show forth more perfectly his image and likeness in which we were all created. We witness to the beauty of God's unconditional love and the divine truth that he is love and when we respond to his call to love, we are transformed into the likeness of his being.

God's Revelation of himself is not only true and good, but also *beautiful*. The beauty of God's love is the mystery of reality; it is the true meaning of life, of existence, of being. Just as we are overwhelmed by a beautiful work of art, so God's love overwhelms us, transforms us, brings us to ourselves, and awakens us to respond to God with love.[8] "Before the beautiful—no, not really *before* but *within* the beautiful—the whole person quivers. He not only 'finds' the beautiful moving; rather, he experiences himself as being moved and possessed by it."[9]

> Before creating man, the Creator withdraws as it were into himself, in order to seek the pattern and inspiration in the mystery of his Being, which is already here disclosed as the divine "We". From this mystery the human being comes forth by an act of creation: *"God created man in his own image,* in the image of God he created him; male and female he created them" (*Gen* 1:27).[10]

4

THE TWO CREATIONS ACCOUNTS: WHAT DO THEY SAY ABOUT OUR RELATIONSHIP WITH GOD AND ONE ANOTHER?

What does the Pastoral Letter on Marriage have to say?

In the first account, God creates both male and female at the same time and in the divine image. This act completes creation, and God judges it to be "very good" (Gn 1:31). In this way, Sacred Scripture affirms the fundamental equality and dignity of man and woman as persons created in God's image. The second creation account emphasizes that both sexes are necessary for God's plan. (*Marriage: Love and Life*, 9)

The LORD God said: "It is not good for the man to be alone. I will make a suitable partner for him." So the LORD God formed out of the ground various wild animals and various birds of the air, and he brought them to the man to see what he would call them; whatever the man called each of them would be its name. The man gave names to all the cattle, all the birds of the air, and all the wild animals; but none proved to be the suitable partner for the man. So the LORD God cast a deep sleep on the man, and while he was asleep, he took out one of his ribs and closed up its place with flesh. The LORD God then built up into a woman the rib that he had taken from the man. When he brought her to the man, the man said: "This one, at last, is bone of my bones and flesh of my flesh; this one shall be called 'woman,' for out of 'her man' this one has been taken." That is why a man leaves his father and mother and clings to his wife, and the two of them become one flesh. (Gn 2:18–24)

As Catholics we do not read this passage in a literalistic way, but rather in a spiritual sense, i.e., allegorical, anagogical, and moral. The spiritual senses of scriptural interpretation enable us to probe deeper into the mystery of marital love and communion by asking basic and fundamental questions: What is God trying to reveal to us about marriage in this passage? What is he trying to say to us about unity and love, communion and covenant?

We discover from this passage that man, although created and sustained by God, is no longer alone. Woman is created from the rib or side of Adam. This does not mean that women are somehow inferior or subordinate human beings. "We know that women are neither the slaves nor the property of men—nor *vice versa*. God created Eve as a partner fit for Adam, equal in dignity"[11] and heir with him to the life of grace, which forbids any right to domination or subjugation over one's spouse.

As soon as Adam meets Eve, Adam says with delight: "This one, at last, is bone of my bones and flesh of my flesh."[12] As in the first creation account, this passage also reveals the fundamental equality of each person in the eyes of God. "But equal partnership does not mean sameness. Rather, it is the complementarity of man and woman that makes each of them perfectly suited to be the answer to the other's deepest needs, to make each other complete."[13]

So the second creation account not only reveals God's intention in establishing the marriage union between man and woman, but also reveals the genuine one flesh union by which man is no longer alone, he has his wife as a lifelong companion, helper, and bride.

When we read this passage through a Christological lens, we gain an even deeper insight into the mystery of marital love, the mystical or intimate connection between Christ and his Bride, the Church.

When Christ was hanging from the Cross, the soldiers pierced his side with a lance and out flowed Blood and water. From the rib or side of Christ came forth *Blood* which symbolizes the *Eucharist,* and *water,* which symbolizes *Baptism*. The Eucharist and Baptism are two of the three Sacraments of Initiation; Sacraments that sanctify the soul and give it new life in Christ Jesus. Just as Eve came forth from the side of her husband Adam as helper, bride, and lifelong companion, so too, the Church came forth from the side of Christ as his Bride, companion, and helper in the work of salvation. This is God's "marriage" with humanity. Therefore, WE ARE NOT ALONE!

HOW DOES THIS UNDERSTANDING OF COMMUNION TRANSLATE TO YOUR MARRIAGE HERE ON EARTH? WHAT ARE TWO WAYS TO SEE THE TRINITARIAN IMAGE IN MARRIAGE AND FAMILY LIFE?

What does the Pastoral Letter on Marriage have to say?

First, like the Persons of the Trinity, marriage is a communion of love between co-equal persons, beginning with that between husband and wife and then extending to all the members of the family. Pope John Paul II teaches, "The family, which is founded and given life by love, is a community of persons: of husband and wife, of parents and children, of relatives.[14]

This communion of life-giving love is witnessed within the life of the family, where parents and children, brothers and sisters, grandparents and relatives are called to live in loving harmony with one another and to provide mutual support to one another. The *Catechism of the Catholic Church* teaches that "the Christian family is a communion of persons, a sign and image of the communion of the Father and the Son in the Holy Spirit." (*Marriage: Love and Life*, 37; CCC 2205)

The Trinitarian image in marriage in family life can be seen in a second way. Just as the Trinity of persons is a life-giving communion of love both in relationship to one another and to the whole of creation, so a married couple shares in this life-giving communion of love by together procreating children in the conjugal act of love. (*Marriage: Love and Life*, 37)

A child was once asked, "Why do we go to Mass?" The child responded, "To show respect and give worship to God." "And what happens to us when we do this?" asked the teacher. The child said, "It makes us more united to God and to one another; it gives us grace to love God and others more and more each day; and it enables us to live in communion with God kind of like living in a family here on earth."

Essentially, what this child had articulated was the nature of the Trinity and how the family mirrors our relationship to God in three Persons. The communion of love, the relationship that exists within the Trinity, consists of the Father, the Lover who begets and loves the Son; the Son, the Beloved who returns the Father's love; and the Holy Spirit, who is the Love that proceeds from the Father and the Son.

It was from within this overflowing communion of love that each us received our existence. At the moment of conception, God's image and likeness is made manifest in the human person. The very presence of the new child evangelizes to the world that the imprint of God—Father, Son, and Holy Spirit—is the source of all life and that divine and human love bring us into this world so as to share in the communion of love in Heaven with the Lover, Beloved, and Love.

What does the Pastoral Letter on Marriage have to say?

Here one can see that the Father, the Son, and the Holy Spirit give themselves entirely to one another in a life-giving exchange of love. Thus, the Trinity is a loving and life-giving communion of equal Persons. The one God is the loving inter-relationship of the Father, the Son, and the

Holy Spirit … "The divine image is present in every man. It shines forth in the communion of persons, in the likeness of the unity of the divine persons among themselves."[15] (*Marriage: Love and Life*, 36)

Think about what a child experiences when he or she is born into this world, the moment when the father and mother gaze into the child's eyes. The child experiences for the first time what it means to belong to a communion of love, to be in relationship, to be a part of a family. It is from this experience that we all desire to become a part of the larger community of humanity and to seek beyond ourselves the eternal communion of love for which we have all been created.

Dorothy Day once commented after the birth of her first child that, "No human creature could receive or contain so vast a flood of love and joy as I often felt after the birth of my child. With this came the need to worship, to adore. I had heard many say that they wanted to worship God in their own way and did not need a Church in which to praise Him, nor a body of people with whom to associate themselves. But I did not agree with this. My very experience … my whole make-up, led me to want to associate myself with others, with the masses, in loving and praising God."[16]

The birth of her child made her realize that love grows through love, and as Pope Benedict XVI said in his encyclical *Deus Caritas Est*: "Love is 'divine' because it comes from God and unites us to God; through this unifying process it makes us a 'we' which transcends our divisions and makes us one, until in the end God is 'all in all'" (1 Cor 15:28).[17]

God is rich in relationships, communication, and love for all people. The Trinity models to us what life is all about—communication, relationship, and affection. The quality of our Christian life is determined by how much we imitate the interior life of the Trinity.

WHY IS IT IMPORTANT TO BELIEVE THAT GOD IS ONE IN THREE PERSONS: A COMMUNION OF LOVE?

What does the Pastoral Letter on Marriage have to say?

As Pope John Paul II teaches, all human persons are created in the image of God, who is a communion of love of three persons, and thus all are called to live in a communion of self-giving love: "to say that man is created in the image and likeness of God means that man is called to exist 'for' others, to become a gift"[18] … "In the 'unity of the two,' man and woman are called from the beginning not to exist 'side by side' or 'together,' but they are also called to exist mutually 'one for the other.'"[19] (*Marriage: Love and Life*, 10–11)

If God is defined merely by function of what God does rather than what God is—a loving relationship of Persons—then our understanding of the family loses its meaning as a relationship of persons who exist to love and to be loved. The family, like the Trinity, is not merely defined by what it does, but rather by what it is: a relationship of persons called to communion with God and one another. There is a temptation to embrace the modern idea of the human person strictly as an individual, in contrast to seeing our identity in terms of relationship. Cardinal George commented that:

If we are individuals for who relationships are just added on, rather than persons who are born related, then we start with rights and not duties and obligations to others. Since rights have to be protected, we get into a legal framework that is almost adversarial. Society becomes brittle and violent. Natural community, such as marriage, is much weakened. People's mobility and pursuit of one's own dreams, even in conflict with others, have become something of a priority in our culture. This doesn't foster the kind of relationship that is necessary to live humanely … while there is conflict to a certain level, the highest level is one of harmony and peace, mutual love and love of God.[20]

What does the Pastoral Letter on Marriage have to say?

To be created in the image and likeness of God means, therefore, that human beings reflect not the life of a solitary deity, but the communal life of the Trinity. Human beings were created not to live solitary lives, but to live in communion with God and with one another, a communion that is both life-giving and loving. (*Marriage: Life and Love*, 36)

Have not we all, perhaps, felt most alone when we embrace the world's ideology of individualism, and fail to foster our marital relationship? In our relationships with family members, friends, and co-workers, are we not most alone when, in our selfishness, we seek to divide rather than unite; manipulate and dominate rather than surrender to charity, generosity, and kindness; and to control rather than embrace humility?

When we choose to fashion God in our own image and likeness do we not distance ourselves from others, especially our spouses, and compete with others so as to assert our own wills, desires, ambitions, and appetites, over and against those of our spouses or neighbors?

Today human beings not only create their own gods they seem to claim themselves as gods and want to transform the world, excluding, putting aside or simply rejecting the Creator of the universe. Man no longer wants to be the image of God but the image of himself; he declares himself autonomous and free. Obviously, that reveals *an inauthentic relationship with God*, the consequence of a false image that has been constructed of him, like the prodigal son in the Gospel parable who thought that *he could find himself by distancing himself from the house of his father*.[21]

Thomas Merton once commented, "People who know nothing of God and whose lives are centered on themselves, can only conceive one way of becoming real: cutting themselves off from other people and building a barrier of contrast and distinction between themselves and other men. They do not know that reality is to be sought not in division but in unity, for we are members one of another."[22]

By sending his only Son and the Spirit of Love in the fullness of time, God has revealed his innermost secret: God himself is an eternal exchange of love, Father, Son, and Holy Spirit, and he has destined us to share in that exchange. The Trinitarian God, who is utterly transcendent yet radically immanent, reveals to us that just as the Father, Son and Holy Spirit do nothing apart from each other, so too are we called to interact with others as though we are interacting with God himself and participating in the divine exchange of love.

What is so unique about this communion of love that we share in, is that it does not remain turned in on itself, but instead it gives generously, infinitely without boundaries or limits. Discouraging words and actions that tear at the very heart of this exchange/communion and unity are not only debilitating to the spiritual life and to marriage, but in the end, they leave us alone and isolated from God and others.

This is a time of preparation for Heaven. By seeing and loving in others what Christ sees and loves in us, we not only imitate the dynamic Trinitarian life—communication, relationship, and affection—but we communicate to the world that "love grows through love … [and] through this unifying process it makes us a 'we' which transcends our divisions and worldly understandings of love and makes us one."[23]

If our faith is based in this Trinitarian mystery that is fundamentally a mystery of communion, then all of our earthly efforts and activities must work toward building up the human community (family) that is a reflection of God's rich, Trinitarian life.

The Workout

1. What words have I spoken to you today that express our human need for union?

2. How does our marital union help our community?

3. In what ways are we the living image of the beauty of God's love?

4. Reflect privately on the memory of moments when you saw your spouse with delight as Adam first did for Eve. Name three of these and describe how you felt and how you saw the goodness in him or her.

5. Express the love you felt at the birth of your first child. If you do not have children, share with one another some of the ways you have brought joy and happiness into the lives of others, i.e., in-laws, friends, co-workers, etc.

LET US PRAY

Eternal Trinity, you have made the blood of Christ so precious through his sharing in your divine nature. You are a mystery as deep as the sea; the more I search, the more I find, and the more I find the more I search for you. But I can never be satisfied; what I receive will ever leave me desiring more. When you fill my soul I have an ever-greater hunger and I grow more famished by your light. I desire above all to see you, the true light, as you really are.

By this light I shall come to know that you, eternal Trinity, are Table and Food and Waiter for us. You, eternal Father, are the Table that offers us food, the Lamb, your Only-Begotten Son. He is the most exquisite Food for us, both in his teaching, which nourishes us in your will, and in the Sacraments that we receive in Holy Communion, which feeds and strengthens us while we are pilgrim travelers in this life. And the Holy Spirit is a Waiter for us, for he serves us this teaching by enlightening our mind's eye with it and inspiring us to follow it.

When we come up into your presence, these many things we talk about now without understanding them will cease, and you alone will remain everything in everyone, and then we will sing as one an eternal hymn of praise and we too will become one with you.[24]

*W*HAT *W*ENT *W*RONG?

Unit One: Week Two Exercise

LEARNING GOALS

- ❧ To come to a deeper awareness of the effects of Original Sin and the consequences of the Fall.

- ❧ To answer some fundamental questions: "Why does God allow sickness, death, suffering, pain, natural disasters, and evil?

THE CONSEQUENCES OF WANTING MORE THAN WHAT WAS OFFERED: ORIGINAL SIN AND ITS EFFECT ON MARRIED LIFE

What does the Pastoral Letter on Marriage have to say?

While marriage has remained the good gift that God created it to be, and so has not been a blessing forfeited because of the Fall, Original Sin has had grave consequences for married life. Because men and women became wounded by sin, marriage has become distorted. (*Marriage: Love and Life*, 29)

Original Sin introduced evil and disorder into the world. As a consequence of the break with God, this first sin ruptured the original communion between man and woman. Nonetheless, the original blessing of marriage was never revoked. (*Marriage: Love and Life*, 2)

In the beginning, man and woman existed in the state of original holiness, without sin, suffering, sickness, or death. After God had created Adam and Eve and brought them together in the communion of love, God gave Adam a divine command: "You are free to eat from any of the trees of the garden except the tree of knowledge of good and bad. From that tree you shall not eat; the moment you eat from it you are surely doomed to die" (Gn 2:16–17).

The "tree of the knowledge of good and evil"[25] symbolically evokes the insurmountable limits that man, being a creature, must freely recognize and respect with trust. Man is dependent on his

Creator, and subject to the laws of creation and to the moral norms that govern the use of freedom. (CCC 396)

According to Origen of Alexandria, "The violence at the heart of the human condition began with the question by the cunning serpent, 'Did God really tell you not to eat from any of the trees in the garden?'"[26]

In this particular passage, God reveals the instigator of all evil: Satan, God's nemesis, an angel consumed by pride and cast out of Heaven. We read in Revelation how Satan, who after being defeated by St. Michael, went on to wage warfare against those who keep God's Commandments.[27]

In Genesis, "we see the original vision of God for union between men and women that was so intimate, with a love so pure that there was the deepest trust and intimacy. We find no shame here in the full revelation of their hearts and bodies offered as gift to one another. But Satan filled with pride, jealousy, and envy sought to attack the root of this intimacy between men and women, and between man and their Creator."[28]

Satan incessantly tempts us to desire to reach beyond the limits of our present existence, not only to ascend to God and become like God, but indeed to become equal to God.

The serpent asked Eve, "Did God really tell you not to eat from any trees in the garden?"[29] In eating the forbidden fruit, Eve fell prey to the inordinate desire of pride, the overreaching desire for that which is not of God, the unrestrained desire for power over her Creator.

She essentially desired to "become like God," because the serpent had assured her that "You certainly will not die! No, God knows well that the moment you eat of it your eyes will be opened and you will be like gods who know what is good and what is bad."[30]

HOW THE DESCENDING STEPS OF PRIDE DISTORTED
THE PURE LOVE BETWEEN MAN AND WOMAN

By choosing to turn toward the serpent, toward their own selfish desires, and away from God, Adam and Eve denied the very otherness of God and their status as creatures, which inevitably led to a denial or refusal of God's love. In desiring what God had forbidden them, Adam and Eve envied God and in effect, defiantly declared, "I want it because you have it" or "I want it all the more because you told me I couldn't have it."

Adam and Eve freely acted on their inordinate desire to become like God. This Original Sin marked human nature with an "inclination to evil"[31] known as concupiscence.[32] In terms of the relationship between man and woman, concupiscence manifests itself in the desires of lust and domination.[33] Concupiscence is, in effect, an infatuation with death, instead of an orientation of self-giving and self-sacrificial love. Consequently, man has an ever-increasing desire toward a selfish love.

> As a break with God, the first sin had for its first consequence the rupture of the original communion between man and woman. Their relations were distorted by mutual recriminations;[34] their mutual attraction, the Creator's own gift, changed into a relationship of domination and lust;[35] and the beautiful vocation of man and woman to be fruitful, multiply, and subdue the earth was burdened by the pain of childbirth and the toil of work.[36] (CCC 1607)

Instead of a self-giving, self-sacrificial love, Original Sin caused the inordinate, sinful desire among spouses to dominate and subjugate the other for personal gain or satisfaction.

This not only happens in marriage but also in all of our relationships. Pride seeks to demean, humiliate, and control others in order to fortify ourselves. In order to have a happy, healthy, holy, and lasting marriage, spouses need to be aware of the effects of Original Sin, specifically concupiscence and the negative consequences it can have for marriage.

"WHERE ARE YOU, WHAT HAVE YOU DONE?"

When God confronted them, the man blamed the woman by saying, "The woman whom you put here with me—she gave me fruit from the tree, so I ate it," and Eve in turn said, "The serpent tricked me into it, so I ate it."[37] This is best described as scapegoating, which is the denial of or disavowing responsibility. How often do we experience this in our own lives? How often is this one of the primary causes of broken marriages?

By disobeying the divine command, Adam, Eve, and their descendents came under the power of the Evil One. Prior to the Fall, Adam and Eve were naked without shame. After the Fall, they became ashamed of their nakedness and hid themselves, because they were filled with guilt and disgrace. They were expelled from the Garden of Eden, subjected to death, and condemned to servile work on earth.

IT WAS NOT SUPPOSED TO BE THIS WAY; GOD'S PLAN WAS PERFECT, BUT WE DISRUPTED IT BY WANTING TO BE LIKE GOD

The Church understands moral and physical evil to be a consequence of man freely choosing sin. Human suffering is a consequence of man's disobedience. Man has himself brought about the evil from which he suffers. As darkness is nothing but the absence of light, so too evil is merely the defect of goodness. (St. Aug., *In Gen. as lit.*)

Evil is the absence of good. It may be described as the sum of the opposition to the desires and needs of human beings and the cause of the sufferings with which life abounds. There is no area of human life in which its presence is not felt, and the discrepancy between what is and what ought to be has always called for explanation. It should be observed that evil is of three kinds—physical, moral, and metaphysical.

IF SUFFERING IS A CONSEQUENCE OF EVIL, THEN AS CHRISTIANS, WHAT DO WE DO WITH SUFFERING? HOW DO WE MAKE SENSE OF IT? WHAT IS ITS PURPOSE?

Viktor Frankl wrote a compelling book called, *Man's Search for Meaning.* A Jewish psychiatrist, he spent many years in a Nazi concentration camp, where he devoted himself to helping his fellow prisoners. He was later asked how they survived, how they found meaning in the chaos. He said, "If you found meaning in suffering, you survived. To live is to suffer, therefore if life has meaning, suffering has meaning too. If suffering does not have meaning, then life does not have meaning. Suffering ceases to be when one finds meaning in it."

Pope Benedict XVI posed a question in his inauguration homily that we ask all too often:

> How often we wish that God would make show himself stronger, that he would strike decisively, defeating evil and creating a better world. All ideologies of power justify themselves in exactly this way, they justify the destruction of whatever would stand in the way of progress and the

liberation of humanity. We suffer on account of God's patience. And yet, we need his patience. God, who became a lamb, tells us that the world is saved by the Crucified One, not by those who crucified him. The world is redeemed by the patience of God. It is destroyed by the impatience of man.[38]

Suffering, like life itself, is a mystery, and it takes a lot of patience to see God's providence unfold. We would all like to see evil destroyed and suffering cease. God, however, has a plan in everything and is patient with us, because he desires all to be saved and come to the knowledge of truth. Yet, as Pope Benedict XVI observed, we fail to see God's loving plan because of our impatience. We cannot fully understand this plan, and, in consequence, we must await its fulfillment in faith, hope, and charity.

> But the possibility of conversion entails that we learn to read the events of life in the light of faith … In the presence of suffering and grief, true wisdom is to let oneself be called from the precariousness of existence and to read human history with God's eyes, who, always and only wanting the good of his children, by an inscrutable plan of his love, sometimes allows them to be tried through suffering to lead them to a greater good.[39]

In his book, *God's Answer to Suffering*, Peter Kreeft says that instead of asking, "Life what is your meaning? We eventually come to realize that life is questioning us by name … What is your meaning?" As Christians, we find our true identity and meaning only when we include God in the equation. Only when God is part of the equation can we make sense of suffering. Christianity is the only religion that can make full sense of suffering. Why? Because we have a God who endured it and gave it redemptive value.

Suffering is often devalued by our modern world. Many people seem to cling to a utopian ideal of living without pain and suffering. Peter Kreeft asserts that, "When the world is teaching ways to get out of suffering, Christ Jesus is offering us a way and inviting into suffering, as the way to salvation."

What kind of world would exist if all suffering were eliminated? We all suffer, because we are human beings knowing what it means to be happy. Happiness and suffering are like love and hate. They are not opposites; they are components of the same reality. Happiness always presumes the possibility of being able to suffer, and suffering can be the beginning of happiness. It is hard to see God's plan in suffering when we are experiencing it. It is sometimes easier when we have made our way through it. Finding meaning in suffering can be a redemptive source of spiritual growth. With the combination of grace and human effort, we can begin to cope with and embrace suffering in a positive spirit.

What God is trying to reveal to us in Scripture, is that the meaning of human suffering (the Cross) and the meaning of life (the Resurrection) are of the same reality. We cannot have one without the other. Without suffering crises and problems, many of us will never discover the true meaning of our lives. Without faith in God, ourselves, and other human beings, no one will ever be able to discover meaning in suffering.

What counts is not so much the suffering but our attitude toward it. Suffering often cannot be eliminated or changed, but our attitude toward it can be. That is why when we are confronted with the questions like "Why?" and "Why me and not someone else?" we must ask ourselves the more important questions like "What can I do with it?" and "What can I make from the situation in which I find myself?"

Our faith tells us that God is always with us, especially when we experience suffering and darkness. God's presence does not eliminate the suffering, but his grace helps us cultivate the right attitude toward it. Make no doubt about it there will be difficulties in your marriage. With the passing of time, physical and/or emotional health may fail; financial difficulties may arise or the stress of daily life may become a burden; common interests and tastes may change over the years; disagreements or arguments may arise; and idiosyncrasies may get the best of you. We, however, "would have a poor idea of marriage and of human affection if we were to think that love and joy come to an end when faced with such difficulties. It is precisely in these moments that our true sentiments come to the surface, in order to show a true and profound affection that is stronger than human weakness."[40]

Jesus taught us that the afflictions we experience in the flesh are always transformed when we apply the fruits of the Spirit, such as patience, perseverance, fortitude, and love. God knows it is hard sometimes, but if you keep Christ at the heart of your marriage, pray constantly together and for one another, and share your faith together in the sacramental life of the Church (esp. the Eucharist), you will always be strengthened, consoled, and healed in difficult times and given fresh opportunities for proving and strengthening your love for one another.

If we allow the wounds of Christ to shed light and meaning upon our wounds, we will come to recognize that through suffering (the Cross), the human heart is strengthened and the soul begins to embrace the love and compassion of God, in Christ Jesus, who is our hope and salvation.

What does the Pastoral Letter on Marriage have to say?

Conflict, quarrels, and misunderstandings can be found in all marriages. They reflect the impact of Original Sin, which "disrupted the original communion of man and woman."[41] They also reflect modern stresses upon marriage: the conflict between work and home, economic hardships, and social expectations.

Nevertheless, God's plan for marriage persists, and he continues to offer mercy and healing grace. We bishops urge couples in crisis to turn to the Lord for help. We also encourage them to make use of the many resources, including programs and ministries offered by the Church, that can help to save marriages, even those in serious difficulty. (*Marriage: Love and Life*, 25)

The Scottish writer, George MacDonald, asked why God allows suffering, why he sometimes seems so distant. He said, "As cold as everything looks in winter, the sun has not forsaken us. He has only drawn away for a little, for good reasons, one of which is that we may learn that we cannot do without him."

Sometimes the storm arises around us or within us. And it may seem at times that our frail craft (souls) cannot take any more. At times we have the impression that God is heedless of our fate. The waves of temptation and despair may be breaking over us daily, personal weaknesses, illness, professional or financial difficulties can overwhelm us. When we are confronted with such pain and sorrow, we have to realize that Jesus is carrying us and calling all of us in the midst of our trials and tribulations to carry one another; to share with them the words of Jesus, "Be still, do not be afraid … If difficulties arise, then the grace of God will come more abundantly as well. If there are many difficulties, there will be many graces from God. Divine help is always proportionate to the obstacles … it is good that there are difficulties, because then we will obtain more help from God."[42]

The *Workout*

1. When you were engaged you were overjoyed that this was the right person for you. After marriage, your expectations may have changed. What were they then? What are they now?

2. Original Sin makes self-giving love more difficult without God's grace. Pride seeks to demean, humiliate, and control others. How has sin affected your marriage?

3. What were effective and fruitful ways that you were able to reconcile with your spouse?

4. How have you experienced God's grace in your life? In your marriage?

5. What are some practical ways that you can bring about change/conversion in your marriage?

LET US PRAY

Lord, help us treat each other with respect, and remind us often of what brought us together.
Help us to give the highest priority to the tenderness, gentleness, and kindness
that our connection deserves. When frustration, difficulty, and fear assail our relationship,
as they threaten all relationships at one time or another, help us to focus on what is right
and holy between us, not only the part which seems wrong. In this way, with the help
of your grace, we can ride out the storms when clouds hide the face of the sun
in our lives … remembering that even if we lose sight of it for a moment,
the sun is still there. Make us aware everyday that if each of us takes responsibility for the
quality of our life together, it will be marked by abundance and delight.
For we are taught that "where two or three are gathered together in
your Name, there you will be in their midst." Be forever with us
Lord so that we may be one with you forever in Heaven. Amen.

God's Original Plan Restored

Unit One: Week Three Exercise

LEARNING GOALS

- God would not leave us in our sin; he comes to save us and restore us back to life in Jesus Christ. A marriage that is deeply rooted in Christ is the way to a happy, healthy, holy, and lasting marriage.

- The vocation of marriage is directed toward a person's own salvation and that of others, primarily his or her spouse and children. Moreover, in marriage, couples are called to seek the goodness, integrity, holiness, and salvation of each other. Couples will do this perfectly if they follow the example of Jesus Christ.

- To show that marriage is built upon mutual love, understanding, generosity, forgiveness, humility, reverential service, and, most importantly, self-sacrificial love that mirrors Christ's unconditional love for his Bride, the Church.

GOD'S ORIGINAL PLAN IS RESTORED IN CHRIST JESUS

What does the Pastoral Letter on Marriage have to say?

In restoring to marriage its original meaning and beauty, Jesus proclaims what the Creator meant marriage to be "in the beginning." He does so because marriage will be made into the visible embodiment of his love for the Church. In his espousal of the Church as his Bride, he fulfills and elevates marriage. He reveals his own love "to the end" (Jn 13:1) as the purest and deepest love, the perfection of all love. In doing this he reveals the deepest meaning of all marital love: self-giving love modeled on God's inner life and love. (*Marriage: Love and Life*, 30)

After the fall, man was not abandoned by God. On the contrary, God calls him and in a mysterious way heralds the coming victory over evil and his restoration from his fall.[43] This passage in Genesis is called the *Protoevangelium*: ("first gospel"): the first announcement of the Messiah and Redeemer, of a battle between the serpent and the Woman, and of the final victory of a descendant of hers. (CCC 410)

The *Protoevangelium* is the famous passage in which God promised Adam and Eve of their eventual redemption: "I will put enmity between you and the woman, and between your seed and her seed; he shall bruise your head, and you shall bruise his heel."[44]

The *Protoevangelium* foreshadows the New Eve (Mary) and the New Adam (Jesus Christ). "As a new Eve Mary believed, not the serpent of old, but the messenger of God, with a faith wholly free of doubt. She gave birth to the Son, appointed by God to be *the firstborn among many brothers*, that is, among those who believe; with a mother's love she cooperates in their birth and development."[45]

According to Hans Urs Von Balthasar, the *first Adam* freely chose the path into the violent state of Original Sin, a state that "disfigured" the perfect order of God's universe and distorted the "likeness" of God that humanity possessed in the beginning. In consequence, each individual now experiences alienation, isolation, suffering, evil, and ultimately death.

Unable to reverse the violence at the heart of the human condition, man must seek redemption through the perfect obedience and love of the *Second Adam*, Jesus Christ, who alone is able to reconcile the human person with God and restore what was lost due to man's disobedience.[46]

> The human race—every one of us—is the sheep lost in the desert which no longer knows the way. The Son of God will not let this happen; he cannot abandon humanity in so wretched a condition. He leaps to his feet and abandons the glory of heaven, in order to go in search of the sheep and pursue it, all the way to the Cross. He takes it upon his shoulders and carries our humanity; he carries us all—he is the good shepherd who lays down his life for the sheep … Let us pray for one another, that the Lord will carry us and that we will learn to carry one another.[47]

Just as every person comes into this world wounded and fallen because of Original Sin, you, as a couple, entered into marriage wounded and fallen, with your defects and shortcomings, sins, and failures.

Yet there is hope! In order to have a healthy, happy, holy, and lasting marriage, you must recognize and accept the reality of your fallen state so that you may continually strive for sanctity by uniting yourselves ever more closely to Christ the Way, the Truth, and the Life. This can only happen if you remain *One in Christ*.

JESUS UNMASKS THE VIOLENCE DUE TO SIN AND SHOWS US THE WAY TO RECONCILIATION AND TRUE LOVE

St. Paul, like all of the saints, knew his own sinfulness, and yet he had hope in the risen Christ. He knew the problem of sin and yet he proclaimed that "where sin increased, grace overflowed all the more."[48] Jesus Christ comes to "unmask" the violence due to sin and to show us how to overcome pride through humility, envy through generosity, concupiscence through chastity, and scapegoating through responsibility, forgiveness, and unconditional love.

In Jesus Christ, God comes to save us:

- To heal our wounded nature, forgive our sins, and reconcile us to God.

- To accomplish this on the Cross through self-sacrificial love.

- Through his Cross and Resurrection, to lead us on the path of salvation.

God created man out of love, redeems him in love, and calls him to love—the fundamental and innate vocation of every human being. As we said in the first lesson, our unity with Christ and one another should reflect the inner life of the Trinity: a perfect communion of love. In marriage, you are being called to manifest this perfect communion of love. Speaking about communion and love, St. Paul urges us "to live in a manner worthy of the call you have received."[49]

WHAT IS YOUR VOCATION?

What does the Pastoral Letter on Marriage have to say?

In marriage a man and a woman are united with each other, and the two become one flesh, so that they each love the other as they love themselves and cherish each other's bodies as their own. This union is an image of the relationship between Christ and his Church:

He who loves his wife loves himself. For no one hates his own flesh but rather nourishes and cherishes it, even as Christ does the church, because we are members of his Body.

> For this reason a man shall leave [his] father and [his] mother and be joined to his wife, and the two shall become one flesh. This is a great mystery, but I speak in reference to Christ and the church. (Eph 5:31–32)

The Church Fathers expressed this truth when they described the relationship between Adam and Eve as a "type," or mysterious foreshadowing, of the relationship between Christ and the Church. The kind of relationship of love that is foreshadowed in the relationship between Adam and Eve is fulfilled in the relationship between Christ and his Church.

The Sacrament of Matrimony renews the natural institution of marriage and elevates it so that it shares in a love larger than itself. Marriage, then, is nothing less than a participation in the covenant between Christ and the Church. In the words of the Second Vatican Council,

> Spouses, therefore, are fortified and, as it were, consecrated for the duties and dignity of their state by [this] special sacrament; fulfilling their conjugal and family role by virtue of this sacrament, spouses are penetrated with the spirit of Christ and their whole life is suffused by faith, hope and charity; thus they increasingly further their own perfection and their mutual sanctification, and together they render glory to God.[50]

Because the call of Adam and Eve to become one flesh is realized on a more profound level in the creation of the Church as Christ's Bride, one can only see the depth of the meaning of marriage in relation to Christ and his love for the Church as his Bride. Marriage is a call to give oneself to one's spouse as fully as Christ gave himself to the Church. The natural meaning of marriage as an exchange of self-giving is not replaced, but fulfilled and raised to a higher level. (*Marriage: Love and Life*, 31)

A vocation is a call from God to serve him in a particular state. Marriage is one of the three states of life in which a Catholic may serve God, the others being priesthood, religious life, or the state of "single blessedness."

> The Lord has his plan for each of us, he calls each one of us by name. Our task is to be listeners, capable of perceiving his call, to be courageous and faithful, so that we may follow him, and in the end, be found as trustworthy servants who have used well the gifts entrusted to us. The origin and goal of this plan is God's love. God loves us, so that we can love him in return. "He loves us, he makes us see and experience his love, and from God's loving us 'first,' love can also arise as a

response within us." A vocation is always situated in the context of this love. "Before the creation of the world, before our coming into existence, the heavenly Father chose us personally, calling us to enter into a filial relationship with him, through Jesus, the Incarnate Word, under the guidance of the Holy Spirit."[51]

You have responded to God's invitation to love and said "yes" to one another on your wedding day to the vocation of marriage. So what does it mean to enter into and live out the vocation of marriage?

We know that each one of us has been created by God with a unique purpose and an eternal destiny: to love, know, and serve God so as to be happy with him in Heaven. God has called you in Christ Jesus to fulfill a certain mission in life—a mission that you began at Baptism and that continues to unfold in your lives individually and communally through the sacramental life of the Church.

It is a mission of holiness, a mission of deepening your relationship with God and neighbor, and a mission that has as its goal eternal life. This is called Christian discipleship. For the Christian disciple, holiness means imitating the Master, Jesus Christ, and conforming one's will to the Father's with the aid of the Holy Spirit. According to St. Thomas Aquinas, we all share the universal vocation to love with the divine love, with the love of charity. The more we love, the better we will fulfill this vocation.

In marriage, your personal mission/vocation takes on an added dimension and includes not only your own holiness but also that of your spouse. As Christian disciples, you have embraced a special call, a vocation that has as its end, eternal life with God. But you will not accomplish this alone. As a married couple, you have the awesome responsibility of helping one another (and your children) get to Heaven.

How will you do this? The means to achieving this end consists of living out your vocation faithfully with the help of God's grace that you had received on your wedding day in the Sacrament of Matrimony. It also requires three essential ingredients that we learn from Jesus Christ.

1. To love and to be loved.
   Jesus said: "Love one another as I have loved you; No one has greater love than this, to lay one's life down for one's friends."[52]

2. To forgive and to be forgiven.
   Jesus said, "So will my heavenly Father do to you, unless each of you forgives his brother from his heart."[53] Peter approached the Lord and asked, "Lord, if my brother sins against me, how often must I forgive him? As many as seven times?" Jesus answered, "I say to you, not seven times but seventy-seven times."[54] What is demanded of the disciples is limitless forgiveness.

3. To serve and to be served.
   Jesus said, "The Son of Man did not come to be served but to serve and to give his life as a ransom for many."[55]

What does the Pastoral Letter on Marriage have to say?

By the power of the Holy Spirit, spouses become willing to do the acts and courtesies of love toward each other, regardless of the feelings of the moment. They are formed by the self-giving love of Christ for his Church as his Bride, and so they are enabled to perform acts of self-giving love to the benefit of themselves, their families, and the whole Church. The Sacrament of Matrimony, like the Sacrament of Holy Orders, is a sacrament "directed toward the salvation of others; if [these sacraments] contribute as well to personal salvation, it is through service to others that they do so."[56] Those who receive these sacraments are given a special consecration in Christ's name to carry out the duties of their particular state in life. (*Marriage: Love and Life*, 34)

What then does it mean to love, forgive, and serve one another out of reverence for Christ so that your vocation will be formed by a self-sacrificial and unconditional love that follows in the footsteps of Christ?

St. Paul's Letter to the Ephesians states:

> Be subordinate to one another out of reverence for Christ. Wives should be subordinate to their husbands as to the Lord. For the husband is head of his wife just as Christ is head of the church, he himself the savior of the body. As the church is subordinate to Christ, so wives should be subordinate to their husbands in everything. Husbands, love your wives, even as Christ loved the church and handed himself over for her to sanctify her, cleansing her by the bath of water with the word, that he might present to himself the church in splendor, without spot or wrinkle or any such thing, that she might be holy and without blemish. So (also) husbands should love their wives as their own bodies. He who loves his wife loves himself. For no one hates his own flesh but rather nourishes and cherishes it, even as Christ does the church, because we are members of his body. "For this reason a man shall leave (his) father and (his) mother and be joined to his wife, and the two shall become one flesh." This is a great mystery, but I speak in reference to Christ and the church. In any case, each one of you should love his wife as himself, and the wife should respect her husband.[57]

Christopher West has this to say about this Scripture passage:

> While we must admit that some men throughout history have pointed to this Scripture verse to justify their fallen desire to dominate women, St. Paul is in no way justifying such an attitude. He knows it to be the result of original sin, which is why in this passage he's actually restoring God's original plan before sin. He does so by pointing out what marriage was all about in the first place. It was meant to foreshadow the marriage of Christ and the Church. St. Paul simply draws out the implications of this analogy.
>
> He starts by calling both husbands and wives to be subject to one another "out of reverence for Christ" (v. 21), out of reverence for the "great mystery" that spouses participate in by imaging Christ's union with the Church. In the analogy, the husband represents Christ, and the wife represents the Church. So, he says, as the Church is subject to Christ, so should wives also be subject to their husbands (v. 24).
>
> Another translation uses the word, "submission." I like to explain this word as follows. "Sub" means "under," and "mission" means "to be sent forth with the authority to perform a specific service." Wives, then, are called to put themselves "under" the "mission" of their husbands. What's the mission of the husband? "Husbands, love your wives, as Christ loved the Church and gave Himself up for her" (v. 25). How did Christ love the Church? He died for her. (How many men here would die for their bride?) Christ said he did "not come to be served but to serve," and "to give his life as a ransom for many" (Mt 20:28).
>
> What, then does it mean for a wife to "submit" to her husband? It means let your husband serve you. Put yourself under his mission to love you as Christ loved the Church. As John Paul II says: "The wife's 'submission' to her husband, understood in the context of the entire passage of the letter to the Ephesians, signifies above all the 'experiencing of love.' This is true all the more so since this 'submission' is related to the image of the submission of the Church to Christ, which certainly consists in experiencing His love" (*Theology of the Body*, September 1ˢᵗ, 1982).

What woman would not want to receive this kind of love from her husband? What woman would not want to be subject to her husband if he truly took his mission seriously to love her as Christ loved the Church?[58]

In 1930, Pope Pius XI taught:

The submission of the wife neither ignores nor suppresses the liberty to which her dignity as a human person and her noble functions as a wife, mother, and companion give her the full right. It does not oblige her to yield indiscriminately to all the desires of her husband, which may be unreasonable or incompatible with her wifely dignity. Nor does it mean that she is on a level of persons who in law are called minors, and who are ordinarily denied the unrestricted exercise of their rights on the ground of their immature judgment and inexperience. But it does forbid such abuse of freedom as would neglect the welfare of the family; it refuses, in this body which is the family, to allow the heart to be separated from the head, with great detriment to the body itself and even with risk of disaster. If the husband is the head of the domestic body, then the wife is its heart; and as the first holds the primacy of authority, so the second can and ought to claim the primacy of love.[59]

Pope John Paul II echoed this understanding:

"Above all it is important to underline the equal dignity and responsibility of women with men. This equality is realized in a unique manner in that reciprocal self-giving by each one to the other and by both to the children which is proper to marriage and the family."[60] This can only become a reality in marriage if couples submit to one another out of reverence for Christ who never ceases to "abide with them in order that by their mutual self-giving, they will love each other with enduring fidelity, as Christ loved the Church and delivered Himself for it."[61]

The vocation of marriage is truly a path to holiness which is built upon mutual love, understanding, generosity, forgiveness, humility, reverential service, and, most importantly, self-sacrificial love that mirrors Christ's unconditional love for his Bride, the Church.

Pope Benedict XVI sees love as an important, indeed the primary element in a vocation. It is at the origin of every vocation, and every vocation finds its fulfillment in love. Thus, he describes marriage as a vocation insofar as it is to be formed by true love.

"If you are ... married, God has a project of love for {you} as a couple and as a family ... The love of a man and woman is at the origin of the human family and the couple formed by a man and a woman has its foundation in God's original plan (cf. *Gen* 2:18–25) ... In your prayer together, ask the Lord to watch over and increase your love and to purify it of all selfishness. Do not hesitate to respond generously to the Lord's call, for Christian matrimony is a true and proper vocation in the Church."[62]

We conclude with a passage from Tertullian on the Sacrament of Marriage:

Where can I find words to describe adequately the happiness of that marriage which the Church fortifies, which the oblation confirms and the blessing seals? The angels proclaim it and the heavenly Father ratifies it ... What kind of yoke is that of two Christians, united in one hope, one desire, one discipline, and one service? Both are children of the same Father, servant of the same master; nothing separates them either in spirit or in the flesh; on the contrary, they are truly two in one flesh. Where the flesh is one, so is the spirit. Together they pray, together they worship God, they teach each other, exhort each other, encourage each other. They are both equal in the Church of God, equal at the banquet of God, equal in trials, persecution and consolations.[63]

The Workout

1. Do we agree that the long-range purpose of our marriage is to help each other reach our goal of eternal life in Heaven? How have we been doing this? If we have not, what can be our first three steps?

2. What specific change of heart or change in behavior is necessary for us to walk more fully in the way of the Lord, in order that we may live our marriage in Christian discipleship?

3. Share with each other one or two occasions where you have experienced a profound impact of God's providential care in your lives.

4. Do we have difficulty sharing our faith and ideas on religion? If so, what are three ways we can overcome this?

LET US PRAY

May God grant us both Love … to afford each other a special quality of time together.
Joy … in the accomplishments of one another.
Understanding … that our interests and desires will not always be the same.
Friendship … based on mutual trust.
Courage … to speak of a misunderstanding and to work on a solution before the setting of the sun.
Compassion … to comfort each other in pain and sorrow.
Foresight … to realize rainbows follow rainy days.
Awareness … to live each day with the knowledge that there is no promise of tomorrow.
Hope … knowing that God has prepared a place for those who believe in him
and place their trust in him. May God bless us and keep us in the palm of his hand. Amen.

ℱaithful, ℱruitful, and ℱorever

Unit One: Week Four Exercise

WHAT DOES "MARRIAGE" MEAN?

The Catholic Church teaches that:

> The marriage covenant, by which a man and a woman form with each other an intimate communion of life and love, has been founded and endowed with its own special laws by the Creator. By its very nature it is ordered to the good of the couple, as well as to the generation and education of children. Christ the Lord raised marriage between the baptized to the dignity of a sacrament (cf. CIC, can. 1055 § 1; cf. *GS* 48 § 1). (CCC 1660)

What does the Pastoral Letter on Marriage have to say?

As the Second Vatican Council reminds us, marriage is not a purely human institution: "the intimate partnership of life and the love which constitutes the married state has been established by the creator and endowed by him with its own proper laws ... For God himself is the author of marriage."[64] Moreover, God has endowed marriage with certain essential attributes, without which marriage cannot exist as he intends.

The Church has taught through the ages that marriage is an exclusive relationship between one man and one woman. This union, once validly entered and consummated, gives rise to a bond that cannot be dissolved by the will of the spouses.[65] Marriage thus created is a faithful, privileged sphere of intimacy between the spouses that lasts until death.

Marriage is not merely a private institution, however. It is the foundation for the family, where children learn the values and virtues that will make good Christians as well as good citizens. The importance of marriage for children and for the upbringing of the next generation highlights the importance of marriage for all society. (*Marriage: Love and Life*, 7–8)

This communion of persons has the potential to bring forth human life and thus to produce the family, which is itself another kind of communion of persons and which is the origin and foundation of all human society. It is precisely the difference between man and woman that makes possible this unique communion of persons, the unique partnership of life and love that is marriage. A man and woman united in marriage as husband and wife serve as a symbol of both life and love in a way that no other relationship of human persons can. (*Marriage: Love and Life*, 11)

FROM THIS EXPLANATION WE COME TO DISCOVER THE DEFINITION OF MARRIAGE AND ITS PROPERTIES

Granted, "marriage" means different things to different people, and amidst the world's cultures we find some variety in the relationships that bear this name. For Catholics (whatever the country or culture), however, "marriage" is a technical term with a particular meaning. The Church has long embraced the concept of natural law, which is the understanding that God created the universe in such a way that a certain moral law is embedded into his creation, a code that is discernible through the use of reason, which God also created. Revelation further clarifies God's moral law, but certain acts—murder, for example—are known to be wrong through the natural law alone, even by people unaware of the Judeo-Christian tradition. From the perspective of natural law, marriage is a lifelong, faithful relationship between one man and one woman who are open to children.

The *Catechism of the Catholic Church* also teaches that "marriage is based on the consent of the contracting parties, that is, on their will to give themselves, each to the other, mutually and definitively, in order to live a covenant of faithful and fruitful love."[66] The term, "covenant," is one we probably learned in our religious education classes as children, and it indicates a particular kind of relationship, a relationship that looks to God himself as its model.

When we think of a contract as opposed to a covenant, we may think of a lease agreement, which usually spells out in detail the rights and responsibilities of the parties involved. Contracts articulate the obligations and enjoyments that are expected. The duration of the agreement is also spelled out. A "parachute clause" may be included that establishes the terms allowing one or the other party to abandon the agreement and dissolve the relationship of landlord/tenant. Civil marriage is a form of contract.

Certain understandings of "marriage" have much in common with a lease arrangement. If marriage is viewed as a contract, one can analyze how each party has or has not lived up to the obligations of the contract and deduce whether or not there is reason to continue with it. If marriage is viewed as a contract, one can reasonably enter into it with the assumption that if x, y, or z should occur, the marriage may be dissolved.

This is *not* the case in Christian marriage. Christian marriage is not a contract but a covenant. A covenant does not establish a "deal," but rather a *sacred bond* into which each party enters with the firm intention to share in the free, total, faithful and fruitful love of God.

MARRIAGE VOWS

Very rarely in life are we are called upon to utter a vow. A *vow* is nothing less than a *sacred oath*, sworn in such a way that we put our personal salvation on the line as part of the process. We are committing to something, not just as an agreement, but as a way of deepening our relationship with the Lord. We trust that since God is God, he will give us the grace we need to complete our part of the agreement. And if we fail, we trust that he will not abandon us, but will help us to regroup and move forward.

Christian spouses are not joined by passing emotions or infatuation (even if these played a role in courtship). They are joined by God himself in an unbreakable bond, a covenant of love, through the firm and irrevocable act of their own consent. Consider the words of the priest, spoken after the couple has pronounced their vows: *"Therefore let no one separate what God has joined."* God is the active agent in joining the couple, who participate in effecting the Sacrament through their mutual and free consent.

For the baptized, the marriage bond is sealed by the Holy Spirit, and once consummated, it is absolutely indissoluble. Since it is God who seals, not the husband and wife, they cannot dissolve the bond, even by mutual consent. This is what takes Christian marriage beyond what we experience in contractual agreements.

Consider the very words of the Marriage vows:

> I, _____, take you, _____, to be my wife/husband. I promise to be true to you in good times and in bad, in sickness and in health. I will love you and honor you all the days of my life.[67]

This simple promise contains profound meaning. No one either has or ever will make this kind of commitment to you (other than God himself). Therefore, since marriage is the mirror of God's love for us, the closest we will ever come to understanding what God's love for us is like, is by living out faithfully the essential properties of the marriage covenant: fruitful, faithful, and forever.

PROPERTIES OF CHRISTIAN MARRIAGE

Fruitful: Openness to Children

Remember on your wedding day when the priest or deacon asked you, "will you accept children lovingly from God and bring them up according to the law of Christ and His Church?" I'm sure you answered in the affirmative! A relationship that mirrors God's relationship with us must be fruitful, and look beyond itself. The self-sacrifice and unselfish giving that are associated with parenting connect the married couple with Christ's unselfish pouring out of himself for us on the Cross.

> Children are the Incarnation of married love; the material overflowing of two becoming one. Love is always life-giving, always open to the other, always expansive. Those who love find no greater joy than to extend love to others. Children are the natural expression of the love of the spouses—the visible sign of the fruitfulness of self-emptying—and a means of ever deepening joy in marriage.[68]

More on this topic in Unit Three, Exercise Four.

Forever: Indissolubility

Remember the second intention that the priest or deacon asked you at your wedding? "Will you love and honor each other as husband and wife for the rest of your lives?" For most couples, this is the motivating feature of marriage. If your health is good, you will be together forty, fifty, even sixty years! It is wondrous to give yourself to another for life, and to experience another giving him- or herself to you. It is an expression of absolute faith and trust. Couples who have lived to celebrate their fiftieth wedding anniversary set a beautiful example and cannot help but inspire those who know them.

- *How do they do it?* Any couple that makes it this far will be clear on one thing: *it takes work.* Marriage can never be put on auto-pilot. We all know couples whose marriage seems like an empty shell. In most cases, lack of attention to the relationship brought them to this point. Different couples choose different ways to "keep it fresh," but they must keep it fresh if they are to flourish. People grow and change as they get older, and married couples must grow and change *together*.

   Make no doubt about it there will be difficulties in your marriage. Never forget, however, why you fell in love with each other and never focus on the negative aspects, such as each other's defects, shortcomings, or idiosyncrasies. Always try to draw the good out of each other. Pray together and participate in the Sacraments so that you might receive the graces to grow in holiness and strength for each other.

   > "Marriage is like a fine wine; it improves with age and appreciates in value. Torrents of worries and difficulties are incapable of drowning true love because people who sacrifice themselves generously are brought closer together in the long run …"[69]

- *Countless marriages fade, because too much attention is paid to the children.* Children are God's blessing and help to hold a family together. Parents are invested in the lives and development of their children, and this helps to cement their relationship. They have a common "project," a little one into whom they can pour their love and energy. Children bring joy to life, and the stewardship of children is a serious parental responsibility. *But sometimes this comes at the cost of the spousal relationship.* Some couples even think it is *virtuous* to sideline their relationship so that they can focus entirely on their children. Here is a maxim that deserves to be posted on every couple's bathroom mirror: The greatest gift parents can give their child is to love their spouse. Time away from the children focused on nurturing the couple's relationship will come back to benefit the children many times over. Guilt about this must be swatted away. Otherwise, you may wake up twenty-five years later and realize you do not even know the person sleeping next to you.

   > Having children helps us recognize who we are; they reveal our inability to be always loving and patient and kind in our marriage and in our parenting. We find ourselves out of balance with no ability to make things right on our own. We reach the end of ourselves and turn to God for help because he is our only lasting source of hope. (Dr. David Stoop and Dr. Jan Stoop, *The Complete Marriage Book*)

   When you learn to "hang in there" with each other, you're giving a priceless gift of loving security to your children. A familiar bit of advice on parenting is directed to both mom and dad: "The best thing you can do for your children is to love each other." Children are watching us all the time, and when we model a relationship that hangs in there through life's normal conflict and challenges, we're demonstrating to them that they too, will have a place to hang securely in life, despite everyday difficulties. Marriage teaches us how to love, and children learn that lesson from watching. (Elisa Morgan and Carol Kuykendall, *When Husband and Wife Become Mom and Dad,* p. 32)

I'm convinced that a marriage of priority and integrity will be one of the best offerings you can provide for your children. You may still need to give extra time and attention to the needs of your kids, especially at certain seasons of their development. However, your kids must also see their mom and dad taking time for each other through regular date nights, daily connection times, appropriate expressions of romance, and even a commitment to time away for replenishing your relationship. I'm sure you've heard the true statement: "Do your kids a favor and love your spouse." (Jim Burns, *Creating an Intimate Marriage*)

If you are always pushing your spouse aside for time with the children, you may want to consider just what you're teaching your children. By the way you treat your spouse, are you modeling for your children how you hope they will treat their future spouses? Probably not. Spending time with your spouse not only draws the two of you closer together, but it also teaches your children that the marital relationship has to be our number one human relationship. (Dr. Debbie L. Cherry, *Child-Proofing Your Marriage,* 82)[70]

❧ *Many couples make it a point never to go to bed angry with each other.* Disputes arise in every relationship, and many disagreements require some length of time before they are resolved. Anger, however, can be managed, especially once the first wave of the emotion subsides and our rational side can be engaged. Just because disagreement occurs, it does not mean that anger must accompany it. If anger appears, it must be relinquished (by an act of the will, if necessary) for the sake of the marriage. Choose your words carefully, so as not to inflict unnecessary damage. The phrase, "familiarity breeds contempt," sometimes manifests itself in a marriage relationship, and couples need to be on guard against lashing out in ways that "score points" but create deeper wounds that require further healing.

❧ *There are to be no "winners" and "losers" in a dispute involving married persons.* Flexibility and the art of compromise must be learned. Seeking win-win resolutions to conflict is an essential component of healthy marriages.

One evening, [my husband] Jack came home late as usual, and as usual I started my normal whining and haranguing: "Why are you late again? Why can't you ever be on time for dinner? You must waste time earlier in the day and then we have to suffer." You name it, I said it. Then one of the children looked at me and said, "Why are you always mad at Daddy?" It was like a slap in the face. I was stunned! After all, it was *his* fault. Why blame me for being angry? I don't recall what my reply was, but I'm sure it was self-serving. Almost immediately the Holy Spirit spoke to me: "When you stand before your heavenly Father, he will not ask you about Jack's shortcomings, but he will ask you about your attitudes and responses." *Wow! Even though he interrupts our schedule and upsets our lives, I'm supposed to be loving and kind and supportive?* The Holy Spirit answered me sweetly, "Yes."

I didn't hear an audible voice, but in my heart I knew I had received a rebuke from the Lord and it was my responsibility to make things right. I didn't change overnight, but with the Lord's help it was a beginning point. That encounter has never left me, and when I begin to step over the line, I ask him to take control and bring me back. I learned that the blame game has no place in a marriage." (Jean Bishop, *The Best Thing I Ever Did for My Marriage*)[71]

28

ॐ *The physical side of marriage is one of its great blessings.* Every individual has his or her own level of desire for physical touch and affection, and the frequency of conjugal relations is something that ebbs and flows throughout the course of married life. People thrive when they are treated with healthy doses of physical affection, and many wither when physical touch is withheld.

ॐ *Counseling is sometimes necessary even in the healthiest of marriage relationships.* Some couples fear it, thinking that it is the first step to divorce, or they are too proud to admit that they need help in sorting out their differences. Counseling is not a sign of failure, but a sign of health in a marriage. Summoning the courage to confront issues that get in the way of happiness and joy in the relationship is worth every bit of the embarrassment it may cost. In marriage counseling, *the couple* is the client (not one or the other, husband or wife), and a good marriage counselor works to help them improve the health of their relationship. Sometimes additional individual counseling is also beneficial. But take this to heart: Get counseling as soon as one person desires it. (*If one of you says you need it, then you need it! This is not an issue open for discussion*).

There are many books on the market that couples can peruse for ideas on how to support and nourish their marriage. *What* a couple chooses to do is probably less important than *keeping* the issue in front of them, never taking their relationship for granted, and always looking for ways in which they can grow in their love for each other.

People are living longer these days, which can certainly add to both the joy and the difficulty in marriage's lifelong commitment. God's relationship with us is permanent, and since marriage reflects that relationship, marriage is a permanent state as well. The lifelong aspect of marriage is essential to the Catholic understanding of the Sacrament. It is also indisputably an ideal for merely secular marriages.

Faithful: Exclusive

The expectation of fidelity in marriage is standard across cultures, and this reality is an expression of the natural law. Even before marriage, when dating, couples expect both emotional and physical fidelity. So-called "open marriages" may sound like fun to some, but they almost never work out.

We are spiritually wired for fidelity, even if our physical nature, which is wounded and fallen due to Original Sin, seems to desire a variety in sexual partners. Infidelity in marriage is a result of Original Sin and its consequences, namely, concupiscence, which is the inclination to evil pleasures. Concupiscence presents a struggle between the flesh and the spirit. There are two opposing forces: one which is carnal and the other which is spiritual. The carnal must be controlled by the spiritual so that the person is not brought to destruction but rather to the fullness of life in God. Infidelity is most likely to occur when a person is spiritually dead and desires only the things of the flesh rather than the things of the spirit, which are life-giving.

A few things to keep in mind:

ॐ *Be clear in your communication with each other about your own needs and desires for physical intimacy.* Marriage gives couples a kind of "right" to each other's body, but that right is not to be exercised against the will of the other. "No means no." At the same time, to refuse the advances of your spouse requires a good reason, and you should both work to be as responsive to each other as possible. Not everyone is on the same cycle or rhythm, but together you can achieve a physical harmony that will provide a wonderful way for you to express your love for one another. One of the benefits cited by couples who practice Natural Family Planning is that moving away from an "any time, any place" mentality deepens their respect for each other and intensifies the awe and wonder accompanying the conjugal act.

- ❧ *Avoid pornography.* Period.

  Please see article*: "Pornography: What's the Problem" in the appendix on page 209. Recommended Movie*: *Fireproof: Never Leave Your Partner Behind* by Kirk Cameron and Erin Bethea.

  > "Within marriage, addiction to pornography can destroy intimacy. Eventually, the husband or wife who views pornography can lose the ability to relate on a personal and intimate level with the real person of his or her spouse. Being accustomed to "satisfaction on demand," he or she may no longer be able to participate in an authentic sexual relationship that involves communication and spiritual intimacy. Men or women who view pornography can become used to the "perfect" bodies they see in porn and begin to view their spouse as unattractive in comparison. A person who views porn will likely also develop an unhealthy view of sexuality, and a spouse may be unwilling to do the things demanded of them. Consequently, the spouse's refusal may sometimes result in rape or sexual abuse. How can spouses not feel rejected and betrayed when their marriage partner seeks fulfillment from the images of strangers rather than from the human being who loves them?" (Refer to article: "Pornography: What's the Problem?" by Mark J. Houck)

- ❧ *Be honest with yourself regarding the way television shows and movies can take you to an unhealthy place, and then avoid those that are an occasion of sin.*

- ❧ *Carefully find a friend or two you can trust, with whom you can have open and frank discussions, to help keep you honest about situations that might lead to trouble.* Secrets are the friend of infidelity. Conversation helps us to avoid playing games. Discerning our motivations can be difficult. Having friends as sounding boards is wise. (*You can serve the same role for them.*)

- ❧ *Make regular examinations of conscience; receive the Sacrament of Penance on a regular basis.*

- ❧ *Watch/monitor your thoughts and keep a check on sexual fantasies.*

- ❧ *Be vigilant and use common sense in situations where you might be tempted.* Watch your use of alcohol, especially when in social settings where your spouse is not present with you. Avoid any emotional attachment with coworkers of the opposite sex, especially your boss! The main reason why people become emotionally attached to people other than their spouses is a lack of emotional and physical intimacy with their spouses. Emotional infidelity will almost inevitably lead to the sin of adultery.

- ❧ *Maintain a vigorous prayer life both individually and with your spouse.* The channels of grace can get clogged, and regular prayer helps keep the flow moving.

- ❧ *If jealousy plays a troublesome role in your marriage relationship, seek professional help to seek resolution.*

Faithfulness means you are *exclusively* bonded in the most intimate way. It means being emotionally faithful as well as physically faithful. This does not mean that we do not have other important, or even essential, relationships in our lives. In fact, you cannot demand that your marriage relationship provide for *all* of your relationship needs—that is too much to expect and is a recipe for disaster. But your marriage is your primary relationship. Energy spent protecting this sanctuary is well worth the effort.

Closing Thought on this Issue

People sometimes look at the declining number of priests and wonder if the celibate priesthood has a future. The discipline of priestly celibacy comes under scrutiny in our society, and many people are even cynical about it. People, even *religious* people, comment that it is simply unnatural to take on the discipline of celibacy. They maintain that it is just too hard and unrealistic to expect anyone to refrain from sex, let alone from the kind of intimate, exclusive relationship that marriage offers.

It is a concern worth noting. However, (*this a bit tongue-in-cheek*), given how many married people behave, it is monogamy that might appear to be unnatural. Even given the concepts of natural law and marriage outlined above, the success rate of priests maintaining their promise of celibacy is much higher than the success rate of spouses maintaining their marriage vows! To be sure, priests struggle like everyone else to be faithful to their promises, some with greater success than others. The Catholic divorce rate, nevertheless, far surpasses the rate of priests leaving the priesthood.

So what is there to say about this? In the end, priests and married persons rely on *supernatural* grace to help us live our vocations. Alone, without God's help, we are likely to fail. There are just too many forces at work that threaten our values and too little societal support for them. But for those who place their lives and relationships in God's hands, living out their vocation with intention and openness to the working of the Holy Spirit, there is reason to trust that we will be given what we need to make a go of it (even if the road is bumpy at times).

The *Workout*

1. What did marriage mean to us on our wedding day? What does it mean to us now?

2. If we are now one flesh, then when we hurt our spouse, we hurt ourselves. Think of a time in the past when your spouse hurt you. Did you "forgive" in a timely manner? Did you pray to God for assistance? What can we do to open it up to God's healing grace?

3. If times get rough, what sort of language do we use? How do we act? What are some things that we can do to strengthen our love and faithfulness?

4. Do we believe that God's grace can bring life out of struggles, trials, and difficulties in our marriage?

5. How "open to life" is our attitude toward children?

6. How can we bring balance and harmony in our marriage as parents? Is there anything we need to change?

7. What is entailed in emotional faithfulness?

8. What is a vigorous prayer life and how is it similar to the physical training needed for competition?

Of Putting Up with Other's Faults

What we cannot change in ourselves or in others we ought to endure patiently until God wishes it to be otherwise. Perhaps it is this way to try our patience, for without trials our merits count for little. Nevertheless, when you run into such problems you ought to pray that God may find it fitting to help you and that you may bear your troubles well. If anyone who is spoken to once or twice will not listen and change his ways, do not argue with him, but leave it all to God, for he knows well how to turn bad things into good.

He knows how to accomplish his will and how to express himself fully in all his servants. Take pains to be patient in bearing the faults and weaknesses of others, for you too have many flaws that others must put up with. If you cannot make yourself as you would like to be, how can you expect to have another person entirely to your liking? We would willingly have others be perfect, and yet we fail to correct our own faults.

We want others to be strictly corrected, and yet we are unwilling to be corrected ourselves. Other persons' far-ranging freedom annoys us, and yet we insist on having our own way. We wish others to be tied down by rules, and yet we will not allow ourselves to be held in check in any way at all. It is evident how rarely we think of our neighbor as ourselves!

If everything were perfect, what would we have to endure from others for God's sake? But now God has so arranged things that we may learn to bear each other's burdens, for no one is without faults, no one is without burdens, no one is wholly self-sufficient, and no one has enough wisdom all by himself. That being the case, we must support and comfort each other; together we must help, teach and advise one another, for the strength that each person has will best be seen in times of trouble. Such times do not make us weak; they show what we are.[72]

On Kindness in Marriage

A couple was celebrating their fiftieth wedding anniversary, and because the husband was known to be somewhat moody and eccentric, the wife was asked—out of earshot of her spouse—how she managed to put up with his behavior. "It's simple," she replied. "On my wedding day, I decided I would choose ten of my husband's faults and promised myself I would overlook them for the sake of our marriage." The well-wisher remarked, "That was a wonderful idea. Say, if you don't mind my asking, what were some of the faults you chose?" "To tell the truth," the woman replied, "I never got around to listing them. But every time my husband did something that really upset me, I used to say to myself, 'Lucky for him that's one of the ten!'"

LET US PRAY

Heavenly Father, may the covenant of love in which we have entered into be strengthened
by your grace and may we grow in true devotion and spiritual commitment.
Keep us faithful to you, O God, and to one another with a genuine love.
When selfishness shows itself, grant generosity; when mistrust is a temptation, give moral strength;
when there is misunderstanding, give patience and gentleness; if suffering becomes a part of our lives,
give us a strong faith and an abiding love. We ask this through Jesus Christ our Lord. Amen.

Group Workout

Unit One:
What Do We Believe about Christian Marriage?

- The human family as a reflection of God's rich, Trinitarian life.

- The consequences of Original Sin and the restoration of fallen humanity in Christ.

- Perseverance in the midst of adversity, sickness, poverty, suffering, and spiritual infidelity.

- Following Christ in the vocation to marriage.

- Living out the essential properties within the covenant of marriage: faithful, fruitful, and forever.

MONTHLY GROUP MEETING: FIRST UNIT

1. **Prayer (10 minutes including reflection on prayer)—St. Catherine of Siena Prayer from Unit One, Exercise Three.**

   Everyone please read the following prayer together aloud.

   Eternal Trinity, you have made the blood of Christ so precious through his sharing in your Divine Nature. You are a mystery as deep as the sea; the more I search, the more I find, and the more I find the more I search for you. But I can never be satisfied; what I receive will ever leave me desiring more. When you fill my soul I have an ever-greater hunger and I grow more famished by your light. I desire above all to see you, the true light, as you really are.

   By this light I shall come to know that you, eternal Trinity, are Table and Food and Waiter for us. You, eternal Father, are the Table that offers us food, the Lamb, your only-begotten Son. He is the most exquisite Food for us, both in his teaching, which nourishes us in your will, and in the sacraments that we receive in Holy Communion, which feeds and strengthens us while we are pilgrim travelers in this life. And the Holy Spirit is a Waiter for us, for he serves us this teaching by enlightening our mind's eye with it and inspiring us to follow it.

   When we come up into your presence, these many things we talk about now without understanding them will cease, and you alone will remain everything in everyone, and then we will sing as one an eternal hymn of praise and we too will become one with you.[73]

   Icebreakers: Write and share with your table-group what part of the prayer struck you and why.

2. (15 minutes) Life of a Blessed or Saint couple: This week's couple …

Have a couple read it aloud to the group, alternating paragraphs.

Blessed Luigi Beltrame Quattrocchi & Blessed Maria Corsini[74]

*L*uigi, a lawyer and civil servant, died in 1951 at the age of 71; Maria, who dedicated herself to her family and to several charitable and social Catholic movements, died in 1965 at the age of 81.

Stephania, their first daughter, now deceased, became a Benedictine nun with the name Sr. M. Cecilia. Both sons became priests; one is now 95 years old, the other, 91. Another daughter, Enrichetta, dedicated herself first to caring for her parents, then for her brother, a diocesan priest of Rome; she is now in her 80s.

The Beltrame children recall that their parents led a simple life, like that of many married couples, but always characterized by a sense of the supernatural. Cardinal José Saraiva Martins, Prefect of the Congregation for the Causes of Saints, said that they "made a true domestic church of their family, which was open to life, to prayer, to the social apostolate, to solidarity with the poor and to friendship".

Luigi was born on 12 January 1880 in Catania and grew up in Urbino. Luigi's uncle, Luigi Quattrocchi, who was childless, asked Luigi Beltrame's parents if he and his wife could raise the young Luigi in their home. Though Luigi kept his ties with his parents and siblings, he lived with his aunt and uncle, from whom he acquired his second surname. After his basic preparatory education, he enrolled in the Faculty of Jurisprudence at La Sapienza University in Rome. He obtained a degree in Law which enabled him to enter the legal service of the Inland Revenue Department. He went on to hold a number of posts on the boards of a variety of banks and national reconstruction authorities like IRI and the Bank of Italy, retiring as an honorary deputy attorney general of the Italian State. He was a friend of many political figures, such as Fr. Luigi Sturzo, Alcide de Gasperi, and Luigi Gedda, who worked for Italy's rebirth after the Fascist period and World War II.

His meeting with Maria Corsini in her family home in Florence was to shape his future, as they were married on November 25, 1905 in the Basilica of St Mary Major in Rome. Maria was born on June 24, 1884 in Florence to the noble Corsini family. She received a solid cultural formation helped by her family's involvement in the cultural life of the city of Florence. She loved music and was a professor and writer on educational topics as well as a member of several associations, including Women's Catholic Action.

The couple had four children. One year after their wedding, Luigi and Maria had their first son, Filippo. Then, Stefania and Cesare were born. Filippo (today Don Tarcisio) is a diocesan priest. Cesare (Fr. Paolino) left home in 1924 to become a Trappist monk. Stefania, in 1927, entered the Benedictine cloister in Milan and took the name Cecilia.

At the end of 1913, Maria was again expecting a child, her last, Enrichetta. Because of her difficult pregnancy, the best gynecologists advised her to have an abortion in order to "try to save at least the mother". The possibility of survival then with that diagnosis, was barely five percent. Luigi and Maria refused to do it; they put their whole trust in the Lord's Providence. Maria's pregnancy was one of suffering and anguish. God responded beyond all human hope and thus Enrichetta was born; both she and her mother were safe. This experience of faith clearly shows how the relationship between husband and wife grew in Christian virtue, certainly helped by attending Mass and receiving Holy Communion.

Before marriage, Luigi, though he was exceptionally virtuous, honest, and unselfish, did not have a strong faith. Family life was never dull. There was always time for sports, holidays by the sea and in the mountains. Their house was always open to their numerous friends and those who knocked at their door asking for food. During the Second World War their apartment in Via Depretis, near St Mary Major, was a shelter for refugees. Every evening they prayed the Rosary together and the family was consecrated to the Sacred Heart of Jesus, solemnly placed on the mantelpiece of their dining room. They also kept the family holy hour on the eve of the first Friday of the month, and participated in the night vigil prayer, weekend retreats organized by the Monastery of St Paul-Outside-the-Walls, as well as graduate religious courses at the Pontifical Gregorian University, etc.

Maria, who took her maternal and household duties seriously, also found time to pray and write, besides keeping up her demanding apostolic activities, such as supporting the establishment of the Catholic University of the Sacred Heart with Armida Barelli and Fr. Agostino Gemelli and taking part in the General Council of the Italian Catholic Women's Association. She was a volunteer nurse for the Red Cross during the war in Ethiopia and the Second World War, catechist, UNITALSI volunteer with Luigi, and together with him and her children, started a scout group for youth from the poor parts of Rome. They were involved in several forms of marriage and family apostolate.

In the midst of all of her busy daily activities, the flourishing of the first three children's vocations took place, whose developments were followed with love and firmness for a greater generosity and faithfulness to the call of God. In addition, she was willing to offer her fourth child, Enrichetta, to the Lord, if this were asked of her. Then Maria together with her husband, Luigi, undertook a programme for their total response to any call from God, which in the end was the "difficult vow of the most perfect", offered to the Lord in humble obedience to their spiritual father. As is well-known, this vow means the renouncing of marital relations, which the two decided together after 20 years of marriage, when Luigi was 46 years old and Maria 41 (cf. "Maria Corsini e Luigi Beltrame Quattrocchi", by Mons. F. Di Felice in *L'Osservatore Romano*, Italian edition, August 24, 2001).

In November 1951, Luigi died of a heart attack in his home on Via Depretis. After 14 years as a widow, Maria joined Luigi. On 26 August 1965, she died in Enrichetta's arms at their house in the mountains, at Serravalle. In 1993, their daughter, Sr. Maria Cecilia, was united to her parents.

They were a couple who knew how to love and respect each other in the ups and downs of married and family life. They found in the love of God the strength to begin again. They never lost heart despite the negative part of family life: the tragedies of the war, two sons as chaplains in the army, the German occupation of Rome, and lived to see the reconstruction of Italy after the war as they moved forward with the grace of God on the way of heroic sanctity in ordinary life.

The cause for Beatification for Maria and Luigi Beltrame Quattrocchi was opened on 25 November 1994 and, on 21 October 2001, the Holy Father John Paul II raised the married couple to the honour of the altars. On 28 October 2001, the relics of Luigi and Maria were transferred to their crypt in the Shrine of Divino Amore (Divine Love) at Rome.

Reflect on the life of Blessed Luigi Beltrame Quattrocchi and Blessed Maria Corsini:
What struck me about the life of this couple? What can we take from their lives to help strengthen our own marriage?

3. Process/discussion on the material read for homework in Unit One.

Have the couples answer the following questions:

a. At what event did married love move from the natural to the supernatural?

b. How do Catholics interpret the creation of Eve from the rib of Adam?

c. What does it mean for a couple to live in a communion of self-giving love?

d. What are three effects of Original Sin?

e. What is the purpose of suffering?

f. Name three reasons Jesus came to save us.

g. Who is the Bride of Christ?

h. How do Catholics interpret the passage "Wives be submissive to your husbands'" differently than some Protestant denominations?

i. What is a vocation? Why is marriage called a vocation?

j. What are the three properties of Christian marriage?

_____

_____

k. What is the difference between a contract and a covenant?

_____

_____

Group Activity: (25 minutes) (Leaders prepare ahead of time)

A. Hand each group of couples a bag of small household or garage items (such as a sponge, garden gloves, ice cream scoop, egg separator, oil changing funnel, paper towel, picture hanger, etc.).

B. Working in their small groups, have each team member select one item and creatively explore a way to explain a quote from one of the lessons comparing it to the household item they received. (Give each group 10 minutes to work)

C. Have each team present the comparisons to the group.

- For example, the person who has a picture hanger can say,

    Quote from Lesson: "God himself is an eternal exchange of love, Father, Son, and Holy Spirit, and he has destined us to share in that exchange."

    "The picture hangar has a purpose, but without a wall to hang it on and a picture to hang on it, it doesn't really add beauty to the house. Without the Trinity, it is more difficult for us to see God. The actions of Jesus our Redeemer and the Holy Spirit, the Sanctifier, help us experience the love of our Father. Similarly, communion and self-sacrificing love is necessary to the beauty of the family. If one person is off on their own or lost in their own selfishness, not supporting the other, or plugged into the others, then we don't reflect the beauty of God's Trinitarian love as we are called to do."

- Or a simpler example, using a paper towel—Quote: "God's Revelation of himself is not only true and good, but also *beautiful*."

    "Every time I clean the bathroom mirror and faucet with a paper towel, I'll try to remind myself that I need to clean up my soul in order for God's grace to shine in me. That way I will better reflect the beauty of God to my family."

4. Videos: USCCB video on *Marriage: Life and Love* (10 minutes) and video: *Growth in Christ.* (9 minutes)

5. Sharing real life examples on the Unit One topics. Practical applications. (15 minutes)

Table talk in small groups.

a. Share an example of a family you have seen that exemplifies God's Trinitarian love. What do they do that reveals this?

b. Original Sin has led to a distorted version of relationships that affects marriage today. How has Original Sin affected society's understanding of marriage? (e.g., same-sex unions, cohabitation, etc.) (Reference *Marriage: Life and Love*, 22–28)

    c.   Share with the small group a time when you have seen that suffering has strengthened a marriage. Examples can be from your own life or someone else's.

6. Private couple time/ Couple resolution. (15 minutes)

    a.   Couples discuss in private: Out of this unit's lessons and today's discussion, which area should we examine more closely to help our marriage? Consider the exercises from the unit. Which were most challenging? How might God be asking us to "stretch" this workout with a new resolution this week? What would be a good resolution for us to strengthen our marriage this week?

    b.   Our personal resolution for this unit (please write it in the space below).

_____

_____

7. Large Group sharing on practical applications. (10 minutes)

    a.   What can we take away with us today to improve our marriages?

    b.   Leaders can offer open discussion OR have couples down write their answers, turn them in, and read some of them aloud to the group.

8. Warm Up before Unit Two: prepare our minds and hearts.

    a.   Please review the Learning Goals for each of the four exercises in Unit Two.

    b.   Next group workout you should be able to answer the following questions:
        i.   What is a Sacrament and what is its purpose?
       ii.   Christ links what two things in the Sacrament of Matrimony?
      iii.   How does marriage help spouses get to Heaven?
      iv.   What would make marital love incomplete? Guess again.
       v.   What are four effects of Holy Communion?
      vi.   What are five ways frequent recourse to the Sacrament of Penance can improve a marriage?
     vii.   What invisible events occur during the Sacrament of Baptism?

9. Closing Prayer. (5 minutes) Suggested Prayer at end of Unit One, Exercise Two.

10. Social Time.

We Are Not Alone

Unit Two: Week One Exercise

While C.S. Lewis[75] was teaching at Oxford, one of his students said that "we read to know we are not alone." There is a lot of truth and wisdom in his statement. Our experience of reading novels, autobiographies, works of fiction, and history provide us with the assurance that we all share something in common and that we can learn from one another and grow from one another's experiences. Reading is a powerful medium that can foster interpersonal relationships, friendships, and marriages.

When we read Sacred Scripture, God promises us that we are not alone. The Word of God is truly a living Word, and when we read it, we come to discover who we are in relation to God and one another. Jesus came among us to lead us back to God and to lead us out of our sins and selfishness and into greater self-sacrifice and unconditional love. One of the greatest fears today is to be alone, unloved, unwanted, uncared for, alienated, and isolated. Even in some marriages, spouses can find themselves alone, unloved, and isolated. Why? As we spoke about during the first week, Original Sin has left us wounded with an inclination to sin, and when we give into our own selfishness, especially in marriage, we find ourselves alone and alienated from our spouse and ultimately from God.

Chapter 1 of St. John's Gospel reveals:

> In the beginning was the Word,[76] and the Word was with God, and the Word was God. He was in the beginning with God. All things came to be through Him, and without Him nothing came to be. What came to be through Him was life, and this life was the light of the human race; the light shines in the darkness and the darkness has not overcome it … And the Word became flesh

and made His dwelling among us, and we saw His glory as of the Father's only Son, full of grace and truth.[77]

We read how God the Father sent his Only-Begotten Son into the world to dispel our fear of being alone, unloved, unwanted, and isolated from God and one another because of sin. Through the Word of God, we know with certainty that Jesus promised that he would never to leave us and would be with us until the end of time. But now, after his Ascension, how does Jesus remain with us? We know that he established the Church, the visible sign of unity and salvation for the world and that as members of his Body, we share in his life-giving Sacraments. St. Leo the Great said, "What was present in Christ has passed over into his Sacraments." So the Sacraments of the Church are God's way of saying, "I am present among you in a real and tangible way."

"The sacraments are efficacious[78] signs of grace instituted by Christ and entrusted to the Church, by which divine life is dispensed to us"[79] through the work of the Holy Spirit. There are seven Sacraments of the Church.

The Latin word *sacramentum* simply means an oath or pledge or promise to give something, like the covenant promises of the Old Testament. In the early Church, it became associated with an action: the rituals of Christian worship. Around the year 112, a Roman governor named Pliny the Younger recorded that the Christians in his province of Bithynia met before dawn to sing hymns and bind themselves by oath to Christ, as they shared "an ordinary kind of food."[80] Every time we receive a Sacrament, we too bind ourselves by oath to Christ who never ceases to sanctify us and invite us into communion with him.

The *Greek* word most often used for a Sacrament, *mysterion,* stresses the invisible power of the sacramental sign; this term finds its root in the Greek verb "*to close one's eyes.*" It stresses the invisible effects of the Sacrament. Because they are external or perceptible promises of the immense reality of grace, of God's covenant of mercy with his children, Sacraments are signs, but they are effective signs, not merely symbolic ones. They cause what they signify. We see them prefigured throughout the Old Testament and thus fulfilled and instituted by Jesus Christ in the New Testament.

Each Sacrament consists of matter and form. The matter is essentially the physical element, such as water for Baptism, and the form is the words that are said by the minister or ministers of the Sacrament. Through the Sacraments, God communicates something to us that we cannot necessarily see, but we know by faith that this grace has the power to transform our wounded nature. Grace can be defined as a free and unmerited gift of God by which he generously strengthens, elevates, and sanctifies our sinful nature and enables our free wills to choose his life-giving Commandments. Through grace, God grants us a share in his divine nature, or as St. Peter said so well, "His divine power has granted to us all things that pertain to life and godliness … that through these you may … become partakers of the divine nature." So why would God chose this way of communicating himself to us? Or better yet, why would God choose to save us this way?

To say that God became flesh speaks volumes. God became flesh in order to take on our sinful human nature and crucify it to the Cross. By dying in the flesh as a human being, Jesus, both God and man, raised our corruptible nature and clothed it with immortality. St. Bernard once said, "Through flesh came sin and death, so through the flesh our salvation must come."

When you really think about it, Catholicism is a very sensual (corporeal/physical) religion. God utilizes tangible, visible, ordinary, and humble elements of the natural world, such as bread, wine, olive oil, and water in order to communicate his grace to us.

David Lang, author of *Why Matter Matters*, illustrates the importance of material reality in the life of a Christian. He states that God, in his great wisdom, has joined together the material and spiritual realities so as to design a sacramental universe where humble, ordinary natural materials signify divine mysteries and thus convey grace for our salvation.

> It is through this conjunction of matter and form that we grasp the meaning of a sacrament and what it accomplishes. We learn that, by God's almighty power, using these humble signs as instruments, the recipient of the sacrament enters into either a different, or else deeper, supernatural relationship with God and other people. The recipient may be empowered to carry out some new tasks that will be meritorious toward everlasting happiness in heaven. (This is what happens most notably in the Sacraments of Baptism, Confirmation, Holy Orders, as well as Matrimony, but each sacrament has its own unique or special purpose.) If received worthily, every sacrament imparts to the soul the gift of an enhanced participation in God's very own eternal life.[81]

Pope Benedict XVI said that "God touches us through material things, through gifts of creation that he takes up into his service, making them instruments of the encounter between us and himself."

In the Sacrament of Baptism, water is used as the basic element and fundamental condition of all life. But remember, it truly effects what it signifies. When the priest or deacon pours water over the person's head and says, "(name) … I baptize you in the name of the Father, and of the Son, and of the Holy Spirit," the person becomes a new creation and is cleansed of Original Sin; he or she becomes a member of the Church and is incorporated into the Mystical Body of Christ. He or she receives the seven gifts of the Holy Spirit and the virtues of faith, hope, and love. He or she shares in the priestly, prophetic, and kingly role of Christ and is sealed with an indelible mark on his or her soul for eternal life.

What does the Pastoral Letter on Marriage have to say?

> Through Baptism, men and women are transformed, by the power of the Holy Spirit, into a new creation in Christ.[82] This new life in the Holy Spirit heals men and women from sin and elevates them to share in God's very own divine life. It is within this new Christian context that Jesus has raised marriage between the baptized to the dignity of a sacrament.[83] He heals marriage and restores it to its original purity of permanent self-giving in one flesh (See Mt 19:6). (*Marriage: Love and Life*, 30)

It is interesting to note that olive oil is used in four of the seven Sacraments: Baptism, Confirmation, Holy Orders, and the Anointing of the Sick. Olive oil has many functions in the natural world, but sacramentally, it is associated with giving strength and consolation, mission and mercy.

> In popular etymologies a connection was made, even in ancient times, between the Greek word *"elaion"*—oil—and the word *"eleos"*—mercy. In the various sacraments, consecrated oil is always a sign of God's mercy. So the meaning of priestly anointing always includes the mission to bring God's mercy to those we serve. Even the name that we bear as "Christians" contains the mystery of the oil.

> In four sacraments, oil is the sign of God's goodness {mercy} reaching out to touch us: in baptism, in confirmation as the sacrament of the Holy Spirit, in the different grades of the sacrament of holy orders and finally in the anointing of the sick, in which oil is offered to us, so to speak, as God's medicine—as the medicine which now assures us of his mercy and goodness, offering us strength and consolation, yet at the same time points beyond the moment of the illness towards

the definitive healing, the resurrection (cf. Jas 5:14). Thus oil, in its different forms, accompanies us throughout our lives.[84]

Remember the Good Samaritan and how he came along and helped the man half dead? When he saw him, he did not walk away, but instead felt compassion for him. Going over to him, the Samaritan soothed his wounds with olive oil and wine and bandaged them. He brought him to the inn, a symbol of the Church, and paid whatever it took to get him well. This is what Jesus does to us. He welcomes us into this world, wounded and destined for death. He feels compassion for us and desires to cleanse us in the waters of Baptism and confirm us with his life-giving Spirit. As we make our journey through life as prodigal children, Jesus meets us along the way to reconcile us back to God through the Sacrament of Confession. He knows that we need more than just physical food to nourish our bodies, so he gives us bread and wine for the journey, medicine of immortality, which are his Body and Blood in order to feed our souls. When we are sick and dying, he comforts us with the oil of mercy and soothes our wounds of sin, alienation, and the fear of being alone. Many of us, finally, are called to share in a particular vocation in the life of the Church, such as the priesthood, religious life, or marriage.

The Pope said that the priest's mission is to combine, to link the earthly and spiritual realities that appear to be so separate … that is, the world of God far from us, often unknown to human beings, and our human world. The priest is both the dispenser of holy gifts from God and the one who offers humanity's gifts to God. The priest's mission then is to be a mediator, a bridge that connects us to God, to his redemption, to his true light, to his true life.[85] Of course, priests come from families who foster the seed of vocation through prayer, support, and much love.

Marriage is a very special and unique vocation because as husband and wife you have been given the gratuitous grace on your wedding day to make manifest to the world around you Christ's love for his Bride, the Church. As a married couple, you have embraced a special call, a vocation that has as its end, eternal life with God. But you will not accomplish this alone. Once you enter into marriage, you will have the awesome responsibility of helping your spouse and children get to Heaven.

How will you do this? The means to achieve this end consist of living out the vocation of marriage with the continual help of God's grace, which you received in the Sacrament of Matrimony.

Remember, after God created man and saw that it was not good for man to be alone, he gave life to woman from the flesh of man: "That is why a man leaves his father and mother and clings to his wife, and the two of them become one body,"[86] a communion of love. Jesus, though he was in the form of God, emptied himself, and from his wounded side flowed the great Sacrament of Salvation, the Church, to draw all people into God's divine life. Therefore, we are not alone. All of the Sacraments are visible signs of God's grace; they are the means by which we know that we are not alone in our sin and suffering, our failures and our shortcomings, our temptations and trials. If a couple is cooperating with God's grace regularly in the Sacraments, they can be guaranteed to overcome any difficulty, because anything is possible with God.

> "The purpose of the sacraments is to sanctify men, to build up the Body of Christ and, finally, to give worship to God. Because they are signs they also instruct. They not only presuppose faith, but by words and objects they also nourish, strengthen, and express it. That is why they are called 'sacraments of *faith*.'"[87] (CCC 1123)

> Sacraments are "powers that comes forth" from the Body of Christ,[88] which is ever-living and life-giving. They are actions of the Holy Spirit at work in his Body, the Church. They are "the masterworks of God" in the new and everlasting covenant. (CCC 1116)

The Workout

1. What has been your experience of the Sacraments and how have they been transformative in your life? In your marriage?

2. Can you remember times in your marriage when God's grace healed or strengthened you? What was it like?

3. What can you do to be more faithful to the grace that God gives you in the Sacraments?

LET US PRAY

Blessed are you, Lord God of all creation, for you open our eyes, our hearts,
and our minds to your presence in our love and in our world.
Do we ever see and hear and know how close you are to us?
Help us to open our hearts to the power of your grace working in
and though the Sacraments for our strength and healing, consolation, and salvation.
We ask this through Christ our Lord. Amen.

The Visible Sign of an Invisible Reality

Unit Two: Week Two Exercise

LEARNING GOALS

- To explore the meaning and theology of the Sacrament of Matrimony.

- To recognize the effects of grace given through the Sacrament of Matrimony.

WHAT DOES IT MEAN TO SAY THAT THE SACRAMENT OF MATRIMONY IS A VISIBLE SIGN OF AN INVISIBLE REALITY?

What does the Pastoral Letter on Marriage have to say?

In restoring to marriage its original meaning and beauty, Jesus proclaims what the Creator meant marriage to be "in the beginning." He does so because marriage will be made into the visible embodiment of his love for the Church. In his espousal of the Church as his Bride, he fulfills and elevates marriage. He reveals his own love "to the end" (Jn 13:1) as the purest and deepest love, the perfection of all love. In doing this he reveals the deepest meaning of all marital love: self-giving love modeled on God's inner life and love. (*Marriage: Love and Life*, 30)

As we said in the last chapter, God, in his great wisdom, has joined together the material and spiritual realities in a sacramental universe where humble, ordinary natural materials signify divine mysteries and, thus, convey grace for our salvation. Each Sacrament contains a matter and form by which God communicates his grace to us through his Church. So if we take a closer look at marriage, what would be the matter and form of this Sacrament? How does God convey grace in Matrimony, and who is the minister of this Sacrament?

In all of the Sacraments, the priest is the ordinary minister[89] who validly confers or administers the Sacrament. But marriage is a little different. In the Latin rite of the Catholic Church, the man and woman are the ministers of the Sacrament. The matter and form consist in the act of consent by which a man and woman mutually give and accept each other in order to establish an irrevocable covenant, which by its very nature is ordered to their own well-being and to the procreation and education of children. Marriage is based on the mutual consent of the two parties, that is, on their will to give themselves, each to the other, mutually and definitively. After the exchange of vows, if it is between two baptized persons, Jesus bestows his divine grace upon the couple and binds them together in Holy Matrimony. For a Catholic, marriage must be celebrated in the Church,[90] before a priest or deacon and two witnesses, with the approval of the Church.

> In every contract two elements are to be distinguished, the offering of a right and the acceptance of it; the former is the foundation, the latter is the juridical completion. The same holds true of the sacramental contract of marriage; in so far, therefore as an offering of the marriage right is contained in the mutual declaration of consent, we have the matter of the sacrament, and, in so far as a mutual acceptance is contained therein, we have the form.[91]

The couple's irrevocable commitment to each other exchanged in the wedding vows is subsequently fulfilled by a total and unreserved gift of self within the conjugal act. The consummation of marriage thus gives concrete expression to the wedding vows, confirming and strengthening the spouses' total and free consent. Consummation is the realization of the couple's mutual, unitive, and fruitful love. Moreover, a marriage once consummated by the two-in-one-flesh union of the spouses becomes absolutely indissoluble because, as Jesus says, "What God has joined together, no human being must separate."[92] Although not required for validity, consummation, nevertheless, completes the meaning of the Sacrament and renders a validly contracted sacramental marriage indissoluble.

"THIS ONE, AT LAST, IS BONE OF MY BONE AND FLESH OF MY FLESH."

Man and woman communicate love through their physical bodies. Man is made for woman and woman is made for man. This is referred to as the complementarity of the sexes. They complete one another physically and spiritually. "As a consequence [of God's plan for marriage], husband and wife, through the mutual gift of themselves, which is specific to them alone, develop that communion of persons, in which they perfect each other, so that they may cooperate with God in the generation and rearing of new lives."[93]

Remember what Adam said when God created his wife, Eve: "This one, at last, is bone of my bones and flesh of my flesh."[94] The day you exchanged your vows with your spouse, you became one flesh. What does this mean? God chose to reveal in the most intimate way how man and woman become one flesh: The bride comes forth from the bridegroom, and, consequently, the two not only complete one another but complement one another, in that where the flesh is one, so is the spirit. So you could say that, as a result of your exchange of vows, you have finally found your lifelong companion, your true love. None of this could be possible without God and his divine grace.

As Christians, we believe that it takes three to get married: God, man, and woman. Without God, marital love is incomplete. The presence of Jesus at the Wedding Feast at Cana is a sign that he not only blesses the love between man and woman but also transforms it into a Sacrament, a visible sign by which he gives us grace. In creation, God instituted marriage, and Jesus, the God-Man, confirmed it and raised it to the dignity of a Sacrament. Human love, being elevated to the supernatural order, is infinitely deepened and enriched in the Sacrament of Matrimony. Through this Sacrament, God irradiates and enlightens human love by his divine love, thus transforming something good into something holy.

By taking water and changing it into wine at the Wedding Feast at Cana, Jesus demonstrated the transforming power of God's grace. Wine was regarded as an indispensable element in meals and celebrations (especially marriages), so when the host ran out of wine, Jesus not only performed a miracle that allowed the festivities to continue, but most importantly, he also showed us that what was human, the love of husband and wife, is now divine. Thus, husband and wife are joined in a covenant of unconditional love and sealed with an indissoluble bond by God's divine grace so as to resemble the union of Christ with his Church.

THE SACRIFICE OF CHRIST ON THE CROSS, RE-PRESENTED AT EACH MASS, IS A MODEL FOR THE SELF-GIVING THAT TAKES PLACE IN MARRIAGE

This is God's divine plan. God's divine plan for marriage manifests the sacramental union of man and woman, which symbolizes the intimate union between Christ, the Bridegroom, and his Bride, the Church. In the Sacrament of Matrimony, our Lord, who died for our salvation, gives couples a grace that will daily sustain and increase their love for one another. This grace will help you want to prefect yourself and your beloved, to overcome your selfishness, and to give yourself completely.

The Wedding Feast at Cana and all sacramental marriages are thus intimately related to the Sacrament of the Eucharistic. We heard how Eve was taken from the side of Adam to symbolize oneness, unity, and communion between the spouses. The miracle at the wedding feast pointed to a greater and more awesome mystery: the communion of love that would become a reality for those who share in the Body and Blood of Christ. The Blood that came forth from the side of Christ as he hung from the Cross enables us to share intimately in the divine life of God.

"For the miraculous transformation of water into wine at Cana prefigures the transubstantiation at Mass, when our Lord, acting through his priest, changes wine into his Precious Blood. And just as the male-female couple at Cana were united in one flesh to each other, so also we become spiritually one with Christ by receiving his Body and Blood physically (under the appearances of bread and wine) in Holy Communion."[95] Just as the new life of a child is begotten by the husband's "seed of life" in the womb of his wife, so is the spiritual growth of the Church's members actualized by the Groom Christ's flesh (the Bread of Life). The Mass therefore takes on the aspect of a wedding banquet.[96]

The reception of Holy Communion should be a mystical experience that sustains us and provides lasting and meaningful spiritual support and consolation. But most importantly, the sacrifice of Christ on the Cross, re-presented at each Mass, is a model for the self-giving that occurs in marriage. Husbands and wives offer themselves to each other, surrendering themselves for the sake of the good of the other. When married couples worship together, there is a spiritual communion that takes place when kneeling side-by-side, heads bowed in prayer. The bond of love is renewed; souls are opened to the Spirit's healing. And so, the Eucharist must be at the heart of your lives, because communion with God here on earth is a foretaste of what our communion will be like with God in Heaven. Your communion on earth with Christ in the Eucharist will strengthen your communion in marriage.

When we are properly disposed to receive the Sacraments, especially the Eucharist, God's grace can purify our human nature of all our selfishness and self-love, perfecting us and making us holy. The grace that was given to you on your wedding day is a grace that keeps on giving. Never take it for granted and never underestimate the transformative power it can have in your marriage. Jesus said, "Ask and it will be given to you; seek and you will find; knock and the door will be opened to you."[97]

What does the Pastoral Letter on Marriage have to say?

By using the image of the relationship between bridegroom and bride to explain the relationship between Christ and the Church, the Scriptures are appealing to a natural human relationship that is already well known. All of us know something about the depth, the intimacy, and the beauty of the gift of self that occurs in the marriage of husband and wife. The Scriptures also show us, however, that Christ's love for the Church surpasses natural human love. Christ's love for the Church is a love of complete self-giving. This love is most completely expressed by his Death on the Cross. Christian marriage aspires not only to natural human love, but to Christ's love for the Church:

> Husbands, love your wives, even as Christ loved the church and handed himself over for her to sanctify her, cleansing her by the bath of water with the word, that he might present to himself the church in splendor, without spot or wrinkle or any such thing, that she might be holy and without blemish. (Eph 5:25–27)

Christian spouses are called to this imitation of Christ, an imitation that is possible only because, in the Sacrament of Matrimony, the couple receives a participation in his love. As a Sacrament, marriage signifies and makes present in the couple Christ's total self-gift of love. Their mutual gift of self, conferred in their promises of fidelity and *love to the end*, becomes a participation in the *love to the end* by which Christ gave himself to the Church as to a Spouse (see Jn 13:1).

> When Christian couples receive the grace of the Sacrament of Matrimony, Christ dwells with them, gives them the strength to take up their crosses and so follow him, to rise again after they have fallen, to forgive one another, to bear one another's burdens, to "be subject to one another out of reverence for Christ, and to love one another with supernatural, tender, and fruitful love."[98]

By the power of the Holy Spirit, spouses become willing to do the acts and courtesies of love toward each other, regardless of the feelings of the moment. They are formed by the self-giving love of Christ for his Church as his Bride, and so they are enabled to perform acts of self-giving love to the benefit of themselves, their families, and the whole Church. The Sacrament of Matrimony, like the Sacrament of Holy Orders, is a Sacrament "directed toward the salvation of others; if [these sacraments] contribute as well to personal salvation, it is through service to others that they do so."[99] Those who receive these sacraments are given a special consecration in Christ's name to carry out the duties of their particular state in life. (*Marriage: Love and Life*, 32–34)

THE EFFECTS OF GRACE GIVEN
THROUGH THE SACRAMENT OF MATRIMONY:

- ❧ Helps you grow in holiness.

- ❧ Deepens your relationship with one another and with God.

- ❧ Gives you strength to overcome difficulties and to find in them opportunities for spiritual and personal growth.

- ❧ Guides you in making important decisions together.

- ❧ Enables you to communicate openly and honestly with one another.

- ❧ Helps you to turn away from the sin and temptation we all face throughout our lives.

- ❧ Shows you truly how to love and forgive as God loves and forgives.

The Workout

1. Remember when we said, "I do" to each other in our wedding vows? How have we strengthened those vows over the years? How have we undermined them through our words and actions?

2. What are some acts of courtesy we can do for each other that can help strengthen the grace we received on our wedding day?

3. What does it mean that we are called to love like Christ loves? What are some practical examples?

4. Remember a time when your spouse acted with total self-giving. How did you respond?

5. What can we do to remind ourselves during the day of the graces available for our marriage?

LET US PRAY

Our Father, who art in Heaven, hallowed be thy name. Thy kingdom come;
thy will be done on earth as is in Heaven.
Give us this day our daily bread; and forgive us our trespasses,
as we forgive those who trespass against us; and lead us not into temptation,
but deliver us from evil. Amen.

$\mathcal{O}$NE IN $\mathcal{B}$ODY AND $\mathcal{S}$OUL

Unit Two: Week Three Exercise

LEARNING GOALS

  ❧ To discover a new appreciation for the Eucharist and its intimate connection with the Sacrament of Matrimony.

  ❧ To understand why the Mass is at the heart of our lives as Catholics.

The Sacrament of Holy Communion is one of the Sacraments that will sustain and strengthen your marriage.

What does the Pastoral Letter on Marriage have to say?

A family matures as a domestic church as it ever more deeply immerses itself within the life of the Church. This especially means that fathers and mothers, by their example and teaching, help their children come to an appreciation of the need for continual conversion and repentance from sin, encouraging a love for and participation in the Sacrament of Reconciliation.

Moreover, since it is Christ's presence within the family that truly makes it a domestic church, their participation in the Eucharist, especially the Sunday Eucharist, is particularly important. In the Eucharist, the family joins itself to Jesus' sacrifice to the Father for the forgiveness of sins. Furthermore, it is in receiving Holy Communion that the members of the family are most fully united to the living and glorious Christ and so to one another and to their brothers and sisters throughout the world. It is here, in the risen and Eucharistic Christ, that spouses, parents, and children express and nurture most fully the love of the Father and the bond of the Spirit. (*Marriage: Love and Life*, 41–42)

There was a woman who had painstakingly journeyed from complete atheism to the Catholic Faith. She looked into many non-Christian religions and Christian denominations and had come to understand that belief in God is more rational than atheism.

One day she asked an evangelical clergyman to help her find God. The best he could do was to say that God is everywhere. The woman said that his answer left her feeling upset and discouraged. She said it was no use telling her that God was everywhere; she wanted to find God somewhere. The Italian author, Luigi Santucci, had a profound, yet simple way to express how God, in Christ Jesus, at the Last Supper decided to stay and live among us forever.

> At this point I see his eyes wandering around over the remains of the bread on the table-cloth, and then shining with an ineffable inspiration: this, this would be his hiding place. That's where he would take refuge.
>
> That night they wouldn't capture him in his entirety; they'd think they'd done so, they'd think they'd dragged him away from his companions … he had hidden himself in that bread. Rather as in Galilee, when they wanted to seize him and kill him or make him king, he had the knack of hiding himself and disappearing from sight. So he stretched out his hand over the already broken bread, broke it into smaller bits and, raising it in the air, pronounced the words: "This is my body, it's been given for you."
>
> He really did leave to his followers a Christ that no-one could ferret out and wrench from their hands. A little earlier Jesus had washed their feet; he degraded himself with the muddiest part of their physical being. Now he wanted to do more: he wanted to go down into their souls … and gradually melt into all the fibers of their body.
>
> The primary significance of the Eucharist isn't mystical but physical, almost a clinging to the material being of his friends who would stay on and live. He said "This is my body" with a tenderness that first and foremost exalted it itself. Not "This is my spirit" or "This is generalized goodness or well-being" possibly they wouldn't have known what to do with such things.
>
> It was necessary to them that he should remain with the only thing we really know and attach our hearts and memories to: the body; and that it should be a desirable, acceptable body.
>
> That evening Christ measured out for us all the millions of evenings before we'd see him face to face; he measured out the long separation. He knew that men forget things within a few days … That's why he looked over that table-cloth for the easiest, most familiar and most concrete thing: bread. So as to quench hunger and give pleasure. Above all so as to stay … he had to throw between himself and me that never-ending bridge of bread … "Do this in memory of me."[100]

As the *Catechism* points out, the Eucharist is "the memorial of the love with which he [Christ] loved us 'to the end,'"[101] even to the giving of his life. In his Eucharistic presence he remains mysteriously in our midst as the one who loved us and gave himself up for us,[102] and "he remains under the signs that express and communicate this love."[103]

On the day of Passover, the Apostles would have taken the lamb to the Temple and offered it as a sacrifice. They would have prepared the water for the ablutions, the bitter herbs (which were representative of the bitterness of slavery), the unleavened bread (in memory of their ancestors who had to interrupt their baking in the sudden flight from Egypt), and the wine. And then, while they were eating, surrounded by those whom Jesus had chosen and who believed in him, he would have given them his final teaching: the institution of the Eucharist, the visible sign of God's sacrificial love and mercy; and the institution of the new and everlasting priesthood, the office that would perpetuate and make present this ongoing sacrifice for future generations.

This is what eventually led the woman, who was searching for God somewhere, into the Catholic Church. She found the Blessed Sacrament on the altar to be the "somewhere" of God's encounter with us. God desires to make himself present within the "somewhere" of our existence.

There are many people who can accept that God is everywhere, but who cannot conceive of encountering God somewhere. Many people today are embracing a New Age or Pantheist ideology, which essentially teaches that "All is God" and that the "sacredness of nature" or the universe is the only thing deserving the deepest kind of reverence, while they desperately try to search for the "god" within themselves. This obviously denies any personal relationship with a Creator God. Materialism (another threat to finding God somewhere) goes so far as to deny the reality of the transcendent and asserts we should view everything, people and material things (creation), as ends in themselves without God as the final end/cause of existence. (This ideology has devastating consequences: it leads us to use, manipulate, and destroy the gifts of God's creation and most importantly, the precious gift of human life.)

As Catholic Christians, nevertheless, we evangelize and witness to our secular, materialistic culture that God became incarnate in a particular culture and religion, was born of a Virgin, and died for our salvation so as invite us to enter into communion with him.

At Mass, we come together as the People of God, as his Body, the Church, in a particular place, at a particular time, to make present now what happened then in the Upper Room and on the Cross.

Our Lord suffered on the Cross on the first Good Friday, but his sacrifice is made actual at every moment of history. His sacrifice is not just something that occurred two thousand years ago; it is a drama as real now as then.

What happens is that the Mass incorporates us into the present redeeming act of Christ or as Pope Benedict XVI said … "introduces us into the Being of Christ, into Divine Being." That is why we use the expressions *to reenact, to re-actualize, and to re-present.*

Our Lord took the occasion of the Last Supper to create the somewhere of his presence for those who love him. The somewhere is his Church, the Body of Christ; and those who gather around the priests of the Church, who have been ordained to offer this sacrifice to the Father, become the living signs of unity and salvation in the world.

Jesus will be sacramentally present in his Church until the end of the world. As Catholics, we truly believe that Jesus' words over the unleavened bread and cup of wine at the Last Supper transform the wine into his own Blood and the bread into his Body.

And when the Apostles drank from the cup and ate the bread, they actually partook of the Body and Blood of the Son of God, under the appearance of bread and wine. Thus the New Covenant was ratified. So the Sacrament of the Eucharist not only signifies a family bond between God and his people, but also actually affects it. Consequently, the Eucharist is a sign that makes us family, part of the Mystical Body of Christ destined as people to become partakers of the divine nature.

We all have a desire for this union, for this sanctification, because by participating in the very life of the Creator, we are being transformed into the likeness of his being and we know that if he does not remain spiritually and physically in us and we in him, he becomes an abstraction, a concept, or nice idea that is unable to raise us up out of our sinfulness now or in eternity. Consequently, we end up losing our way and become abandoned once again to our foolish and sinful ways.

Again and again, we participate in the Holy Sacrifice of the Mass, because we know what it means to be satisfied and yet to remain hungry—hungry for the life and union that is promised to those who live and would die for the Body and Blood of Jesus Christ.

Attending Mass on Sundays and Holy Days of Obligation is an absolute requirement for Catholics. The mandate is enshrined in the Third Commandment as well as in the first of the seven "Precepts of the Church." Those who believe that Christ becomes truly present in the Eucharist and that this Sacrament re-presents his sacrifice on Calvary through the actions of the priest at the Altar cannot imagine absenting themselves from Mass.

(The following excerpt is from Dorothy Day's Autobiography: *The Long Loneliness*. The chapter "Love Overflows" speaks about her experience of being a mother, her conversion to the Catholic Faith, and the importance of practicing the Catholic Faith, especially on Sunday).

> "*Thou shall love the Lord thy God with thy whole heart and with thy whole soul and with thy whole mind.*" This is the First Commandment. The problem is how to love God? We are only too conscious of the hardness of our hearts, and in spite of all that religious writers tell us about feeling not being necessary, we do want to feel and so know that we love God.
>
> "Thou wouldst not seek Him if thou hadst not already found Him," Pascal says, and it is true too that you love God if you want to love Him. One of the disconcerting facts about the spiritual life is that God takes you at your word. Sooner or later one is given the chance to prove his love. The very word "*diligo*," that Latin word used for "love," means "*I prefer.*" It was all very well to love God and His works, in the beauty of His creation which was crowned for me by the birth of my child. Forster [her husband] had made the physical world come alive for me and had awakened in my heart a flood of gratitude. The final object of this love and gratitude was God.
>
> No human creature could receive or contain so vast a flood of love and joy as I often felt after the birth of my child. With this came the need to worship, to adore. I had heard many say that they wanted to worship God in their own way and did not need a Church in which to praise Him, nor a body of people with whom to associate themselves. But I did not agree to this. My very experience ... my whole make-up, led me to want to associate myself with others, with the masses, in loving and praising God.
>
> Without even looking into the claims of the Catholic Church, I was willing to admit that for me she was the one true Church. She has come down through the centuries since the time of Peter, and far from being dead, she claimed and held allegiance of the masses of people in all cities where I had lived. They poured in and out of her doors on Sundays and Holy Days, for novenas and missions. What if they were compelled to come in by the law of the Church, which said they were guilty of mortal sin if they did not go to Mass every Sunday? They obeyed that law. They were given a chance to show their preference. They accepted the Church. It may have been an unthinking, unquestioning faith, and yet the chance certainly came, again and again, "*Do I prefer the Church to my own will,*" even if it was only the small matter of sitting at home on Sunday morning with the papers? And the choice was the Church.
>
> I had known enough of love to know that a good healthy family life was so near to Heaven as one could get in this life. There was another sample of Heaven, of the enjoyment of God. The very sexual act itself was used again and again in Scripture as a figure of the beatific vision ... It was through a whole love, both physical and spiritual, I came to know God.

From the time Tamar Teresa was born I was intent on having her baptized. What driving power joy is! When I was unhappy and repentant in the past I turned to God, but it was my joy at having given birth to a child that made me do something definite. I wanted Tamar to have a way of life and instruction. We all crave order, and in the Book of Job, hell is described as a place where no order is. I felt that belonging to the Church would bring that order into her life which I felt my own had lacked … I felt that only faith in Christ could give the answer. I knew little about the Sacraments, and yet here I believed, knowing that without them Tamar would not be Catholic. Tamar was baptized in July … in the Church of Our Lady, Help of Christians, the seed of life was implanted in her and she was made a child of God.[104]

What does the Pastoral Letter on Marriage have to say?

In the Eucharist, Catholic married couples meet the one who is the source of their marriage. "In this sacrifice of the new and eternal covenant, Christian spouses encounter the source from which their own marriage covenant flows, is interiorly structured and continuously renewed."[105] Pope Benedict XVI explains how, in the Eucharist, the very meaning of marriage is transfigured: "the imagery of marriage between God and Israel is now realized in a way previously inconceivable: it had meant standing in God's presence, but now it becomes union with God through sharing in Jesus' self-gift, sharing in his body and blood."[106]

Moreover, Pope Benedict points out that the sacramental mysticism he mentions is "social in character."[107] The Eucharist "makes the Church" because "those who receive the Eucharist are united more closely to Christ. Through it Christ unites them to all the faithful in one body—the Church."[108] In the Eucharist, spouses encounter the love that animates and sustains their marriage, the love of Christ for his Church. This encounter enables them to perceive that their marriage and family are not isolated units, but rather that they are to reach out in love to the broader Church and world of which they are a living part.

Marriage continually sends the believing Catholic back again to the Eucharist. Here is where the gratitude that has become a life-giving habit in a marriage can be fully and completely expressed. "Eucharist," after all, means "thanksgiving." In the Eucharist one thanks God the Father for his supreme gift, the gift of his risen Son, who, in turn, bestows most fully the divine life and love of the Holy Spirit.

Marriage is a school for gratitude. By celebrating the Sacrament of Marriage, "Christian spouses profess their gratitude to God for the sublime gift bestowed on them of being able to live in their married and family lives the very love of God for people and that of the Lord Jesus for the Church."[109] (*Marriage: Love and Life*, 54–55)

If someone gives you a gift the natural response is to say "thank you." But if someone gives you the gift of their life, a simple "thank you" would never be enough. Jesus' act of self-sacrifice requires an infinite amount of thanksgiving. All of us were destined for death because of sin, but because of God's gracious mercy and the sacrifice of his only Son, we are now destined for eternal communion with the Blessed Trinity in Heaven. That is why the Eucharist in Greek means "thanksgiving."

In the Eucharist, God gave us the perfect act of thanksgiving, worship, praise, adoration, and reparation for sin until he comes again in glory. This action, the offering of Christ's sacrifice to the Father, is the perfect act of thanksgiving. God gives this act of thanksgiving to us because our thanksgiving by itself can never be enough. Although our thanksgiving adds nothing to his greatness, it allows us to grow in his grace.

When Jesus said, "This is my Body," he literally meant, "This is myself." Each time we receive Holy Communion and share in this feast, we experience a sense of joy at the thought of knowing that God desires our company; he desires to share not just a part of himself, but his entire life with us, in conversation, friendship, and communion.

Ronald Knox relates a story of a priest who after distributing Communion in St. Peter's Square with thousands of people crying out *Padre, Padre, per favore,* (Father, Father, please), remarked:

> Throughout the long history of the Church, through a whole series of dramatic successes and failures, despite the stupidity and wickedness of so many Christians, the command *do this in memory of me* has been and continues to be obeyed.

> It is as though Christians, in all of their sin, have realized from the beginning that the spiritual life depends upon the Eucharist the way that physical life depends upon food, oxygen, and water.

> Those people in St. Peter's Square embodied a truth that is deep in our Catholic Tradition, though too infrequently stated: "The Eucharist is not a luxury, but a necessity, for without it, we would, in the spiritual sense, starve to death."

WHAT ARE SOME OF THE EFFECTS OF HOLY COMMUNION?

ல் You experience communion with Christ himself.

ல் You participate in Christ's saving Death and Resurrection.

ல் It increases your love for others, especially your spouse, impelling you to serve one another out of reverence for Christ.

ல் It reinforces the unity of the Church as the Mystical Body of Christ.

ல் It removes venial sins and helps to preserve you from mortal sin.

ல் It diminishes sinful love of self and strengthens you against temptation.

> When a soul has understood the greatness of … life, when it has grasped that the wellspring of it is to be found in union with Christ through faith and charity, it aspires to the perfection of that union; it seeks the fullness of life that it should, in accordance with the thought of God, possess within itself.

> It is indeed true that all the efforts of human nature, left to itself a distance from Christ, are not able to advance us one step in the achieving of that union, in the birth and development of the life it brings forth. It is God alone who gives us the seed germ and the growth; we care for the plant, we water it, but the fruits of life are produced only because God causes the sap of his grace to rise within us.

> God gives us incomparable means of keeping alive this sap within us, "He who eats my flesh and drinks my blood remains in me and I in him … and I will raise him up on the last day."[110]

The Workout

1. Describe God as you perceive him. What can each of us do to make our relationship with God more personal? What can each of us do to strengthen our relationships within the Church community?

2. What has been our experience of going to Mass? Have we experienced the power of Christ truly present in the Eucharist?

3. If we attend Mass regularly with our spouse and/or children, have we experienced God's healing grace? If we have not been attending Mass every Sunday, why not? How we can plan better to commit to Mass each week?

4. In trials and temptation, how has Jesus in the Eucharist given us the strength to move forward, to root out our vices and avoid sin?

LET US PRAY

Lord, we thank you for being veiled in the mystery of the host,
so fully present that you yourself teach us to pray and help us to live.
Lord you know how weak and distracted we are and how we consider everything more important
than you; but again and again you guide us back to the Church where you dwell,
so that we may be fed once again with your Body and Blood in order for you to change us
and shepherd our soul into eternal life. Amen.

"Father, Forgive Them"

Unit Two: Week Four Exercise

LEARNING GOALS

- ❧ To discover a new appreciation for the Sacrament of Penance and its intimate connection with the Sacrament of Matrimony.

- ❧ To understand why regular Confession is crucial to the success of marriage and one's spiritual life.

The Sacrament of Matrimony is another very powerful Sacrament that will assist you in marriage and help heal the wounds of sin and division.

What does the Pastoral Letter on Marriage have to say?

When Christian couples receive the grace of the Sacrament of Matrimony,

> Christ dwells with them, gives them the strength to take up their crosses and so follow him, to rise again after they have fallen, to forgive one another, to bear one another's burdens, to "be subject to one another out of reverence for Christ," and to love one another with supernatural, tender, and fruitful love. (CCC 1642)

> The imitation of the love of Christ for the Church also calls for a healing of the relationship between man and woman. (*Marriage: Love and Life*, 33–34)

Confession is a Sacrament in which Jesus Christ himself, through the actions of the priest, forgives the sins committed after Baptism. It is important for all people but an essential tool for married persons. We all need to forgive and to be forgiven, and this Sacrament will heal the wounds in you and in your marriage.

Many people avoid Confession because they feel embarrassed or humiliated by the thought of acknowledging actions of which they are not proud. We sometimes prefer to bury our sins under the rug, trying to forget about them, and just move on. Or we might believe we can ask God to forgive us in the sanctuary of our own prayer, and just leave it at that.

For venial sins, this is indeed the case. We need not receive sacramental absolution in order to be forgiven. Mortal sins, however, *require* that we confess them to a priest and receive absolution. But just because Confession is not necessary for the forgiveness of venial sins does not mean that it is not helpful. In fact, it is more than helpful.

Those who only receive this Sacrament when they really need it (i.e., when they have committed a *mortal* sin), can find it extremely difficult to break the inertia of not going, and actually enter the confessional. How much easier and less threatening Confession can be if received regularly, perhaps once a month. In the end, it is much easier to make a special trip for Confession after a serious sin if receiving the Sacrament is regular practice anyway.

Those who confess their sins regularly report positive effects on their spiritual lives and in their relationships. Holding ourselves accountable and acknowledging our faults and failures, our weaknesses and misdeeds, is an immensely human act. It places us in touch with our souls and puts us into an incredibly receptive spiritual posture. People who do not go to Confession regularly rarely make thorough examinations of conscience. They generally just wait and respond only if something they have done starts to bother them or makes them feel uneasy. If the nagging will not go away, they seek to do something about it. An examination of conscience helps us to recognize the sins that do not bother us so much and that we might otherwise ignore. All sin damages our relationship with God and with one another, and even the sins we "forget" will have lasting effects on our spiritual and relational life.

Conscience and Confession: Coming Back to God

FRANCIS CARDINAL GEORGE, OMI, March 30, 2003

About 80 years ago, the noted English journalist and thinker, G.K. Chesterton, came into the Catholic Church. Surprised by his conversion, some of his friends asked him, "Why?" Chesterton answered, "To get my sins forgiven." The forgiveness of sins begins with baptism. We enter the baptismal font creatures of God and emerge disciples of Jesus Christ. Our relationship to God changes because we are in Christ. That baptismal relationship cannot be abolished, but it can be broken, become merely formal, no longer life-giving, if we deliberately sin grievously after baptism, Christ has given the Church another sacrament, a "second baptism." In the sacrament of penance or reconciliation, Christ uses the ordained priest and the ministry of the Church to get rid of people's sins after baptism. Sin confessed and adequately repented is abolished and the sinner can begin again his or her life in Christ. Sin which is not deadly or mortal is also forgiven, of course, through the Eucharist and through asking for forgiveness in our daily prayer.

Jokes are sometimes made about Catholic guilt. But guilt is healthy if it is a sign that one has taken responsibility for one's life and actions. Guilt becomes morbid or obsessive only if one is never able to escape from one's sins. Practicing Catholics acknowledge their failures, as measured by objective moral norms, but they know the forgiveness of God. Only when people feel they cannot be forgiven does life become a horror story.

Penance is the sacrament we need and use all through our lives as Christ's disciples in order to be fully reconciled with God when our sins distance us from him or even break our relationship to him. In the beautiful words of St. Francis de Sales, penance is "the sacrament of reconciled friends." It is the sacrament of ongoing conversion, for there are depths in the personalities of each one of us which have still to be brought under Christ's sway.

We discover where we are in our journey toward holiness in examining our conscience. Such an examination helps us to see us as God sees us. Even though it seems discouraging to dig into our sinfulness and lay it before the Church, it is also liberating to discover how God is working constantly to transform us and how whatever we do, no matter how sinful it might be, can be healed by God's mercy. Recalling our sins by name, preparing for the sacrament by examining the state of our lives frankly and honestly before God is necessary for conversion, for turning from our sins and back to God. The examination of conscience is thorough when it looks not only at our actions but also at our thoughts and words and omissions (see the *Catechism of the Catholic Church*, 2041 ff.) and does so using the Gospel and the moral teaching of the Church as a sure and certain norm.

The basic requirements for a good Confession, besides consciousness of one's sins, is the intention to return to God, as the prodigal son in the Gospel wants to return to his father. (Luke 15:11–32) What the prodigal son finds on his return is a self-righteous brother, who doesn't believe in forgiveness, and a merciful father, who is eager to forgive. But not even God can forgive someone who is not sorry for his sins. A profound sorrow for our sins and a desire to make amends are part of the contrition necessary to receive the sacrament of reconciliation. Another part of contrition is the resolution, out of the love one has for God, not to sin again. Without such a resolution not to sin again, our contrition can be a mere feeling or sentiment which vanishes as quickly as it comes and leaves us captive to habits of sin.

How does one receive the sacrament of penance? After examining his conscience, the penitent approaches a priest with contrite heart and lays his or her sins before the Church. It is customary to begin the confession of sin by asking the priest for his blessing. Then the penitent says how long it has been since his or her last good confession. Sometimes the priest will read a brief passage of Scripture to remind the penitent of God's desire to forgive our sins. Then the penitent confesses all the grave sins committed since his or her last confession and often adds venial sins that particularly trouble the penitent. Those who have difficulty in confessing should simply ask the priest for help.

The priest hearing the confession may ask a question in order to clarify something that has been confessed. This is not out of curiosity but only to help the penitent make a complete and integral confession. The priest receiving a confession in Christ's name is bound in the strictest way and without exception never to reveal anything he has heard in a sacramental confession. Respect for the penitent's conscience governs the rules for the sacrament. This "seal of confession" enrages some people and has been attacked by enemies of the Church over the centuries. It is being attacked in some state legislatures today.

The priest may give his penitent some spiritual advice. He will ask the penitent to accept some small penance and then he will wait for the penitent to express sorrow for his sins. This can be done in one's own words, rejecting sin, expressing love of God and one's firm purpose not to sin gain. There are, however, set acts of contrition which mention all this, and it is useful to memorize one of them. I still use the act of contrition I learned in the second grade.

The priest then declares: "Through the ministry of the Church, may God give you pardon and peace; and I absolve you from yours sins, in the name of the Father and of the Son and of the Holy Spirit." To these words of absolution, the penitent responds "Amen." Here the compassion and boundless mercy of our heavenly Father meet our honest contrition. We are forgiven and set free. As Pope John Paul II has written on Penance and Reconciliation, "Our faith can give us certainty that at that moment every sin is forgiven and blotted out by the mysterious intervention of our Savior." The absolution is not some general declaration that God forgives sins. It is, rather, an act of Christ which restores full friendship and communion with God by judging the sins and the repentance of the particular penitent who has just confessed. The priest may conclude with a few verses of Scripture or with a prayer to the Blessed Virgin Mary on behalf of the penitent whom he tells to go in peace.

Various booklets are available to help one prepare for and receive the sacrament of reconciliation. The United States Conference of Catholic Bishops has produced an excellent guide, "Celebrating the Sacrament of Penance: Questions and Answers" (800-235-8722). A useful and cost-free leaflet produced locally is "Short Guide for Confession," available from the Midwest Theological Forum (630-739-9750). Both leaflets are available also in Spanish.

Only if we are fully reconciled to God can we become effective peacemakers among ourselves. The world needs peacemakers. The world needs reconciled and forgiven sinners. The world needs saints, and God is eager to make saints. In an address to Americans several years ago, the Holy Father said, "To those who have been far away from the sacrament of reconciliation and forgiving love, I make this appeal; come back to this source of grace. Do not be afraid! Christ himself is waiting for you. He will heal you, and you will be at Peace with God."

Sincerely yours in Christ,

Francis Cardinal George, OMI
Archbishop of Chicago

The three words, "I love you," are probably the three most important words in a marriage. The three words, "I am sorry," run a close second. Sacramental Confession prepares us for working through the reconciliation we need in all of our relationships, especially the marriage relationship. Even the healthiest marriages experience hurt and sin, and learning to express contrition for sins, even if those "sins" are small ones, is an essential part of married life.

What are some of the effects of sacramental Confession?

- It forgives sin, thereby restoring sanctifying grace.

- It remits eternal punishment caused by mortal sin.

- It imparts actual grace to avoid sin in the future.

- It reconciles the penitent person with the Church.

- It remits part of purgatorial punishment.

- It gives peace of conscience and spiritual consolation.[111]

Pope Pius XII outlined some of the benefits of frequent Confession in his encyclical, *Mystici Corporis Christi* (June 29, 1943):[112]

- Genuine self-knowledge is increased.

- Bad habits are corrected.

- Conscience is purified.

- Christian humility grows.

- The will is strengthened.

- Lukewarmness and spiritual neglect are resisted.

- Self-control is increased.

> Spouses are therefore the permanent reminder to the Church of what happened on the Cross; they are for one another and for the children witnesses to the salvation in which the Sacrament makes them sharers. Of this salvation event marriage, like every Sacrament, is a memorial, actuation, and prophecy: "As a memorial, the Sacrament gives them the grace and duty of commemorating the great works of God and of bearing witness to them before their children. As actuation, it gives them the grace and duty of putting into practice in the present, towards each other and their children, the demands of a love which forgives and redeems. As prophecy, it gives them the grace and duty of living and bearing witness to the hope of the future encounter with Christ."[113]

$\mathcal{T}$HE $\mathcal{W}$ORKOUT

1. How have we experienced forgiveness in our marriage? Has it been difficult? If so, why?

2. How has the Sacrament of Penance healed the wounds of sin and division in our marriage? If we have not been to confession in a while, what is keeping us from going?

3. Scripture tells us that God's grace is sufficient for us. Do we believe that God's grace in the Sacraments will be the source of nourishment, strength, healing, and salvation for us?

4. Do we truly believe that being forgiven by God can help us forgive one another? How can this work in our marriage?

5. How do we provide emotional and spiritual support to each other in marriage when we confront trials, arguments, and disagreements? How can we improve on this?

6. How easy or difficult has it been to say, "I'm sorry"? Think of some examples when it was difficult or when it was easy to say, "I'm sorry."

LET US PRAY

"Love is patient, love is kind. It is not jealous, (love) is not pompous, it is not inflated,
it is not rude, it does not seek its own interests, it is not quick-tempered, it does not brood over injury,
it does not rejoice over wrongdoing but rejoices with the truth. It bears all things,
believes all things, hopes all things, endures all things. Love never fails."[114]

O God, whose mercy is endless and whose treasury of compassion inexhaustible,
look kindly upon us and increase your mercy within us,
that in difficult moments we might not despair nor become despondent,
but with great confidence submit ourselves to your most holy will which is love and mercy itself. Amen.

*G*ROUP *W*ORKOUT

Unit Two:
Espoused Forever in the Sacraments of the Church.

- What was present in Christ has passed over into his Sacraments.

- The Sacrament of Matrimony: a foretaste of the wedding banquet in Heaven.

- The Sacraments of the Church that assist and support marriage: Communion and Confession and Cardinal George's article on Confession.

- Fostering vocations in the family, the Church, and society: A call to service for the sake of mission.

MONTHLY GROUP MEETING: SECOND UNIT

1. Prayer (10 minutes including table reflection)—Reflection on 1 Corinthians 13:1–8.

Leader slowly and carefully reads the prayer aloud. Couples follow along. Ask each person to underline or write down a phrase that stood out for him or her:

> If I speak in human and angelic tongues but do not have love, I am a resounding gong or a clashing cymbal.
>
> And if I have the gift of prophecy and comprehend all mysteries and all knowledge; if I have all faith so as to move mountains but do not have love, I am nothing.
>
> If I give away everything I own, and if I hand my body over so that I may boast but do not have love, I gain nothing.
>
> Love is patient, love is kind. It is not jealous, (love) is not pompous, it is not inflated,
>
> it is not rude, it does not seek its own interests, it is not quick-tempered, it does not brood over injury,
>
> it does not rejoice over wrongdoing but rejoices with the truth.
>
> It bears all things, believes all things, hopes all things, endures all things.
>
> Love never fails.

Icebreakers 1: Write and share with your table-group what part of the prayer stood out to you and why.

Icebreaker 2: Share any successes in resolutions you have had during this unit OR how these first two units have helped your marriage.

2. (15 minutes) Read the life of Blessed Louis Martin and Blessed Marie Zelie Guerin, the parents of St. Therese of the Child Jesus. Have a couple read it aloud to the group, alternating paragraphs.

Blessed Louis Martin and Blessed Marie Zelie Guerin, The Parents of St. Therese of the Child Jesus[115]

On October 19, 2008, World Mission Sunday, Louis Martin and Marie Zelie Guerin, the parents of St. Therese of the Child Jesus, were declared blessed in Lisieux, France, by Cardinal Jose Saraiva Martins, retired prefect of the Congregation for the Cause of Saints. It was only the second time in history that a married couple has been beatified. (The first couple being Luigi and Maria Quattrocchi of Italy, in 2001.) Here are excerpts from their biography, read during the ceremony by Father Antonio of the Mother of God, O.C.D., Vice Postulator:

Louis Martin was born in Bordeaux on August 22, 1823. At the end of his studies in Alençon, he didn't turn toward a military career like his father, but chose the profession of watchmaker. A man of faith and of prayer, for a time Louis wished to enter the priesthood. In 1845, he went to the Swiss Alps to enter a Carthusian monastery, where his first task was to learn Latin. He tried to learn it but in the end gave up. Having finished his watchmaking studies in Rennes and Strasbourg, he returned to Alençon, where he dedicated himself to his work as a watchmaker-jeweler with diligence and honesty.

Zelie Guerin was born at Gandelain, near Saint-Denis-sur-Sarthon, on December 23, 1831. When her father retired in 1844, the family moved to Alençon. Zelie studied under the Sisters of Perpetual Adoration. She received training that made her a very skillful lacemaker. She made the famous Point d'Alençon, and she was in charge of sales for her own lacemaking business. Like her sister Marie-Louise, now a religious at the Visitation convent in Le Mans, Zelie wanted to consecrate herself to the Lord. After a discussion with the Superior of the Daughters of Charity at the Alençon hospital, she understood that it was not the will of God.

A providential meeting united these two young people thirsty for the Absolute. One day, as Zelie crossed the Saint-Leonard Bridge, she passed a young man with a noble face, a reserved air, and a demeanor filled with an impressive dignity. At that very moment, an interior voice whispers in secret, "This is he whom

I have prepared for you." The identity of the passer-by was soon revealed. She came to know Louis Martin.

The two young people quickly came to appreciate and love each other. Their spiritual harmony established itself so quickly that a religious engagement sealed their mutual commitment without delay. They did not see their marriage as a normal arrangement between two middle-class families of Alençon, but as a total opening to the will of God.

From the beginning, the betrothed couple placed their love under the protection of God, who, in their union, would always be "the first served." Their marriage was celebrated at midnight on July 13th, 1858 in the parish of Notre-Dame d'Alençon.

Louis and his spouse decide at the beginning of their marriage to maintain perfect chastity. Shortly thereafter, they welcome into their home a five-year-old boy whose widowed father was crushed by the burden of raising eleven children. However, Divine Wisdom, which leads all with "strength and gentleness," has other views for this couple, and at the end of ten months, on the advice of a priest friend, they change their minds. They now desired to have many children in order to raise them and offer them to the Lord.

The union of Louis and Zelie is blessed by the birth of nine children. The work of both spouses obtained for them a certain wealth, but their family life is not without trials. In this time of high infant mortality, they lose four children at an early age, at a time when they want to have a son to become a priest. But neither the bereavement nor the trials weaken their confidence in the goodness of God's plans, and they abandon themselves with love to His Will. (The surviving children, five girls, will all become nuns, four of them in the Carmelite monastery.)

The education of the children is at the same time joyful, tender, and demanding. Very early, Zelie teaches them the morning offering of their hearts to the good God, the simple acceptance of daily difficulties "to please Jesus." An indelible mark that is the basis of the little way taught by the most celebrated of their children: Therese. One cannot conceive of the growth in holiness of Therese and the religious vocations of her sisters independent of the spiritual life of Mr. and Mrs. Martin, at the heart of their vocation to family life.

Towards the end of 1876, an old growth in Mrs. Martin's breast returns. Discovered too late, the cancer is inoperable. At half past midnight on August 28, 1877, she dies in Alençon. Louis is left with five children: Marie, Pauline, Leonie, Celine, and Therese, who is four and a half years old.

Louis consults with his elder daughters, and decides to move to Lisieux to live close to the family of his brother-in-law, Isidore Guerin, and thus to ensure a better future for his children. Life at the Buissonnets, the new house in Lisieux, is more austere and withdrawn than at Alençon. But the most admirable work of this father, an exemplary educator, is the offering to God of all his daughters and then of himself. In his unshakable submission to the will of God, like Abraham, he places no obstacle to these vocations and considers the offering of his children to the Lord as a very special grace granted to his family.

Shortly after the entry of Therese into the Carmel of Lisieux, during a visit to the parlor of the monastery, Louis tells his daughters that at the Church of Notre-Dame of Alençon (May 1888), as he was reconsidering his life, he had said: "My God, I am too happy. It's not possible to go to Heaven like that. I want to suffer something for you." "And," said he, "I offered myself." Louis doesn't dare pronounce the word "victim," but his daughters understand this. This confidence really strikes Therese, who, several years later, offered herself as a victim to the Merciful Love of God (June 9, 1895).

The last years of the life of Mr. Martin, "the patriarch," as he is affectionately called by those close to him, are marked by several health problems. He knows the humiliation of illness: a cerebral arteriosclerosis with a long hospitalization at the Bon Sauveur in Caen in 1889, where he filled those around him with admiration and respect. Returning to Lisieux in May 1892, from then on paralyzed and almost unable to speak, he dies peacefully on Sunday, July 29, 1894.

On March 26, 1994, the Servant of God, John Paul II, declares the individual heroic virtues of the Martin couple. In 2008, the Medical Commission of the Congregation for the Causes of Saints declared inexplicable by science and general knowledge the healing of the young Pietro Schiliro, of Monza, Italy. Born on May 25, 2002, Pietro suffered from a serious condition following the inhalation of meconium, which led to serious pulmonary complications. The unexpected healing came about on June 29, 2002, after a novena of prayers to the Venerable Servants of God Louis and Zelie Martin. On July 3, Pope Benedict XVI approved the miracle of Pietro's healing, accomplished by God through the intercession of the Venerable Servants of God, Louis and Zelie, "incomparable" parents of Saint Therese of the Child Jesus, and he set October 19, 2008, as the date of their beatification, and July 12 as their feast day on the liturgical calendar.

In his homily, Cardinal Saraiva Martin, the Prefect of the Congregation for the Causes of Saints, said that in a time of crisis for the family, the family has in the Martin couple a true model. He also offered them as a model for people who face illness and death, as Zelie died of cancer, leaving Louis to live on through the trial of cerebral arteriosclerosis. He said that they teach us to face death, abandoning ourselves to God. Here are excerpts from his homily:

> Therese wrote in a letter to Father Belliere, and that many people now know by heart: "God gave me a father and a mother who were more worthy of heaven than of earth". This beatification of Louis Martin and Zelie Guerin, whom Therese defined as "parents without equal, worthy of heaven, holy ground permeated with the perfume of purity" is very important in the Church.
>
> My heart is full of gratitude to God for this exemplary witness of conjugal love, which is bound to stimulate Christian couples in practicing virtue just as it stimulated the desire for holiness in Therese. While reading the Apostolic Letter of the Holy Father, I thought of my father and mother, and now I invite you to think of your parents that together we may thank God for having created and made us Christians through the conjugal love of our parents. The gift of life is a marvelous thing, but even more wonderful for us is that our parents led us to the Church which alone is capable of making us Christians. For no one becomes a Christian by oneself.
>
> Among the vocations to which individuals are called by Providence, marriage is one of the highest and most noble. Louis and Zelie understood that they could become holy not in spite of marriage, but through, in, and by marriage, and that their becoming a couple was the beginning of an ascent together. Today the Church celebrates not only the holiness of these children of Normandy, a gift to us all, but admires, as well, in the Blessed couple that which renders more splendid and beautiful the wedding robe of the Church. The conjugal love of Louis and Zelie is a pure reflection of Christ's love for his Church, but it is also a pure reflection of the "resplendent love without stain or wrinkle, but holy and immaculate" (Ep 5, 27) as the Church loves its Spouse, Christ.

Reflect on the life of Blessed Louis Martin and Blessed Marie Zelie Guerin.

What struck me about the life of this couple? What can we take from their lives to help strengthen our own marriage?

3. Process/discussion on the material read for homework in Unit Two.

   a. What is a Sacrament and what is its purpose?

   _____

   _____

   b. Christ links what two things in the Sacrament of Matrimony?

   _____

   _____

   c. How does marriage help spouses get to Heaven?

   _____

   _____

   d. What would make marital love incomplete? Guess again.

   _____

   _____

   e. What is really happening at Mass? Explain what is offered and what is received.

   _____

   _____

   f. What are four effects of Holy Communion? How is this Sacrament intimately connected with our marriage?

   _____

   _____

   g. What are five ways that frequent recourse to the Sacrament of Penance can improve a marriage?

   _____

   _____

   h. What invisible events occur during the Sacrament of Baptism?

   _____

   _____

Group Activity: (25 minutes) (Leaders bring poster materials or laptop computers to prepare ahead of time)

A. Assign one of the topics from this unit to each group of 3 couples.

B. Write an advertisement for good things. Working in their small groups of 6, give each group 15 minutes to design an advertisement promoting one of the topics of marriage, Confession, going to Mass, or fostering vocations. You can use take-offs from other popular advertisements or sayings, presenting a convincing argument for the teaching of the Church. Design the advertisement on a poster board or on the computer to display for all.

C. Have each team present their advertisements to the group.

4. Video: *Forgiveness*.

5. Sharing real life examples on the Unit Two topics. Practical applications. (15 minutes)

Table Talk in small groups.

a. What do we do to prepare our family for Mass on Sundays?

b. What do you think is the easiest and the most difficult part of going to Confession regularly?

c. What can we do to foster vocations in our homes?

d. What are some ways that forgiveness has improved your relationship with God and each other?

6. Private couple time/ Couple resolution. (15 minutes)

a. Couples discuss in private: Out of this unit's lessons and today's discussion, which area should we examine more closely to help our marriage? Consider the exercises from the unit. Which were most challenging? How might God be asking us to "stretch" this workout with a new resolution this week? What would be a good resolution from this unit for us to strengthen our marriage?

b. Our personal resolution for this unit (Please write it in the space below).

_____

_____

7. Large Group sharing on practical applications. (10 minutes)

What can we take away with us today to improve our marriages?

Leaders can offer open discussion, or else have couples write their answers down, turn them in, and read some of them aloud to the group.

8. Warm Up before Unit Three: prepare our minds and hearts.

    a.   Please review the Learning Goals for each of the four exercises in Unit Three.

    b.   Next group workout you should be able to answer the following questions
- i. What is the "hidden agenda" behind the Commandments?
- ii. How does the Law help a person practice self-control?
- iii. What is sin really? What does sin cost us?
- iv. Is it possible to forgive adultery? Does the Bible say we do not have to forgive this sin?
- v. What is a "married single"?
- vi. What is the secret to melting someone's heart?
- vii. What is a virtue? What five virtues bring unity to marriage?
- viii. What breaks unity in marriage?
- ix. What is the "supreme" gift of marriage?
- x. Are contraception and sterilization really so bad, now that they are so widely accepted?
- xi. What is this "thing" called Natural Family Planning?

9. Closing Prayer. (5 minutes) Suggested Prayer at end of Unit Two Exercise Two.

10. Social Time.

The Moral Life: A Virtual Workout

Unit Three: Week One Exercise

The rich young man asked Jesus, "Teacher, what good must I do to gain eternal life?" Jesus answered, "If you wish to enter into life, keep the commandments"[116]

> Jesus begins with the knowledge that the young man has surely already acquired from his family and from the synagogue: he knows the commandments. These lead to life, which means that they guarantee our authenticity. They are the great signs which lead us along the right path. Whoever keeps the commandments is on the way that leads to God.
>
> It is not enough, however, simply to know them. Witness is even more important than knowledge; or rather, it is applied knowledge. The commandments are not imposed upon us from without; they do not diminish our freedom. On the contrary: they are strong internal incentives leading us to act in a certain way. At the heart of them we find both grace and nature, which do not allow us to stay still. We must walk. We are motivated to do something in order fulfill our potential. To find fulfillment through action is, in reality, to become real.[117]

"When God says, 'Thou shalt not,' He is not trying to take all the fun out of life. He is trying to save us from actions that will harm us, that will distort our natures; that will inevitable make us profoundly unhappy."[118]

Many years ago, a seminarian was out to dinner with a couple of friends and as always the subject of theology or philosophy made its way into the conversation. One of his friends asked him why a person in their right mind would belong to a religious institution, i.e., the Catholic Church that is oppressive in its law. This person felt that the Catholic Church set up too many laws, particularly laws that define what is morally right or wrong. He felt that this type of "control" could ultimately stifle a person's individual growth, which would lead to "oppression." Essentially, he did not understand why a person needed to belong to a Church at all and concluded that all a person needs to do is to follow his or her own conscience and to act or be fundamentally "good."

After listening to him for about fifteen minutes, with much patience and charity, the seminarian replied, "As a human society we are all governed by laws every moment of our lives, whether it is human laws enacted and promulgated by civil authorities for the common good or the laws of nature that govern our bodies and the universe around us. Laws, whether human or divine, are seen as oppressive only when we perceive them selfishly. God has bestowed upon us divine commands, whose sole purpose is to draw us to him. Unfortunately, in our selfishness, we inevitably see them as a threat to our own individual freedom or impinging upon our own personal rights."

Pope Benedict XVI once said, "God's yoke is God's will, which we accept. And this will does not weigh down on us, oppressing us and taking away our freedom. To know what God wants, to know where the path of life is found—this was Israel's joy, this was her great privilege. It is also our joy: God's will does not alienate us, it purifies us—even if this can be painful—and so it leads us to ourselves."[119]

Christ's Law is a law of love, and once we embrace it, it leads to nothing but freedom—freedom in the Spirit to live as children of God. This is the great paradox! How can laws lead to freedom? The freedom that God gave us in the beginning, a freedom that is oriented toward self-surrender and self-giving, has been disfigured due to sin, yet we are still free. Christ died so that we could experience true freedom from the yoke of sin and live as sons and daughters of God. Our freedom, governed by God's laws, is rooted in the Law of Love, a law deeply rooted within us. God's laws are not threatening or oppressive; they do not strip us of our freedom. They are actually life giving, because everything we have and are belongs to God, who is life and love itself.

Fulton Sheen, in his book *Peace of Soul*, asked the question: "Is God hard to find?" He points out an obvious fact that many people often forget or try to avoid: all humanity has a natural desire for God. God is the most obvious fact of human experience and we discover his image in the world of nature and in the people around us. We receive him in Word and Sacrament, but sadly there are people who remain suffocated by their own frustrations and fears, refusing to open the door to God and obey his divine laws. Archbishop Sheen identified three false fears that keep us away from God.

WE WANT TO BE SAVED, BUT NOT FROM OUR SIN

Some people desire some type of salvation, but not from their own personal sins. People who fall into this error are usually more interested in seeking their own interests before those of their spouse, neighbors, or co-workers. They are always ready to point out other peoples' faults and sins or to blame others for their misfortunes and downfalls. They are good at not taking responsibility for their actions, because they consider themselves innocent of any personal sin. They know deep down, however, that something is wrong, and they try to compensate by becoming preoccupied with trying to right wrongs on the outside, i.e., other peoples' lives.

WE WANT TO BE SAVED, BUT NOT AT TOO GREAT A COST

Throughout our lives, we all want to strive for perfection, a desire to be perfect just like our heavenly Father is perfect. Jesus showed us what perfection looks like through his perfect act of obedience and love by which he paid the ultimate price for our sins and reoriented our lives back to him. Many people in this category take this redemption for granted without ever realizing the great love God has for us and the great cost he paid for our salvation. Growing in perfection or holiness without Christ can lead a person to become extremely demanding toward his or her spouse or neighbor. By placing too high expectations upon other people, they become dissatisfied with other peoples' achievements or results. No one can ever meet up to their expectations. These people once again become preoccupied with the defects of others, and as a result, they find it very difficult to love and forgive others. It often happens that the spouse who cannot meet the other person's expectation starts to distance him or herself or push away the other person, because he or she feels a sense of inadequacy or failure. A saint once said, "If we wait to love others who have no defects, or who are only perfect in our eyes, we will never truly love anyone." Only when we come to realize with utter gratitude and thankfulness the sacrifice God made on our behalf, are we able to get out of ourselves and discover what it means to be saved at a great cost. Jesus reminds us that salvation requires much love and patience and that none of us will ever be perfect. Perfection means to grow in holiness and to help others become the saints that God has called them to become. This is only done at a great cost.

WE WANT TO BE SAVED, BUT IN OUR OWN WAY, NOT GOD'S

Upon reflection, the argument made above to the seminarian was in fact a product less of his fear of the Church and more of his fear of Jesus Christ. He, like so many people, fears that Jesus will do just what his name implies, "He who saves us from our sins." This false sense of fear can lead a person to say things such as, "I can work things out for myself … I can define my own morality, what is right and wrong."

But this begs the question: "What or who defines 'good' and how do you know what is right and wrong?" "How are we saved?" Christ is the answer to all of these questions. In answer to the question regarding the Church, the seminarian simply replied, "The Church that Christ instituted and died for should not be seen merely as a bureaucratic structure, with laws that seem oppressive or threatening to our freedom, but rather the Church is made up of people, like you and me, all seeking salvation, happiness, and eternal fulfillment through the divine laws that Christ instituted for our salvation."

So many people today are scared to open themselves up to God who loves us beyond anything we can ever imagine, and who takes nothing from us but gives us everything. Which leads us to discover the real question: "Is God really hard to find or are we just afraid of being found?" What happens when we allow ourselves to be found … to be saved from our sins, according to God's way, at a cost beyond our imagining? Jesus reveals, through his truth and most importantly by his love, that to be found by him leads us to the truth about ourselves, our identity, and our need for salvation. Many people are scared to face the reality about their lives and what is going on inside them. That is why our Lord finds it necessary to say, over and over again throughout Scripture: "Fear not, do not be afraid."

By living in but not of the world, we live as those who have died in Christ. He bids us to join him, to be heralds of this new reality, to live it, and to imprint it on the hearts of all, especially our family and those who are questioning life and the very mystery of God.

Are we not perhaps all afraid in some way? If we let Christ enter fully into our lives, if we open ourselves totally to him, are we not afraid that He might take something away from us? Are we not perhaps afraid to give up something significant, something unique, something that makes life so beautiful? Do we not then risk ending up diminished and deprived of our freedom? ... No! If we let Christ into our lives, we lose nothing, nothing, absolutely nothing of what makes life free, beautiful, and great. No! Only in this friendship are the doors of life opened wide. Only in this friendship is the great potential of human existence truly revealed. Only in this friendship do we experience beauty and liberation. And so, today, with great strength and great conviction, on the basis of long personal experience of life, I say to you, ... : Do not be afraid of Christ! He takes nothing away, and he gives you everything. When we give ourselves to him, we receive a hundredfold in return. Yes, open, open wide the doors to Christ—and you will find true life.[120]

What does the Pastoral Letter on Marriage have to say?

Not only do parents present their children for Baptism, but having done so, they become the first evangelizers and teachers of the faith.[121] They evangelize by teaching their children to pray and by praying with them. They bring their children to Mass and teach them biblical stories. They show them how to obey God's commandments and to live a Christian life of holiness ...

A family matures as a domestic church as it ever more deeply immerses itself within the life of the Church. This especially means that fathers and mothers, by their example and teaching, help their children come to an appreciation of the need for continual conversion and repentance from sin, encouraging a love for and participation in the Sacrament of Reconciliation. (*Marriage: Love and Life*, 40–41)

If God made us in his image, and our family is to reflect the love of God to the world, then we need to show it with our actions. One way to prove to God that you are in his family is by living according to the covenant between God and man, the Ten Commandments.

The Ten Commandments call us to proclaim our faith with our actions: Are we on God's team or not? The Commandments are our invisible team shirt. The People of God follow them. Others do not. Even if we fail we resolve once again to do our best to help our team, and are forgiven. But we do not leave the team. God's team trains through frequent confession. What are these Commandments, and how do we follow them as a team? Are we "exercising" to be God's team?

THERE'S NO BETTER TIME THAN THE PRESENT TO SET THINGS RIGHT WITH GOD

A Guide to Confession

HOW TO GO TO CONFESSION

You always have the option to go to Confession anonymously, that is, behind a screen or face to face, if you so desire.

1. After the priest greets you in the name of Christ, make the Sign of the Cross. He may choose to read some verses of Scripture, after which you say: "Bless me Father for I have sinned. It has been (state how long) since my last confession. These are my sins."

2. Tell your sins simply and honestly to the priest. You might even want to discuss the circumstances and the root causes of your sins and ask the priest for advice or direction.

3. Listen to the advice the priest gives you and accept the penance from him. Then make an Act of Contrition for your sins.

4. The priest will then dismiss you with the words "The Lord has freed you from your sins. Go in peace." And you respond by saying: "Thanks be to God."

5. Spend some time with Our Lord thanking and praising him for the gift of his mercy. Try to perform your penance as soon as possible.

EXAMINATION OF CONSCIENCE

1. *I am the LORD your God. You shall not have strange gods before me.*
   - Do I give God time every day in prayer? Do I seek to love him with my whole heart?
   - Have I been involved with superstitious practices, or have I been involved with the occult?
   - Do I seek to surrender myself to God's Word as taught by the Church?
   - Have I received Communion in the state of mortal sin?
   - Have I deliberately told a lie in Confession or have I withheld a mortal sin from the priest in Confession? Are there other "gods" in my life, such as money, security, power, people, etc.?

2. *You shall not take the name of the LORD your God in vain.*
   - Have I used God's name in vain: lightly or carelessly?
   - Have I been angry with God?
   - Have I wished evil upon any other person?
   - Have I insulted a sacred person or abused a sacred object?

3. *Remember to keep holy the LORD's Day.*
   - Have I deliberately missed Mass on Sundays or Holy Days of Obligation?
   - Have I tried to observe Sunday as a family day and a day of rest?
   - Do I do needless work on Sunday?

4. *Honor your father and your mother.*

- Do I honor and obey my parents?
- Have I given my family good religious example?
- Do I try to bring peace into my home life? Do I care for my aged and infirm relatives?

5. *You shall not kill.*

- Have I had an abortion or encouraged or helped anyone to have an abortion?
- Have I physically harmed anyone?
- Have I abused alcohol or drugs?
- Did I give scandal to anyone, thereby leading him or her into sin?
- Have I been angry or resentful? Have I harbored hatred in my heart? Have I encouraged or condoned sterilization? Have I participated in or approved of euthanasia?

6. *You shall not commit adultery.*

- Have I engaged in any sexual activity outside of marriage? Have I been faithful to my marriage vows in thought and action? Have I used any method of contraception or artificial birth control in my marriage?
- Have I been guilty of masturbation or viewing pornography?
- Do I seek to control my thoughts and imagination?
- Have I respected all people, or have I thought of other people as mere objects?
- Have I been guilty of any sexual activity with people of the same sex?
- Do I seek to be chaste in my thoughts, words, and actions?
- Am I careful to dress modestly?
- Have I practiced *in vitro* fertilization?
- Did I obtain a vasectomy or tubal ligation to avoid having children?

7. *You shall not steal.*

- Have I stolen what is not mine?
- Have I returned or made restitution for what I have stolen?
- Do I waste time at work, school, and home?
- Do I gamble excessively, thereby denying my family of their needs?
- Do I pay my debts promptly?
- Do I seek to share what I have with the poor?
- Have I cheated anyone out of what is justly theirs?

8. *You shall not bear false witness against your neighbor.*

- Have I lied? Have I gossiped?
- Do I speak badly of others behind their back?
- Am I sincere in my dealings with others?
- Am I critical, negative, or uncharitable in my thoughts of others?
- Do I keep secret what should be kept confidential?
- Have I injured the reputation of others by slander?

9. *You shall not desire your neighbor's wife.*

- Have I consented to impure thoughts?
- Have I caused them by impure reading, movies, television, conversation, or curiosity?
- Have I behaved in an inappropriate way with members of the opposite sex: flirting, being superficial, etc.?

10. *You shall not desire your neighbor's goods.*
- Am I jealous of what other people have?
- Do I envy the families or possessions of others?
- Am I greedy or selfish?
- Are material possessions the purpose of my life?

ACT OF CONTRITION

O my God, I am heartily sorry for having offended you, and I detest all my sins because I dread the loss of Heaven and the pains of Hell, but most of all because they offend you, my God, who is all good and deserving of all my love. I firmly resolve, with the help of your grace, to confess my sins, to do penance, and to amend my life. Amen.

A DIFFICULT TOPIC
EMOTIONAL, SPIRITUAL, AND PHYSICAL ADULTERY AND FORGIVENESS

Throughout the Scriptures, adultery (the Sixth Commandment: *Thou shall not commit adultery*) is viewed, in the strict sense, as unfaithfulness to the *marriage* vow. However, adultery is also presented in the wider sense of Israel's betrayal of its covenant with God by means of pacts or agreements with other nations or false gods. God warned them, "do not break my covenant; be faithful in all your words and actions." Israel's regular episodes of "infidelity" are a sad commentary on our own human weakness and susceptibility to temptation.

Many marriage preparation programs make use of an inventory such as FOCCUS (an acronym for "*F*acilitating *O*ngoing *C*ouple *C*ommunication, *U*nderstanding, and *S*tudy). Using this tool, each person individually responds to several hundred statements, checking boxes marked either a) "I agree"; b) "I disagree"; or c) "I'm not sure." One of the statements on the FOCCUS inventory is:

> "I could not under any condition remain married to my spouse if he/she were ever unfaithful to me."

Before going any further, consider what happens when we are unfaithful to *God's* commands? Certainly there are consequences. One of God's commands is that we love our spouse with a deep, abiding, and exclusive love. If we stray, does God take us back? Scriptures say: "If we deny him, he will deny us; but if we are unfaithful he remains faithful, for he cannot deny himself."[122] We may wake up one day and find ourselves in the abyss of "spiritual infidelity," yet God will never abandon us. It is within the context of that assurance that we have the courage to seek Confession; we know that God will take us back if we are truly contrite and repentant of our sin, regardless of how careless or obstinate we have been.

Consider how unfaithful you have been in your relationship with God (how unfaithful we *all* have been). Can you imagine going to God with a contrite heart saying, "sorry," and God turning his back? Thankfully, this is not how God deals with us. Consider the scene in the New Testament where Jesus comes across the woman found committing adultery. What was his response to those who sought to punish her with death? "Let the one among you who is without sin [who has not been unfaithful to God] be the first to throw a stone at her."[123] Remember what they did? They all walked away. "Jesus said, 'Woman, where are they? Has no one condemned you?' She replied, 'No one, sir.' Then Jesus said, 'Neither do I condemn you. Go, [and] from now on do not sin anymore.'"[124]

Trust may be broken, but it can always be restored through prayer, penance, patience, love, and, of course, a forgiving heart that knows no limits to the gift of God's mercy. You are both in this marriage for life. Couples should never even think about adultery. So what do you need to do? In order to steer clear of adultery, couples need to avoid all *occasions of sin* (know each other's friends, co-workers, MySpace and Facebook friends; avoid pornography; avoid alcohol if you know that it will make you vulnerable to sin, etc.). Do not let your guard down, even for a moment. Infidelity in marriage is more the symptom of marital problems needing attention than it is the cause of those problems. It highlights a disease that was likely already present, but perhaps not yet identified.

While perhaps sounding unfair, this is a kind of litmus test to see if you really accept the Catholic understanding of marriage—or … is infidelity your parachute clause? Would physical unfaithfulness be a deal breaker? If so, then you are unprepared to enter into Christian marriage. Think of the marriage vows: "I promise to be true to you in good times and in bad, in sickness and in health. I will love you and honor you all the days of my life." The first time you said these vows should not have been the last. These vows should be repeated throughout your married life, in all your words and actions. Whether you realize it or not, you are a living embodiment of your vows.

$\mathscr{T}$HE $\mathscr{W}$ORKOUT

1. How does our family live the Ten Commandments?

2. How can we help each other live the Commandments of God?

3. How often do we go to Confession? Should we go more often?

4. How can we plan our days and weeks to include a nightly examination of conscience and more frequent Confession?

5. How many of our family members know the Act of Contrition by heart?

6. Do we practice forgiving one another as Christ forgives us? How can we improve?

7. What can we do to build trust and unity in our marriage so as to avoid any infidelity?

8. Do I need to seek forgiveness from my spouse? Is there anything I need to forgive that I have been holding against my spouse?

LET US PRAY

The Act of Contrition

O my God, I am heartily sorry for having offended you, and I detest all my sins because I dread the loss of Heaven and the pains of Hell, but most of all because they offend you, my God, who is all good and deserving of all my love. I firmly resolve, with the help of your grace, to confess my sins, to do penance, and to amend my life. Amen.

Two Become One

Unit Three: Week Two Exercise

LEARNING GOALS

- ❧ To understand God's plan for the unitive dimension of marriage.

- ❧ To explore how to bring more unity and less division to our marriages.

What does the Pastoral Letter on Marriage have to say?

Marriage has two fundamental ends or purposes towards which it is oriented, namely, the good of the spouses as well as the procreation of children. Thus, the Church teaches that marriage is both unitive and procreative, and that it is inseparably both. . .

God clearly made human beings to love and to be loved, to be in relationships wherein the act of giving oneself and receiving the other becomes complete. . .

God established marriage so that man and woman could participate in his love and thus selflessly give themselves to each other in love. A man and a woman who by their very act of consent are no longer two but one flesh (see Mt 19:16ff.) render mutual help and service to each other through an intimate union of their actions.[125] (*Marriage: Love and Life*, 11–12)

Are we becoming one? How are we growing unity in our marriage? Are we each giving our whole self to the other? Do we feel "complete" when we are together? We hope so, since that is God's plan. However in today's busy society, this does not always happen. In Marriage Encounter, they use the term, "Married Singles" to describe people who live separate lives in the same house, and share the same bedroom and children. Living as a "single" while you are married, without continuous efforts at unity is the recipe for sexual tension, or worse. True conjugal love requires that each is continuously giving oneself to the other, freely, with love. When that "all-day love" is missing, and the couple is not "becoming one" in any other way than physically, their sex life can emotionally divide instead of unite them. Looking from the natural view, instead of the supernatural view, it might appear that they have "sexual problems." The truth, however, is that they have not worked at their personal union and actually have *unity* problems first. When the unity problems are resolved, the sex problems will often diminish, because unity usually leads to attraction and affection; that is how man and woman were wired by God.

How do we grow in unity as a couple? What do we need to stop doing that divides us? These are two separate questions that we will address in this exercise.

Man and woman are united in marriage. The Pastoral Letter speaks of marriage as "for the good of the spouses," and indicates that couples "participate in God's love," "selflessly give themselves to each other in love," act in "mutual service to each other," and are "no longer two but one flesh." Marriage must include a unity of minds and hearts. This includes common values and common goals, and working together to obtain them.

WHAT ASPECTS OF LOVE BRING UNITY TO THE MARRIAGE? HERE ARE JUST A HANDFUL:

- *Acceptance:* After some time in marriage, the spouses get to know each others' strengths and weaknesses, virtues and defects. Genuine love includes a merciful attitude toward your spouse's struggles, as well as being his or her "'helpmate" or "encourager" without nagging and criticizing. Try not to exaggerate your spouse's weaknesses and instead offer your strengths in service to them. Frequently, "opposites attract." However, what attracted you at first may later irritate you. Look for the good, accept the good and the bad, and learn to love the whole person—for better or for worse.

- *Understanding*: How often do we only see from our perspective? Try putting yourself in your spouse's place. Think about his or her personal struggles, efforts, and defeats. When we disagree on something, we can try our best to understand each other's situation. Listen carefully to what your spouse is saying, and be slow to judge.

- *Humility:* You are not always right. There are other ways (within moral means) to accomplish things. Marriage can be very difficult when one person always needs to win. Treating your spouse like a child instead of an adult demeans him or her. Humility allows your spouse to be free to grow with the Holy Spirit. The humble person knows when to yield and when to seek forgiveness.

- *Kindness:* Make positive comments to each other. Watch your tone of voice. Speak always with gentleness. It helps to practice thinking kind thoughts about the other when you are apart. Do secret good deeds for your spouse frequently. No matter how long you have been married, acts of kindness can melt a person's heart, just like they did when you were dating. Laugh at your spouse's jokes, do not bring up his or her faults, and pray for him or her. It is God's plan that spouses build up one another in love. Every action and word we speak has a purpose, to build up or to tear down, to do good or to do evil.

- *Joyful diligence in one's family duties:* Quite often affection in marriage is rooted in admiration. Once the "honeymoon is over," people's weaknesses surface, and we have to look for ways to increase our admiration. A good way to continue to earn the respect of your spouse is to fulfill your family duties in a diligent way, with joyful attitude. Joy keeps daily life from becoming a burden and inspires your spouse to be joyful, too. Diligence in your duties, especially when times become difficult, is something that your spouse and children will remember. Actions speak louder than words.

WHAT HOLY PRACTICES BRING UNITY TO THE MARRIAGE?

❧ Continuous struggle to live virtuously.

❧ Regular Confession, which helps us get to know ourselves, seek forgiveness from God, and receive God's helping grace to do better next time.

❧ Regular and intimate prayer.

TWO BECOME ONE FLESH:
WHAT KIND OF CONJUGAL RELATIONS BRING UNITY TO THE MARRIAGE?

❧ Faithful Relations

In marriage, one is to be faithful in one's mind and heart, with one's eyes, with one's emotions, and with one's body. This eliminates intimate conversations with old boyfriends and girlfriends and co-workers of the opposite sex. Faithfulness requires one to keep one's eyes away from pornographic material and to avoid complaining about one's spouse to other friends and flirting with anyone of the opposite sex. Faithfulness is worth quitting a job, changing friends, throwing out the television, or disconnecting the computer.

❧ Naturally Good Sex Life

Magazines and books are everywhere trying to tell couples how to have "good sex." We already discussed how good sex, or conjugal relations, is rooted in the love of spouses. Yet, there is a natural design for the conjugal union that is built within the couple's bodies, that is ignored by many of those so-called-expert manuals. What is right and good about sex within marriage?

Within marriage, spouses are required to give themselves to one another in an act of love, which includes preparing for a loving embrace that is open to the possibility of life. Sexual pleasure is the gift, not the goal, of the sexual union, although spouses should seek to please the other and prepare the other for the fullness of the conjugal act. Thoughtfulness is the key to a selfless union. Couples are not to seek orgasm outside of the genital union, even when a couple is avoiding the fertile time to responsibly avoid pregnancy. Mutual masturbation, oral sex, and withdrawal, are outside of God's plan for unity in sex and marriage. These are violations of marital chastity and forms of lust. God designed man and woman's bodies to find the ultimate union in each act of conjugal love, thus renewing their "I do" of Matrimony with their whole self, body and soul.

A naturally good sex life is supportive of the overall relationship, routinely enjoyable and reaffirming of the other, and always open to new life. When Pope Paul II was giving his series of audiences on the Theology of the Body in 1980, he was heavily criticized by the media for stating that a man can commit adultery in his heart even with his own wife. He was teaching us that a man is not to "use" his wife as an outlet for his disordered sexual desires. A husband is to follow God's original intention in the "nuptial meaning of the body" which is to always be seeking the norm of sincere gift of oneself to his wife in all sexual relations.

The Virtues of Selfless Love-Making in Marriage[126]

The basic premise of Pope John Paul II's book, Love and Responsibility, *is the Personalistic norm: the person is to be respected and not to be used. A person cannot be treated as an object of use or as a means to an end. In its positive form the norm confirms that the person is a good towards which the only proper and adequate attitude is love. Pope John Paul II extends this personalistic principle to the conjugal act in marriage in the following excerpt. It is better advice than a secular therapist can offer.*

Sexual ethics, the ethics of marriage, must examine closely certain facts on which clinical sexology can provide precise information. We have defined love as an ambition to ensure the true good of another person, and consequently as the antithesis of egoism. Since in marriage a man and a woman are associated sexually as well as in other respects the good must be sought in this area too. From the point of view of another person, from the altruistic standpoint, it is necessary to insist that intercourse must not serve merely as a means of allowing sexual excitement to reach its climax in one of the partners, i.e., the man alone, but that climax must be reached in harmony, not at the expense of one partner, but with both partners fully involved. This is implicit in the principle which we have already so thoroughly analyzed, and which excludes exploitation of the person, and insists on love. In the present case love demands that the reactions of the other person, the sexual "partner" be fully taken into account.

Sexologists state that the curve of arousal in woman is different from that in man—it rises more slowly and falls more slowly. Anatomically, arousal occurs in the same way in women and in men (the locus of excitement is in the cerebro-spinal system at S2–S3). The female organism, as was mentioned above, reacts more easily to excitation in various parts of the body, which to some extent compensates for the fact that the woman's excitement grows more slowly than that of the man. The man must take this difference into account, not for *hedonistic*, but for *altruistic* reasons. There exists a rhythm dictated by nature itself which both spouses must discover so that climax may be reached both by the man and by the woman, and as far as possible occur in both simultaneously. The subjective happiness which they then share has the clear characteristic of the enjoyment which we have called 'frui', of the joy which flows from harmony between one's own actions and the objective order of nature. Egoism on the other hand—and in this context it is obviously more likely to be egoism on the part of the man—is inseparable from the 'uti' in which one party seeks only his own pleasure at the expense of the other. Evidently, the elementary teachings of sexology cannot be applied without reference to ethics.

Non-observance of these teachings of sexology in the marital relationship is contrary to the good of the other partner to the marriage and the durability and cohesion of the marriage itself. It must be taken into account that it is naturally difficult for the woman to adapt herself to the man in the sexual relationship, that there is a natural unevenness of physical and psychological rhythms, so that there is a need for harmonization, which is impossible without good will, especially on the part of the man, who must carefully observe the reactions of the woman. If a woman does not obtain natural gratification from the sexual act there is a danger that her experience of it will be qualitatively inferior, will not involve her *fully as a person*. This sort of experience makes nervous reactions only too likely, and may for instance cause secondary sexual frigidity. Frigidity is sometimes the result of an inhibition on the part of the woman herself, or of a lack of involvement which may even at times be her own fault. But it is usually the result of egoism in the man, who failing to recognize the subjective desires of the woman in intercourse, and the objective laws of the sexual process taking place in her, seeks merely his own satisfaction, sometimes quite brutally.

In the woman this produces an aversion to intercourse, and a disgust with sex which is just as difficult or even more difficult to control than the sexual urge. It can also cause neuroses and sometimes organic disorders (which come from the fact that the engorgement of the genital organs at the time of sexual arousal results in inflammation in the region of the so-called little pelvis, if sexual arousal is not terminated by detumescence, which in the woman is closely connected with orgasm). Psychologically, such a situation causes not just indifference but outright hostility. A woman finds it very difficult to forgive a man if she derives no satisfaction from intercourse. It becomes difficult for her to endure this, and as the years go her resentment may grow out of all proportion to its cause. This may lead to the collapse of the marriage. It can be prevented by sexual education—and by this I mean more than merely instruction in sexual matters. For it must be emphasized yet again that physical disgust does not exist in marriage as a primary phenomenon, but is as a rule, a secondary reaction: in women it is the response to egoism and brutality, in men to frigidity and indifference. But the woman's frigidity and indifference is often the fault of the man, when he seeks his own satisfaction while leaving the woman unsatisfied, something which masculine pride should in any case forbid. But in some particularly difficult situations natural pride may not be enough in the long run—everyone knows that egoism may either blind a man and rob him of his pride or, on the contrary, result in a morbid hypertrophy of pride, which causes him to lose sight of the other human being. Similarly, the natural kindness of a woman, who (so the sexologists tell us) sometimes "shams orgasm" to satisfy a man's pride, may also be unhelpful in the long run. These are mere palliatives, and cannot in the end give satisfactory solutions to the difficulties experienced in intercourse. There is here a real need for sexual education, and it must be a continuous process. The main objective of this education is to create the conviction that "the other person is more important than I." Such conviction will not arise suddenly and from nothing, merely on the basis of physical intercourse. It can only be, must be, the result of an *integral* education in *love*. Sexual intercourse itself does not teach love, but love, if it is a genuine virtue, will show itself to be so in sexual relations between married people as elsewhere. Only then can 'sexual instruction' bestow its full benefits: without education in our sense it may even do harm.

This is where the 'culture of marital relations' comes in and what it means. Not the 'technique' but the 'culture'. Sexologists often put the main emphasis on technique, whereas this should rather be thought of as something secondary, and often perhaps even inimical to the purpose which it is supposed to serve. The urge is so strong that it creates in the normal man and woman a sort of instinctive knowledge "how to make love" whereas artificial analysis (and the concept of "technique" implies this) is more likely to spoil the whole thing, for what is wanted here is a certain spontaneity and naturalness (subordinated of course to morality). This instinctive knowledge must subsequently mature into a 'culture of marital relations.'

I must refer here to the analysis of "tenderness" to be found in section 3 of Chapter II. This ability to enter readily into another person's emotions and experiences can play a big part in harmonization of marital intercourse. It has its origin in "sentiment," which is directed primarily towards the "human being" and so can temper and tone down the violent reactions of sensuality, which is so oriented only towards the "body" and the uninhibited impulses of concupiscence. Precisely because a slower and more gradual rise in the curve of sexual arousal is characteristic of the female organism the need for tenderness during physical intercourse, and also before it begins and after its conclusion, is explicable in purely biological terms. If we take into account the shorter and more violent curve of arousal in the man, an act of tenderness on his part in the context of marital intercourse acquires the significance of an act of virtue—specifically, the virtue of continence, and so indirectly the virtue of love (see the analysis in Section 3 of Chapter III). Marriage cannot be reduced to the physical relationship, it needs an emotional climate without which the virtues—whether that of love or that of chastity—become difficult to realize in practice.

❧ Openness to Life.

What does the Pastoral Letter on Marriage have to say?

Conjugal love expresses the unitive meaning of marriage in such a way as to show how this meaning is ordered toward the equally obvious procreative meaning. The unitive meaning is distorted if the procreative meaning is deliberately disavowed. Conjugal love is then diminished. (*Marriage: Love and Life*, 15)

In other words, contraception contravenes both the unitive and the procreative dimensions of marriage, because you cannot have one without the other. Proponents of contraception have long concealed its divisive effect on couples. After decades of practicing contraception, couples have found that their intimacy and unity have diminished greatly. The divorce rate for couples who practice contraception or sterilization is 50%, whereas the divorce rate for couples who use Natural Family Planning is only 3% in many international studies. There's something about the unitive dimension that belongs to God and can only be fulfilled within his plan. Unity becomes much more difficult when we exclude God's plan.

What does the Pastoral Letter on Marriage have to say?

The Church speaks of an inseparable connection between the two ends of marriage: the good of the spouses themselves as well as the procreation of children. The *Catechism of the Catholic Church* teaches that "these two meanings or values of marriage cannot be separated without altering the couple's spiritual life and compromising the goods of marriage and the future of the family."[127] (*Marriage: Love and Life*, 15)

MAN AND WOMAN DIVIDED: THINGS TO AVOID

Couples become divided when they allow sin and meanness to creep into their daily lives. These evils include impatience, criticism, dishonesty, pride, manipulation, envy, and control, and they can take away the freedom of the couple to grow in trust, openness, and genuine loving concern for one another.

Sexual alienation occurs when lust enters the marriage. It can sometimes be present from the beginning, especially if premarital sex or masturbation were regular occurrences. Lust is sexual passion directed toward the gratification of self rather than toward the service of God and spouse. It is one of the capital sins, a sin that makes a couple's sex act divide instead of unite. Lust can be fed by a wife's continuous reading of romance novels, or a husband's entertainment of impure thoughts. Lust de-personalizes sex and takes the love-giving out of the act. Women especially have an inner sense that tells them when they are being "used" for sex instead of being "loved" for themselves as persons. It makes them want to avoid relations with their husbands.

Selfishness and manipulation also weaken the marital union. Communication about the sexual union should always be honest, open, and sincere, with each seeking the good of the other. If a couple finds that their conjugal life is not satisfying to one or both of the spouses, it is probably time to take an inventory of the love, virtue, and grace in your marriage. When the personal life truly becomes "One in Christ," the conjugal life can flourish as well.

The Workout

1. What obvious barriers do we have to our personal unity?

2. What is the first step we can take to resolve these issues?

3. What barriers do we have to our physical unity?

4. What is the first step we can take to resolve these issues?

5. How can we yield to one another without sinning?

6. How can we lead one another to Heaven through our unity?

LET US PRAY

St. Francis Prayer for Peace

Lord, make me an instrument of your peace;
Where there is hatred let me sow love,
Where there is injury, pardon;
Where there is doubt, faith;
Where there is despair, hope;
Where there is darkness, light;
Where there is sadness, joy.

O Divine Master, grant that I may not so much seek to be consoled as to console;
To be understood as to understand;
To be loved, as to love,
For it is in giving that we receive,
It is in pardoning that we are pardoned,
And it is in dying that we are born to eternal life.

Procreation: Our Love Comes Alive Forever

Unit Three: Week Three Exercise

LEARNING GOALS

- To understand God's intention in establishing the bond between the unitive and procreative dimensions of the marriage act.

- To realize that children naturally spring from a couple's love and become the couple's love incarnate.

- To explore the meaning and goodness of procreation as it flows from and for the unity of the couple.

What does the Pastoral Letter on Marriage have to say?

> Children are the supreme gift of marriage ... without intending to underestimate the other ends of marriage, it must be said that true married love and the family life which flows from it have this end in view: that the spouses would cooperate generously with the love of the Creator and Savior, who through them will in due time increase and enrich his family.[128]

> Children are a gift in a myriad of ways. They bring joy even in the midst of heartaches; they give added direction to the lives of their parents. Children, who are the fruit of love and meaningful commitment, are a cause of love and meaning. (*Marriage: Love and Life*, 14)

When you see your first child, it is hard not to know there is a loving God who is behind this awesome power to create life. God created you out of love, to love and for love. God created man and woman to love one another and to reflect his creative love to the world. Pure and selfless love is a reflection of God. Your love as husband and wife is so powerful that it can become a whole new person; a person who looks like the two of you and acts like the two of you. Your children are the sign of your love to the whole world. Procreation is the power and privilege to co-create new life with God. This is a love that surpasses all other forms of human love.

God created man and woman with a power to cooperate with him in bringing new life into existence for all eternity. Even the angels cannot procreate. The animals cannot live for all eternity. Only human beings are given this gift of procreation. The sperm and the egg contributed by the father and mother become, at conception, a whole new and unique human person. At conception, God creates the soul of this person, the seed of life that will grow and live for all eternity. As parents, you have become co-creators with God, collaborators with him in creating life.

Having children is not something "separate" from the conjugal union. God asks you to share his love with one another and bear lasting fruit. The sexual life of the couple is a way of experiencing God's love. This communion of love and life (husband, wife, and child) is a reflection of the Trinity, a communion of three divine Persons. Children are an extension of your mutual self-giving. This conjugal love is so great that it can unify two human beings with God in a way that no human can separate. "The two shall become one flesh. What God has joined together, no human being must separate."[129] This love is not merely natural, it includes the supernatural.

In separating the unitive and procreative dimension of the conjugal union, our modern, secular culture has rejected God's plan for human sexuality. Many people today consider love-making and baby-making to be two separate decisions and thus reduced sex to a form of self-centered pleasure. This is a violation of our very nature and a misuse of a tremendous gift.

The love of God that is designed for self-giving is challenging. It calls us to empty ourselves of our egotism and give ourselves totally. It challenges us to be kind and patient when we do not feel like it. Love challenges us to work through our problems, to be humble, to suffer, to die to ourselves, and to live in service to the family we have brought into the world. When Catholics love, we do not hold back; our love goes all the way—all the way to the divine—all the way to eternity. This self-sacrificial love is what will bring us fulfillment and make us truly happy. This is a love that contemporary culture does not often understand. God's plan, however, is bigger than we are, and sometimes more than our minds can handle.

It is the Church's job to protect God's plan by helping couples understand the truth about marriage and how we were made. Conjugal love is not merely physical or emotional. It is not just a question of biology, nor can it be reduced to a game. Children are blessings, not burdens. Conjugal love is a free, loving, and unconditional gift of one spouse to another that is open to the fruit of God's blessing.

When couples learn the truth about contraception, sterilization, or reproductive technologies, such as IVF, and how they distort conjugal love, they often begin to see how the removal of the procreative dimension from their marriage has harmed the unitive dimension as well. Like two pieces of paper that have been super-glued together, you cannot destroy one without affecting the other. When we stray from God's plan, even the beauty of the person is changed.

What does the Pastoral Letter on Marriage have to say?

Marriage is a unique union, a relationship different from all others. It is the permanent bond between one man and one woman whose two-in-one-flesh communion of persons is an indispensable good at the heart of every family and every society. (*Marriage: Love and Life*, 22)

Conjugal love expresses the unitive meaning of marriage in such a way as to show how this meaning is ordered toward the equally obvious procreative meaning. The unitive meaning is distorted if the procreative meaning is deliberately disavowed. Conjugal love is then diminished. (*Marriage: Love and Life*, 15)

MAN ALWAYS COMES FORTH DIRECTLY FROM THE HAND OF GOD

Artificial birth control severs the link between the most intimate love union and the coming into existence of a new human being.

Every *active* intervention of the spouses that eliminates the possibility of conception through the conjugal act is incompatible with the holy mystery of the superabundant relation in this incredible gift of God. And this irreverence also affects the purity of the conjugal love act, because the union can be the real fulfillment of love only when it is approached with reverence and when it is embedded in the *religio*, the consciousness of our basic bond to God.

To the sublime link between marriage and procreation Christ's words on the marriage bond also apply: "What God has joined together, let no man put asunder." This becomes still clearer when we consider that the mystery of the birth of a man not only should be essentially linked to wedded love (through the conjugal act, which is destined to be the expression and fulfillment of this love), but is always linked to a creative intervention of God. Neither wedded love nor, still less, the physiological process of conception is *itself capable* of creating a human being with an immortal soul. On this point Pope Paul VI quotes the encyclical *Mater et Magistra*: "'Human life is holy,' Pope John XXIII reminds us, 'and from conception on it demands the immediate intervention of God!'" (*Humanæ Vitæ*, 13). Man always comes forth directly from the hand of God and therefore there is a unique and intimate relation between God and the spouses in the act of procreation. In a fruitful conjugal act we can say that the spouses participate in God's act of creation; the conjugal act of the spouses is incorporated into the creative act of God and acquires a serving function in relation to His act.

We thus see that artificial birth control is sinful not only because it severs the mysterious link between the most intimate love union and the coming into existence of a new human being, but also because in a certain way it artificially cuts off the creative intervention of God, or better still, it artificially separates an act which is ordained toward co-operation with the creative act of God from its destiny. For, as Paul VI says, this is to consider oneself not a servant of God, but the "Lord over the origin of life" (*Humanæ Vitæ*, 13).[130]

St. John Chrysostom writes on the unitive and procreative ends of marriage:

I say that husband and wife are one body in the same way as Christ and the Father are one. The two have become one. This not an empty symbol. They have not become the image of anything on earth, but of God Himself. From one man, Adam, he made Eve; then He reunited these two into one, so that their children would be produced from a single source. As if she were gold receiving the purest of gold, the woman receives the man's seed with rich pleasure, and within her it is nourished, cherished and refined. It is mingled with her own substance and she then returns it as a child! The child is a bridge connecting mother and father, so the three become one flesh.[131]

Why My Life Is Better Since Becoming Open to Life[132]

By Jennifer Fulwiler

"You guys aren't really going to have any more after this one, right?" a few people have asked me privately.

"We thought about having another, but the sleepless nights, the diapers, the pregnancy and birth—ugh! Aren't you just so ready to be *done* with all that?" a neighbor asked at the playground last week.

"I do not envy you," a lady at the grocery store said solemnly as I passed by with a cart full of three kids under five and a hugely pregnant belly.

Whenever people say things like this, I have this odd reaction of simultaneously having no idea what they're talking about and knowing exactly what they're talking about. My life seems so completely normal to me that I can't imagine it any other way; yet just a few years ago I would have been horrified by the idea of having so many kids so close together and would have thought it unthinkable not to use at least five different forms of contraception to make sure that no others came along any time soon.

Up until my mid-20's I was firm in my belief that I never wanted to have kids. A combination of events made me reconsider the issue, and by the time we got married I was open to the idea of having some pre-set, small number of kids and had begun thinking about the precise timetables on which I would have them.

Even after my husband and I came to an intellectual agreement with Catholic thought on contraception and agreed to do Natural Family Planning, I viewed my future with trepidation. I'd see women at Mass or on blogs who were pregnant and had lots of kids, or I'd hear about a Catholic couple mis-estimating their fertile period and ending up with a surprise pregnancy, and I'd think, "Ugh. That is not the life I want!"

It is surprising, then, to find that even though our combination of high fertility and high ineptitude at NFP makes me well on the way to being "one of those women," my life is actually much better than it was before. It would have been inconceivable to me to imagine that constantly having my plans derailed by pregnancies and not even having any idea when I'd be done changing diapers would be an *improvement* over my fully controlled, well-ordered life, but it has been.

Lately I've been imagining what I would say to 2003 Jen if I could go back in time and give her a crystal ball to show her what her future would be like. I've been trying to imagine how I would talk her down from the balcony ledge after the crystal ball got to the "four kids in five years—and doing NFP!" part, how I could possibly convince her that this life is not only *not* a recipe for misery, but the true fulfillment of everything she thought she wanted.

I would love to tell you that I'd simply be able to explain that each child is such a joy and a blessing, but that would not have resonated with Old Jen; I might have agreed, but ultimately I would have said that those joys and blessing are just too much hard work. "I just don't see how that kind of life could be anything but miserable for someone like me," I would have said.

Here is what I would say in response, based on five key things I didn't understand then that I understand now through the wisdom of Christian teaching:

1. Each of us is called to a vocation, and we'll never find peace until we find it and throw ourselves into it.

I've talked before about how understanding the concept of vocation revolutionized the way I saw my life. Until I understood this concept, that God has called me to the married life and that therefore my primary purpose on this earth is to be a wife and a mother, I kept thinking that there was something "out there" in the world that was going to bring me fulfillment and joy. I was stuck in the mindset that I needed to hurry up and get these challenging diaper and temper-tantrum years out of the way so that I could get back to living my "real" life, i.e. immersing myself in worldly pursuits in search of fulfillment.

What I could not have imagined is that when I surrendered to the idea that I am a wife and a mother first, that all my other hobbies and interests are important but secondary to that primary calling, it opened the floodgates for a waves of peace and grace to wash over me.

2. The world has nothing to offer us.

At the same time I began to understand my true vocation and attempt to fully embrace it, I also began to really get the Christian concept of, to paraphrase the great theologian Yaya, "WHAT YOU THINK IS OUT THERE AIN'T OUT THERE!" I realized that all of these excellent and important things I was going to do with my life after I was out of that difficult diaper phase were nothing more than all the things I'd been doing with my life before that had just left me restless and endlessly searching for the next big thing.

Slowly I began to realize that the only thing that was ever going to bring me lasting happiness was to discern what God's will was for my life, and to abandon myself to it.

3. "It's not what you do, it's whom you serve."

A product of secular society, I'd fallen into the common notion that the way to find true happiness is to focus on yourself more and other people less. It makes perfect sense, after all: doing pleasurable things for me is fun, sacrifice and hard work are not fun; ergo, the secret to happiness must be to live for myself as much as possible. Right?

How shocked I was to discover that I was wrong—dead wrong. Part of fully understanding the concept of vocation was understanding that a vocation is not to be thought of as "what you do" as much as it is "whom you serve." It was nothing short of revolutionary to hear the concept that God has called every one of us to serve others, that living for yourself is not a valid option; that the key to deep fulfillment, to finding your very purpose in life, is as simple as finding out the specific way in which you're called to serve. Do that, and you will find peace.

It sounded not only too simple to be true, but too difficult. As a spoiled only child the idea of living to serve sounded terrible. But once I actually took a leap of faith and tried it, I had no doubt that this was truth.

4. When you see something as temporary, you don't optimize.

On a practical level, I realized something that should have been more obvious to me given my business background: when you see a situation as temporary, you don't optimize.

Back when I saw pregnancy and birth and babies and diapers and the terrible two's as just a brief phase of life, my mentality was to simply grit my teeth and get through it. I had the luxury of belaboring every inconvenience because I knew in the back of my mind that it would all soon pass.

But once I changed my view to see new life as an inherent part of marriage and made no more long-term plans about exactly when we'd be done having kids, I was forced to confront the difficulties of the baby/toddler years in a new way. Now I was motivated to really get creative and brainstorm with my husband about how we could overcome some of the difficulties of these years and make things run more smoothly. And, due to some combination of natural psychological mechanisms and the grace of God, all those things about having little ones that had seemed like such a big deal just weren't that much of a big deal anymore once I saw it all as a lifestyle instead of a brief phase of life.

5. Life is better when you don't try to control everything.

One of the most frightening things about this lifestyle change—taking the decision about whether or not to have more kids month by month, seeing openness to life as the default, not using contraception even though we're bad at NFP—was the lack of control.

"But what about my plans?!" I'd think. "What about those lists of things I want to accomplish in the next five, ten, twenty years? How can I make progress on that if I don't even know how many kids I'll have and when I'll have them?!"

As I've said before, after a few years of living this way I've come to the shocking conclusion that my plans weren't actually that great. I've seen over and over again that just taking it day by day, discerning what God wants me to do here and now and not worrying about the long-term, is a far more fulfilling way to live.

What I was ultimately searching for with all those grand plans was a sense of accomplishment, a feeling of making a difference, a life of excitement, joy, peace, and happiness. Little did I know that children would never get in the way of any of that, because those things are not the result of well-crafted goals spreadsheets and to-do lists; they are only found in God.

And then, of course, there's this: the "result" of my first surprise pregnancy, snuggling with her grandfather. Children are only burdens when they're theoretical. Once they're here, you don't need any further analysis to know that they are priceless gifts from God, that whatever you had to sacrifice for them to exist was a small price to pay.

A FEW WONDERFUL REASONS TO HAVE CHILDREN

- A child is a new, wonderful, unique, unrepeatable human soul, and the parents become co-creators with God to bring this soul into existence. There is great dignity in the titles: father and mother.

- A child helps the parents grow in Christian virtues. A child requires that parents give up time, resources, sleep, pleasure, and comfort. True love, like Christ's love, is sacrificial. Children increase the parent's love, joy, peace, patience, goodness, kindness, and self-control through their needs and very existence.

- A child renews the human race and makes possible, by its very presence on earth, what was impossible. A child has infinite potential for doing good. Even if the child may not become a doctor that cures cancer or a Nobel Peace Prize winner, each human has the ability to perform countless acts of kindness throughout his/her life that would not have happened otherwise.

- A child is wonderfully entertaining. New parents can gaze for hours as their child puts his feet in his mouth, slobbers, or just sleeps. As their children get older and develop a sense of humor, they are even more entertaining. They learn to make people laugh and give them joy. Few people appreciate your jokes as much as your children do.

- Children are lifelong companions for their parents. Children come to visit you when all others may forget. When you grow old, your children will take care of you with respect others may not give. The more children you have, the more grandchildren you will have to hold.

- A child is God's opinion that life should go on.[133]

The Workout

1. Do we see our children as gifts from God? Do we see our children as a reflection of our love to the world?

2. What sacrifices has your spouse made in order to be a good parent? Do you appreciate what your spouse has given up for love of you and your family? Tell him or her now what you do appreciate.

3. What would you list as the benefits of having children? How have you grown as a person for having children? Have you grown in patience, kindness, or understanding because it was demanded of you? Have you thought less of yourself?

4. Whom do we serve with our marriage? Do we see our vocation as a gift from God that is offered back to him for our salvation?

LET US PRAY

Lord, God, creator of all things and people,
we praise you for your many gifts and thank you for the gift of married love.
We thank you for the happiness you have brought to us through our love.
Thank you for the joy you pour into our hearts in good times
and the comfort of the Holy Spirit during the storms of life.
Please bless our union and make it fruitful for you.
May we experience the fulfillment of love that you have planned for us.
Show us your will, so that we can be a reflection of your love to the world.
Amen.

PLANNING OUR FAMILY GOD'S WAY

Unit Three: Week Four Exercise
"A Double Session Workout"

LEARNING GOALS

- To understand the truth and wisdom of Pope Paul VI's encyclical *Humanæ Vitæ* (On Human Life).

- To expose the lies behind the contraceptive mentality and the devastating effects of the Sexual Revolution.

- To explore the difference between Natural Family Planning and Contraception.

- To help couples understand how to live God's plan in their particular family situation.

- To offer understanding to couples who are naturally infertile.

What does the Pastoral Letter on Marriage have to say?

It is the nature of love to overflow, to be life-giving. Thus, it is no surprise that marriage is ordained not only to growing in love but to transmitting life: "by its very nature the institution of marriage and married love [is] ordered to the procreation and education of the offspring and it is in them that it finds its crowning glory."[134]

Married love itself is ordered to the procreation of children, for, after all, the first command given to Adam and Eve is "be fertile and multiply" (Gn 1:28). (*Marriage: Love and Life*, 14)

Humanæ Vitæ and the Signs of the Times[135]

Placing Pope Paul VI's encyclical on the transmission of human life within its historical context helps us to understand the controversy it engendered.

Dr. Mark S. Latkovic

"*L*ove and marriage go together like a horse and carriage," as the popular 1955 Sammy Cahn song made famous by Frank Sinatra has it. "This I tell you brother, 'You can't have one without the other.'" One could have said just as easily that they go together *with* a *baby* carriage. The twentieth century saw feverish attempts to "rewrite" the meaning of this song—looking for ever new technological means of severing the God-given connection between marriage, love, sex and procreation. If, however, in the Catholic vision, marital love is a matter of total bodily self-giving (including one's fertility) and the *telos* (end) of sex is offspring, how can contraception be morally good?

Contraception and the Culture of Disruption

Of course, contraception is not a new phenomenon; even the ancient world was familiar with primitive forms of it. Sacred Scripture was aware of some forms of contraception as its use of "*pharmakeia*" testifies (see Gal 5:19–21). Such primitive forms were condemned in the *Teaching of the Twelve Apostles* (*The Didache*, 80 AD). St. Augustine in his *Confessions* (Book IV) seems to allude to the use of contraception with his concubine before his conversion ("when children are born against their parents' will"). The Catholic Church, for her part, has always taught that contraception is morally wrong, as Judge John T. Noonan has shown in his massive 1965 book, *Contraception*—even though in the same breath he favored a change in that constant teaching!

Pope Paul VI courageously affirmed this teaching in his landmark but controversial encyclical *Humanæ Vitæ* (*On Human Life*) in July 1968. This encyclical treated not only the morality of contraception, but also the proper understanding of marriage and the principles for the responsible transmission of life.

Much of the ecclesial dissent that ensued after the release of the document had its roots in the cultural and theological ferment of those times, and also in preceding decades, with pro-contraception figures such as Planned Parenthood founder Margaret Sanger preaching the (often eugenicist) "gospel" of abortion and contraceptive sex. Abortion would fuel the sexual revolution, but contraception in large measure would make it possible. We might call the 1960s the decade of "the Great Disruption," to borrow from political scientist Francis Fukuyama, although rightly he includes the 1970s in that disruption.

These were the days of "free love" and "free speech" movements, of calls for an "open Church" and for dialogue with the modern world (often understood as one-way instruction from the world *to* the Church). They were the days of anti-authority views, especially in the secular Western world. The mass media would, as today, disseminate these views into the homes of Americans.

They were also the days of *Griswold v. Connecticut* (what Catholic social thinker George Weigel calls "the Pearl Harbor of the American culture war"), the 1965 U.S. Supreme Court decision legalizing contraception for married couples based on "the right to marital privacy." Its reasoning would lead to the *Roe v. Wade* decision that legalized abortion eight years later. Change was in the air and the Church was expected to keep up with the times and "adapt" her teaching to the modern age.

After all, some argued, didn't the Second Vatican Council (1962–1965) call on Catholics to read the "signs of times"? Wasn't one of these signs the idea that technological fixes such as the progesterone pill would solve many of our problems, from poverty to overpopulation? Couldn't it be argued the Holy Spirit was speaking to the Church through the experience of those married couples who had found the Church's teaching (the rhythm method) not only onerous but outdated, in a world where poverty and population were increasing, where women where entering the workforce in increasing numbers, and people were giving greater attention to sexual pleasure in and outside of marriage?

Christian Marriage, Love and Procreation

Now, in fact, the Church had faced a version of this question before; better, the question had never really gone away and was now resurfacing under new circumstances. What, it was asked in the early-to mid-twentieth century, is the relationship between love and procreation in marriage? The 1917 *Code of Canon Law* spoke of "procreation and [the] raising of offspring" as the "primary end" of marriage (see c. 1013). But many "personalist" theologians thought this language too juridical, too impersonal, and well, downright neglectful of conjugal love.

In their attempts to incorporate love and the more personal elements of the couple's relationship into the understanding of marriage, some of these theologians, such as Herbert Doms, seemed to downplay the procreative good from their definition of marriage. Others, such as Catholic philosopher Dietrich von Hildebrand, were able to maintain faithfulness to the Magisterium and the Catholic tradition yet develop that tradition in positive ways. Von Hildebrand spoke of procreation as the *primary purpose* of marriage and marital intercourse, but of loving communion as their *primary meaning*.

Nevertheless, the personalists firmly accepted the Church's teaching condemning contraception. Indeed, no Catholic theologian denied this teaching before the early 1960s. Even educated American Catholics in the early 1960s fully accepted it, as sociologist Fr. Andrew Greeley noted at the time. The further expansion of such personalist ideas could be found in Pope Pius XI's 1930 encyclical, *Casti Connubii*. Pius XI issued this marvelous but neglected document in the wake of the Anglican Communion's Seventh Lambeth Conference (1930) and its new-found acceptance of contraception in marriage in exceptional circumstances. He structured its treatment according to the traditional Augustinian "three goods" of marriage: offspring, fidelity and the sacrament.

Pius XI spoke of conjugal love in glowing terms, but he also condemned direct abortion, contraception and sterilization in the strongest of language. He reminded the faithful that marriage is naturally ordered to children, even if it is not simply instrumental to them. But that wasn't all the pope said.

At the same time, Pius wrote, "This mutual molding of husband and wife, this determined effort to perfect each other, can in a very real sense, as the [*Catechism of the Council of Trent*, 1566] teaches, be said to be the chief reason and purpose of matrimony, provided matrimony be looked at not in the restricted sense as instituted for the proper conception and education of the child, but more widely as a communion, companionship, and association of life as a whole" (no. 24).

In this beautiful passage, as moral theologian Germain Grisez notes, the Holy Father not only re-presents Trent's teaching, but implies that marriage is intrinsically a vocation and path to holiness, and thus good not only as a means to children.

The Popes, the Pill, and the Pontifical Commission

In the late 1950s, Pope Pius XII was faced with judging the morality of the newly invented birth control pill. Dr. John Rock, a Catholic layman and co-developer of the pill, wrote a book titled, *The Time Has Come: A Catholic Doctor's Proposals to End the Battle over Birth Control* (1963), arguing, in its favor, that the pill was a "natural" contraceptive. Already, the University of Louvain priest-theologian Louis Janssens had argued that the pill could be morally acceptable. Even some bishops were beginning to wonder at this time if the pill could be reconciled with Catholic conjugal morality under certain conditions.

Pius XII, however, saw that the pill was no different in moral character than any other form of contraception, even though it did not interfere with the *physical* integrity of the act of sexual intercourse. This fact—often taken to be the chief criterion for determining the morality of the sexual act in one understanding of the natural law—had led many to think that the Church could and would "make her peace" with chemical contraception.

Thus, Pius XII would prohibit as morally wrong any attempt to render procreation impossible before, during or after the marital act. The pill (when used expressly for contraceptive purposes), although not interfering with the physical performance of the act itself, as a condom does, would render the marital act intentionally closed to procreation.

Even though Pius XII had already condemned the pill, Pope John XXIII established in the early 1960s the Pontifical Study Commission on Family, Population, and Birth Problems—of which Noonan was later made a member—to investigate the issue further. The commission's establishment would explain the Council's silence on the morality of the pill. What was at issue, however, was not the Church's teaching on the immorality of contraception. At issue was only whether the pill should be prohibited as contrary to Church teaching on contraception. (As evidence, see *Gaudium et Spes*, no. 51, footnote 14, which cites passages from *Casti Connubii* and Pius XII strongly condemning contraception, except for the latter's teaching against the oral contraceptive).

The Pontifical Commission would produce four papers meant for the pope's eyes only, but then have them leaked to the media in April 1967, most likely to put pressure on the Holy Father to change the Church's teaching. These papers would make dubious arguments rooted in a moral theory later called proportionalism (which was condemned by Pope John Paul II in his encyclical *Veritatis Splendor*) in its case for the Church to change her teaching on contraception. Included among these papers was the report of a minority of the commission's members that upheld the traditional teaching on contraception.

The "Majority Report" of the Pontifical Commission, coupled with the progressively-minded reading of Vatican II (especially seen in *Gaudium et Spes'* new approach to marriage, with its emphasis on covenant and conjugal love), added to the expectation by many that the Church would do an about-face and accept the pill and other forms of contraception. As we know, such was not the case. Three (long!) years after the close of the Council, Paul VI in *Humanæ Vitæ* would teach that *each and every marital act had to remain open to new human life* (see no. 11); meaning, not that spouses must intend procreation every time, but rather that *contraception is always wrong*.

Humanæ Vitæ and the Development of Doctrine

Paul VI rooted this teaching in a profound truth of natural law, that the two meanings of the marital act (the unitive and the procreative) are inseparable as designed by God (see no. 12). Like *Gaudium et Spes* before him, the pope refrained from using (yet did not deny) the older language of "ends" and their hierarchical ranking. Paul VI had found, with Vatican II, new language ("meanings" of the marital act) to proclaim an old truth: marriage *and* marital love are ordained to the procreation and education of children.

In teaching that man was not permitted to break the connection between the unitive and the procreative meanings, Paul VI was affirming the notion that these two meanings are *interdependent*: that is, if you attack the one, you attack the other because both goods are intrinsic to the nature of the marital act (see no. 13). John Paul II, in his 1981 apostolic exhortation *Familiaris Consortio* (see no. 32) and in his writings on the "Theology of the Body," would develop these ideas in profound ways.

In fact, as Grisez argues, Vatican II, Paul VI and John Paul II, in a remarkable development of the tradition, would treat parenthood as part of the *communion* of married life. Paul VI sums up this development nicely when he writes in *Humanæ Vitæ:* "As a consequence [of God's plan for marriage], husband and wife, through that mutual gift of themselves, which is specific to them alone, develop that communion of persons, in which they perfect each other, so that they may cooperate with God in the generation and rearing of new lives" (no. 8). This vision of marriage and the marital act would find its way into the 1983 *Code of Canon Law*, particularly in the language that speaks of "the good of the spouses" (see c. 1055).

According to Paul VI, however, not all ways of regulating birth are immoral. He taught that recourse to the natural cycles of the reproductive system is fundamentally different in moral character than contraception (see no. 16). For the pope, then, use of periodic abstinence, or what we today call Natural Family Planning or NFP (not to be confused with the unreliable calendar method), was not an attack on the good of human life-in-its-transmission, as is contraception. But the crucial moral difference did not rest on the fact that one was "artificial" (the pill) and the other "natural" (NFP).

One might put the matter this way. For Paul VI, contraception is a choice to impede new human life from coming-to-be by doing something before, during, or after freely chosen intercourse—whether as an end or as a means (see no. 14). NFP, on the other hand, does not involve an intention to impede the transmission of life. It is, rather, the choice to *abstain* during the fertile period.

Simply put, the moral difference between the two ways of regulating fertility is this: contraception (as its name implies) is always *anti*-procreative, while NFP is simply *non*-procreative. Married couples can practice the latter (have sexual relations during the infertile period) when they have a good reason for not bringing new life into the world—and there are such reasons—recalling, too, that conjugal intercourse during the infertile period can realize other legitimate spousal values (the expression of love and affection). But only the choices to welcome more children, to be open to their coming-to-be, and the use of NFP, are exercises in "responsible parenthood" (see *Humanæ Vitæ*, no. 10).

A Call to Commitment

Towards the end of *Humanæ Vitæ*, before the pope offers pastoral directives such as the promotion of chastity, he reflects prophetically on what would be the consequences if contraception became widespread (see no. 17). Sadly, his predictions have become all too true about the "moral fallout" from contraception. Paul VI argued that widespread use of contraception would lead to marital infidelity and a general lowering of moral standards. The Holy Father also warned that contraception would lead to disrespect for women, where men would treat them like sex objects. Finally, he warned of the danger of governments using contraception coercively to solve problems of overpopulation. The "one-child only" policy in China, for example, has proven out the pope's fears. His other "prophecies" would also prove true, borne out by social science data on such problems as rising divorce rates. One might argue just as well—

contrary to popular belief—that there is a real connection between contraception and greater reliance on abortion.

"In preserving intact the whole moral law of marriage," Paul VI writes in *Humanæ Vitæ*, "the Church is convinced that she is contributing to the creation of a truly human civilization. She urges man not to betray his personal responsibilities by putting all his faith in technical expedients. In this way she defends the dignity of husband and wife" (no. 18).

This is the ultimate legacy of *Humanæ Vitæ:* its contribution to building a truly human civilization, a "civilization of love," with a "culture of life" at its heart. This is why we read the document today and why I hope we will keep on reading it for the next forty years. The teaching can surely be a hard one to practice, but assisted by God's grace, it is possible! If only more of us Catholics would give the document a "second chance."

In a spirit of conversion, let us commit or recommit ourselves to the teaching of *Humanæ Vitæ*. Let its inspiring vision of the human person, marriage and conjugal relations serve as an impetus to not only learn about Paul VI's teaching but to boldly live it.

(Dr. Mark S. Latkovic is professor of moral theology at Sacred Heart Major Seminary).

HISTORY OF THE SEXUAL REVOLUTION

The following five points have been taken from the article "*Casti Connubii*: 60 Years Later, More Relevant than Ever," by John F. Kippley.[136]

Most parishioners have utterly no idea that before August 14, 1930, birth control was not a Catholic-Protestant issue. This isn't to say that before that time some theologians, both Catholic and Protestant, had not argued in favor of allowing marital contraception, but the formal teaching of all the Christian churches had held the line. I have found that the simple exposition of the relevant facts can be helpful in leading couples to understand better and then to accept the teaching of *Casti Connubii* and *Humanæ Vitæ*. The entire Church would benefit from a closer look at these landmark encyclicals in the context of the historical circumstances that prompted it and the sexual revolution in which the Church struggles today. What are the relevant facts? I think it is helpful to explain that the modern sexual revolution did not start in 1960 but rather has developed over a period of almost two centuries. The first stage started with Malthus; the second with Margaret Sanger; the third with Lambeth of 1930; and the fourth with the Pill.

Stage 1: Malthus.

I credit the Rev. Thomas Malthus with starting the modern sexual revolution because he provided the scare—the fear that would cast out true love. In his 1798 "An Essay on the Principle of Population," Malthus created the modern "population explosion" scare, saying that unless it were checked, population would outgrow food supplies and result in mass starvation. He recommended only moral means of family limitation, i.e., late marriage and sexual self-control, but his scare would outlive his morality. The discovery of vulcanization of rubber in 1839 led to the production of cheaper, more effective condoms, and armed with this technological breakthrough, the neo-Malthusians of the 1860s substituted condoms for the self-control of Malthus and beat the drums of the population scare. (Fear of the future generally provides a good rationalization for sins of the present.) I call this Stage I of the sexual revolution because at the time it was truly revolutionary to advocate separating the unitive and procreative aspects of marital relations.

In the United States, this led to a reaction led by a Protestant reformer, Anthony Comstock, who persuaded Congress in 1873 to legislate against the distribution and sale of contraceptive devices in federal territories. Many states followed suit, and the conglomerate of anti-contraceptive legislation became known as the Comstock laws.

Here's what I find religiously interesting about these brief historical facts. During the first 400 years of the Reformation, birth control was not a Catholic-Protestant issue. Charles Provan has recently published a small book which contains the anti-contraceptive teachings of 66 Protestant theologians including Luther and Calvin.[137] The Comstock laws were passed by essentially Protestant legislatures for a basically Protestant America, and they remained in effect until Christian unanimity about birth control was shattered in 1930.

Stage 2: Margaret Sanger.

Forerunner to Planned Parenthood

In the years before World War I, Margaret Sanger and others began to wage war on the Comstock laws, and about 1914 she founded her National Birth Control League, the forerunner of today's Planned Parenthood, which she founded in 1939. The contraceptionists frequently advocated a whole new concept of marriage. They denied the divine origin and the permanence of marriage and made efficient contraception the technological cornerstone of "companionate" marriage—a serial polygamy consisting of legal marriage, efficient contraception, divorce when boredom set in, and then remarriage to start the process over. I call this Stage II of the sexual revolution because of the tremendous influence Margaret Sanger had on the practices and moral thinking of her day and even more so today. The pressures she generated were highly influential in removing the legal, religious and social barriers to contraception and then abortion.

PLANNED PARENTHOOD UNVEILED

What is Planned Parenthood?

Planned Parenthood is the world's leading vendor of abortion and contraceptives, as well as a political organization. With almost 880 locations in the United States and lobbying groups and clinics throughout the world, Planned Parenthood sells abortion, contraceptive services, contraceptive sexuality education, and more. Planned Parenthood has become a prominent presence in the Chicago area with the opening of "express" locations targeting minors for abortion and contraceptive services without parental notice or consent. How can parents of teens be prepared? By knowing the facts.

Who Founded Planned Parenthood and Why?

Margaret Sanger (1879–1966) was born into a poverty-stricken family of eleven children. Her second husband was a millionaire who enabled her rise to affluence. After establishing her first birth control clinic as a result of her obsession with total sexual "freedom," she became active in the eugenics movement. Eugenics is a phony science that advocates compulsory "breeding" of the select, contraception among the poor, and sterilization and euthanasia for the "unfit." This became the foundation for the practice of contraception, sterilization, abortion, and euthanasia.[138]

The Founder's Philosophy: In Her Own Words

"Defectives" and the "Unfit": "Birth control itself, often denounced as a violation of natural law, is nothing more than the facilitation of the process of weeding out the unfit, of preventing the birth of defectives or of those who will become defective."

— *Woman and the New Race* by Margaret Sanger

Racism: "[The most] successful educational approach to the Negro is through a religious appeal. We do not want word to get out that we want to exterminate the Negro population, and the minister is the man who can straighten out that idea if it ever occurs to any of their more rebellious members … Remember our motto: if we must have welfare, give to the rich, not to the poor … We are paying for and even submitting to the dictates of an ever increasing, unceasingly spawning class of human beings who never should have been born at all."

— Elisha Drogin, *Margaret Sanger: Father of Modern Society*
(New Hope: CUL, 1989), p. 43, 33, 45, 52.

Planned Parenthood's Mission: In Its Own Words

"Teen[s] 17 and under receive services and supplies at a special discounted price."

— Web listing for Planned Parenthood Express Orland Park.
www.planned-parenthood.org/pp2/clinicDetail.do?ID=368&org=chago&serviceID=0

"If your parents are stupid enough to deny you access to birth control, and you are under 18, you can get it on your own. Call Planned Parenthood."

— *Dallas Observer*, January 30, 1986

"We're trying to shame the medical profession into doing its job. It's a breach of the public trust when you're graduated and licensed as an ob-gyn not to perform abortions."

— Alexander Sanger, CEO of Planned Parenthood of New York City,
The Kokomo (Indiana) Tribune, February 10, 1995

"Planned Parenthood Express is about fast, affordable birth control options. If you're ready for the pill, the patch, the shot, condoms, or just need some trusted information, come to Planned Parenthood Express."

— Press release for opening of Planned Parenthood Express in Schaumburg, IL.
www.plannedparenthood.org/pp2/chago/files/chago/news/ppexpress.xml

Does Planned Parenthood Help Teens & Women Now?

Some women who have been clients of Planned Parenthood have suffered injury or death. In 2002, Diana Lopez, 25, bled to death after her cervix was punctured during an abortion.[139]

Holly Patterson, 18, died in 2003, one week after she underwent an early abortion using mifepristone (RU-486).[140] Although she was impregnated at age 17 by a 24-year-old man, Planned Parenthood did not explore the possibility of statutory rape. Holly's parents didn't know until it was too late.[141]

Additional cases of Planned Parenthood malpractice, unsanitary conditions and more are documented in *The Scarlet Survey* by Kevin Sherlock (Brennyman Books, 1997). *LifeSiteNews.com* is also a great resource to get updated information on life issues.

From 1977 through 2005, Sanger's Planned Parenthood performed 4,068,794 abortions. Planned Parenthood's 2008 annual report states that the organization committed 305,310 abortions in the United States in 2007. This excludes abortions caused by hormonal "contraceptives" such as the birth control pill, the Patch, Depo-Provera, RU-486, or the "morning after pill," which can prevent implantation after a new life is conceived. Of the hundreds of thousands of women it served, Planned Parenthood referred only 4,912 women for adoption in 2007—a ratio of more than 62 abortions committed for each adoption referral.

How Much Money Does Planned Parenthood Receive?

For the fiscal year concluding June 2008, Planned Parenthood Federation of America reported a record income of $1.038 billion, with a profit of $85 million. That year, PPFA received $349.6 million in government grants and contracts. More than one-third of Planned Parenthood's budget comes from taxpayers. In spite of an average of $80 million in "excess of revenue over expenses" annually, Planned Parenthood lobbyists are continually in Congress and state legislatures fighting for more government funding. (Planned Parenthood Federation of America Annual Report 2007–2008)

How Can I Protect My Teens and My Community?

- Foster open communication about relationships and sexuality with your teens. Helpful resources to foster discussion include *www.pureloveclub.net*; *www.teenbreaks.com*; *www.lovematters.com*; *www.sexrespect.com.*

- Clearly and lovingly communicate your expectations about chastity and the sanctity of human life.

- Let your state legislatures, members of Congress and the U. S. President know that you do not want your tax dollars going to Planned Parenthood.

- Contact your school board members and ask them to keep Planned Parenthood out of your local schools.

- Boycott companies that give to Planned Parenthood.

- Pray at abortion clinics or volunteer at a pregnancy resource center to provide positive options to women.

- Contact your Diocesan Respect Life Office for additional resources.

"The greatest destroyer of peace today is abortion."
— *Blessed Teresa of Calcutta (Mother Teresa)*

Assistance for women or couples who face unplanned pregnancies:
Aid for Women, Chicago and Berwyn (312) 621-1100, *www.aidforwomen.org*
The Women's Center, Chicago and Evergreen Park (773) 283-1400
Catholic Charities, Aurora (630) 820-3220
Birthright… *www.birthright.org/*
International Life Services *www.internationallifeservices.org*

Post-Abortion Reconciliation and Healing:

Project Rachel (312) 337–1962, (888) 456–HOPE
www.hopeafterabortion.org
projectrachelchicago@gmail.com

Contact your local parish priest for the Sacrament of Reconciliation.

Stage 3: Lambeth of 1930.

Stage III of the sexual revolution was its embrace by Protestant Christianity. The key event is the Lambeth Conference of the Church of England in 1930. In 1908, the Anglican bishops had reacted to the neo-Malthusian pressures by reaffirming the teaching that it was immoral to use unnatural methods of birth control. So also at their Lambeth Conference of 1920. But the pressures of the 1920s proved too much for them, so on August 14 at their Lambeth Conference of 1930, the Anglican bishops reluctantly accepted marital contraception as morally licit. In doing so, they acknowledged that previously they had always taught the immorality of marital contraception.[142]

This marked the first time in history that a Christian Church had given its acceptance to using unnatural methods of birth control. Furthermore, they were warned by one of their own, Bishop Charles Gore, that accepting contraception would open the door to accepting homosexual sodomy, but Gore voted in the minority. We do not know what would have happened if the Church of England had kept the faith regarding marital love and sexuality. But we can certainly see in hindsight that this was an embrace of the sexual revolution.

In the United States, Lambeth of 1930 was quickly accepted by a committee of the Federal Council of Churches in March 1931, when it endorsed "the careful and restrained use of contraceptives by married people." The general moral atmosphere of the times can be inferred from a March 22 editorial in the *Washington Post*:

"Carried to its logical conclusion, the committee's report, if carried into effect, would sound the deathknell of marriage as a holy institution by establishing degrading practices which would encourage indiscriminate immorality. The suggestion that the use of legalized contraceptives would be 'careful and restrained' is preposterous." However, it was carried into effect, and the deathknell was sounded. The promise of marital contraception in the eyes and mouths of religious-talking people has always been that with very limited family size and unlimited sex, couples would be happier and divorce would become almost unknown. In the light of current American contraceptive marriage with its 50% divorce rate, what can be said except that nature bats last?

Pope Pius XI Responded to Anglicans

It was to the Anglican resolution at Lambeth that Pope Pius XI made reference in his famous and immortal reply in *Casti Connubii* on the last day of 1930:

"Since, therefore, openly departing from the uninterrupted Christian tradition some recently have judged it possible solemnly to declare another doctrine regarding this question, the Catholic Church, to whom God has entrusted the defense of the integrity and purity of morals, standing erect in the midst of the moral ruin which surrounds her, in order that she may preserve the chastity of the nuptial union from being defiled by this foul stain, raises her voice in token of her divine ambassadorship and through Our mouth proclaims anew: any use whatsoever of matrimony exercised in such a way that the act is deliberately frustrated in its natural power to generate life is an offense against the law of God and of nature, and those who indulge in such are branded with the guilt of a grave sin."[143]

Stage 4: The Pill.

The fourth stage of the sexual revolution was the Pill. By 1960, the practice of contraception was well accepted by all the mainline Protestant churches and was more or less universally practiced by all "family planners" except the Catholic and Orthodox Churches, some very conservative or fundamentalist Protestants, and Orthodox Jews. Certainly contraception was practiced by many Catholics in the fifties, but hard data is hard to come by. Large families were in vogue, and without the natural spacing of ecological breastfeeding (which, if practiced correctly, spaces babies an average of two years apart), many couples were having babies every year. There is data indicating that in 1965 rhythm was by far the most widely used form of conception regulation by Catholic "family planners"; trying to read that backwards is hazardous, but I would hazard a guess that before 1960 no more than half and perhaps only a third of Catholic couples in their fertile years were using contraception.

The arrival of the Pill in 1960 marks the fourth stage of the sexual revolution because it brought birth control to the front pages and made it seem all the more acceptable. Since it was totally different in approach from other methods, it was discussed in the papers and popular magazines just as a health matter, and every article conveyed the assumption that birth control was the modern thing to do, almost a social obligation. The morality of birth control as such was not a subject for public debate, but within the Catholic community, the Pill occasioned fierce attacks upon the traditional teaching against all unnatural forms of birth control, and such attacks went largely unanswered in the popular Catholic press: there was little real debate. The teaching of *Casti Connubii* was being seriously muted and undermined, and the result was that more and more Catholics accommodated themselves to the dominant contracepting culture. Thus by 1965, while rhythm was still practiced by 32% of Catholic "family planners," the Pill was being used by 18%, and barrier methods 24%.

Pope Paul VI, in *Humanæ Vitæ*, would teach that each and every marital act had to remain open to new human life, meaning not that spouses must intend procreation every time, but rather that contraception is always wrong. The Pill and all other forms of contraception go against God's plan for life and love.

Many women who have been put on the Pill for medical reasons or because their doctor put them on it at a very early age for no apparent reason have begun to discover the devastating physical, spiritual, and emotional effects of the Pill. Many have stopped taking it and discovered that their bodies will never be the same again.

How does the Pill work? — Dr. Martha Garza
- Inhibits ovulation
- Inhibiting the action of the cilia
- Decreases cervical mucus
- Potential abortifacient

The Harms of Contraception
Predicted by Pope Paul VI

Pope Paul VI in his encyclical *Humanæ Vitæ* predicted four evils that would arise if Church teaching on the regulation of births were ignored and if dissent continued.

First, he stated that widespread use of contraception would lead to conjugal infidelity and the general lowering of morality. Between 1960 and 1996, statistics show that babies born out of wedlock increased by forty-five percent. The divorce rate has doubled from 1965 to 1990 among those who use contraception before they marry and the rate of adultery has increased dramatically since 1965.

> The media frequently reports that 50% of American marriages will end in divorce. This number appears to have been derived from very skimpy data related to a single county or state. However, it appears to be reasonably close to the probable value. The Americans for Divorce Reform estimates that probably, 40 or possibly even 50 percent of marriages will end in divorce if current trends continue. However, that is only a projection and a prediction.[144]

It has been reported that the divorce rate among Catholics is *less than one percent* for couples who pray together, practice the faith regularly, and use a natural approach to family planning.

Second, Paul VI warned that man would lose respect for a woman's physical and psychological equilibrium, and treat her as a "mere instrument of selfish enjoyment." Contraception deceives a woman into thinking that she is liberated and free to choose when and how she will get pregnant, when in reality men have become the real "beneficiaries." The use of contraception diminishes a man's responsibility and commitment, treating a woman merely as an object of desire and lust.

Third, he warned that artificial birth regulations would "place a dangerous weapon in the hands of those public authorities who take no heed of moral exigencies." The FDA, pharmaceutical companies, and several other organizations, such as Planned Parenthood, continue to approve and distribute oral contraceptives, abortifacient drugs (morning after pill), and sterilization devices that do nothing but harm a woman's body, jeopardize the life of an unborn baby, and break up marriages, without any consideration to the moral, physical, or psychological ramifications it has on women, the family, and society as a whole.

Finally, he asserted that contraception would mislead human beings into thinking that they have unlimited dominion over their bodies, turning the human person into the object of his own intrusive power. For example, we may read on bumper stickers today, "Keep your laws off my body." Or hear people chant in protest, "It's my body; it's my choice." With all the new reproductive technology, we are even able to create, change, modify, and manipulate genes, in order to get that perfect baby, as though we were ordering some "thing" off the Internet. Where is God in the equation?

Paul VI in *Humanæ Vitæ* recognizes the state and its responsibility for the well-being of its citizens. In this capacity it is legitimate for the state to intervene to orient the demography of the population. This can be done by means of objective and respectful information, but not by authoritative, coercive measures. The state may not legitimately usurp the initiative of spouses, who have the primary responsibility for the procreation and education of their children. It is not authorized to promote demographic regulation by means contrary to the moral law.[145]

On October 4, 1965, when addressing the U. N. General Assembly, Paul VI challenged his audience: "You must make it possible to have enough bread for humanity's table; and not favor the artificial control of births—something irrational—to decrease the number of guests at the banquet of life."

A man and woman's authentic freedom thus exists when the couple expresses and embraces the act of self-giving or reciprocal love. By practicing their rights according to the natural moral law, they are thus cooperating with the Divine Plan of God, the Creator. Married couples must be open to the transmission of life, without interfering with the Natural Moral Law, which is that law of human conduct that arises from human nature as ordered to its ultimate end. Divine positive law are those laws of human conduct that are found in the revealed word of the Old and New Testaments. Thus according to "the order of nature" where God is the author, Divine Revelation takes priority over anything derived from reason. Consequently, a violation consists of any interference with the order designed by God or acting against what we know to be true expressions of what most fulfills human potential.

The two ends of marriage—love and life—always go hand in hand. Contraception divorces the unitive and procreative end in the conjugal love act. "Thus the innate language that expresses the total reciprocal self-giving of husband and wife is overlaid, through contraception, by an objectively contradictory language, namely, that of not giving oneself totally to the other. This leads not only to a positive refusal to be open to life but also to a falsification of the inner truth of conjugal love, which is called upon to give itself in personal totality ... The difference, both anthropological and moral, between contraception and recourse to the rhythm of the cycle ... involves in the final analysis two irreconcilable concepts of the human person and of human sexuality ... [146]" "Let all be convinced that human life and the duty of transmitting it are not limited by the horizons of this life only: their true evaluation and full significance can be understood only in reference to *man's eternal destiny*"[147]

Contraception and a Woman's Self-Image[148]

by Jennifer Fulwiler

On the rare occasions that I used to think about the prospect of having a large family before my conversion, one of the first things that would come to mind is, "Just think of what my abs would look like! And years and years of nursing babies wouldn't exactly leave me looking like a Victoria's Secret model!" and with a shudder I'd perish the thought. There were other reasons that the prospect of having many children didn't appeal to me. But the issue of what my body would start to look like somewhere around baby number five or six was actually a pretty large factor.

Was I just shallow? I'm not so sure.

I was the product of a culture that takes contraception for granted and believes that the primary purpose of sex is for pleasure. Sure, it can be one of a variety of methods for creating life, but the main reason it exists is just for pleasure.

Given that worldview, it kind of makes sense for a wife to prize preserving her physical appearance over bringing new life into the world. If it's true that a fundamental part of marriage is sex, and sex is for pleasure, and men are visually oriented when it comes to physical attraction, it doesn't seem so unreasonable that a wife would take great pains to look young and fit as long as possible, and perhaps even value that above additional children. This sort of thing also came up back in college when my pro-choice friends and I would rage about these awful pro-lifers who tried to tell women that they should carry an unexpected pregnancy to term. The horror! Didn't these people know what pregnancy does to a woman's body?! This assumed, of course, that there would be circumstances upon which a pregnancy would be totally unexpected (a la the contraceptive mentality), and that any physical trauma to a woman's body would be so terrible as to be a justifying factor in terminating a pregnancy.

Thinking back to those discussions, we so abhorred the idea of what a pregnancy does to a woman's body because *this was our value*. What we looked like physically was so intertwined with our value as human beings that to tell us we should have to carry a pregnancy to term—with all the weight gain and stretch marks and physical changes that would entail—was to say that we should make our very selves less valuable as women.

It is the same pro-contraception worldview that motivates women's magazines to talk about little else other than "how to be SEXY", for pop culture to insist that older women are STILL SEXY, and for well-meaning people to assure women of varying body types such as the overweight or the disabled that they CAN BE SEXY TOO.

And I believe that it's this same worldview that's changed how the ideal woman is depicted. I thought of this as I looked through this beautiful video of women in art throughout the ages. Contrast the soft, mysterious, classically feminine beauty portrayed in ages past to the hyper-sexualized images we see of women today.

For women in our culture, to be "hot" or "sexy" is to have value. There are a variety of theories as to why this is true but, from my experience, it goes back to the acceptance of contraception and the idea that the primary purpose of sex is for pleasure.

None of this had really crystallized for me until, one day last year, I put on a swimsuit to go to the pool with the kids. I checked my appearance in the mirror and with my pale skin and post-baby figure the word "Yeti" came to mind. I chuckled at my glowing wit, made a mental note to cut out the new habit of ice cream after dinner, and threw a towel over my shoulder to head to the pool. But something about that moment nagged at me, and after thinking about it for a while I realized what it was: how very, very different my reaction was to seeing myself looking a little heavy in a swimsuit than it would have been just a year or two before.

What had happened? Years and years of intense focus and worry about my physical appearance had seemingly just melted away into a much more calm, reasonable expectation of what I should look like.

It was then that I realized how much the Catholic Church's teaching on contraception and the purpose of marriage and sex had changed my life. I had thought of my agreement with and acceptance of Church teaching on the matter to be a purely intellectual decision. But I realized that day that it was so much more than that. It had fundamentally changed where I derived my value as a woman, and where my husband and I had derived the value of our marital life.

Shortly after the swimsuit incident my husband and I attended a marriage course required by our parish to have our marriage blessed in the Church. It was offered by a nondenominational Christian group, and in their segment called "Great Sex" they completely separated sex from the creation of life, explaining that sex is a gift from God for our pleasure. The odd, elephant-in-the-room exclusion of having children from the entire discussion impressed upon me how hollow our society's view of sex really is: *Why would we bring up something as un-sexy as pregnancy and having babies? We're trying to talk about sex here!*

I left the course that night feeling sad. Sad for the years I spent mentally compartmentalizing sex and the bringing forth of new life, and the effects that had on my self-image as a woman. Sad for the slightly overweight lady at the table next to me who shifted uncomfortably as the instructors peppily emphasized the importance of staying in shape if you're going to keep things "exciting" in the bedroom. And sad for all the couples who were there because their marriages were troubled, since I'm sure the overly detailed advice they received on how to have a good sex life only added pressure to their stressful situation.

As I listened to the instructors offer tips and tricks for how couples could better bond through the marital act, I couldn't help but think that it seemed like they were just missing it. It almost seemed as if they themselves knew that they weren't exactly hitting the nail on the head with this topic. They offered suggestion after suggestion for how spouses could be romantic, show each other unconditional love, let their partner feel accepted and cherished, etc., involving touch and eye contact and flowers and candy and surprises and back rubs and … whew! I can't even remember them all. Though all of these things sounded nice enough, they seemed so weak and pale compared to the ultimate way of showing your spouse devotion and unconditional love: to implicitly say with every sexual act, "It's OK with me if we should create a life together with this act." What's more romantic than that?

I don't mean to be too hard on the marriage course instructors, who seemed like very sweet people who were genuinely trying to do something good for couples. And I don't mean to alienate or criticize couples who do choose to use contraception. I just wanted to share my thoughts on this aspect of my conversion since it's changed my life in such a big way. Even with challenges like tricky medical issues, financial difficulties and unexpected pregnancy, seeing the world in this new light has brought me more peace than almost anything else I've experienced in my conversion.

What does the Pastoral Letter on Marriage have to say?

Deliberately intervening, by the use of contraceptive practices, to close off an act of intercourse to the possibility of procreation is a way of separating the unitive meaning of marriage from the procreative meaning. This is objectively wrong in and of itself and is essentially opposed to God's plan of marriage and proper human development. It makes the act of intercourse signify, or speak something less than the unreserved self-gift intended in the marriage promises. (*Marriage: Love and Life*, 18–19)

WHAT IS NATURAL FAMILY PLANNING?

What does the Pastoral Letter on Marriage have to say?

Natural Family Planning (NFP) methods represent authentic family planning. They can be used both to achieve and to postpone a pregnancy. NFP makes use of periodic abstinence from sexual intercourse based upon the observations of the woman's natural signs of fertility, in order to space births or limit the number of children when there is a serious reason to do so. NFP methods require that couples learn, accept, and live with the wonders of how God made them. This is essentially different from contraception. (*Marriage: Love and Life*, 21)

The Church supports scientific efforts to aid couples who wish to achieve children. There is a scientific technique for achieving pregnancy that is moral and effective, not to mention organic and virtually cost free.

Natural Family Planning is a term referring to the family planning methods approved by the Roman Catholic Church. In accordance with the requirements for sexual behavior in keeping with the dignity of the human person, NFP excludes the use of other methods of contraception.

Periodic abstinence and the natural infertility caused by breastfeeding are the only methods deemed moral for avoiding pregnancy. When used to avoid pregnancy, NFP limits sexual intercourse to naturally infertile periods: portions of the menstrual cycle, during pregnancy, or after menopause. Various methods may be used to identify whether a woman is likely to be fertile; this information is used to either try to avoid or try to achieve pregnancy.

"NFP is learning about God's gift of fertility, embracing that gift and paying attention to it and monitoring it. It is a discovery of a plan that our loving God has already given us, built into our bodies. It is a natural, harmless way to postpone, avoid, or achieve pregnancy without drugs, artificial hormones or devices. It is a way of life and a different way of looking at life."[149]

Pre-Twentieth Century

Possibly the earliest Christian writing about periodic abstinence was by St. Augustine. In the year 388, he wrote, "Is it not you who used to counsel us to observe as much as possible the time when a woman, after her purification, is most likely to conceive, and to abstain from cohabitation at that time …?"[150] The Manichaeans (the group the early church father St. Augustine wrote of) believed that it was immoral to create any children, thus (by their belief system), trapping souls in mortal bodies. Augustine condemned them for their use of periodic abstinence: "From this it follows that you consider marriage is not to procreate children, but to satiate lust."[151]

Pre-1800s references to periodic abstinence are scarce to nonexistent. The Roman Catholic Church's first recorded official statement on periodic abstinence to avoid pregnancy is from 1853, where a ruling of the Church's Sacred Penitentiary addressed the topic of periodic abstinence to avoid pregnancy. Distributed to confessors, the ruling stated that couples who had, on their own, begun the practice of periodic abstinence—especially if they had "legitimate reasons"—were not sinning by doing so.[152]

In 1880, the Sacred Penitentiary reaffirmed the 1853 ruling, and went slightly further. It suggested that, in cases where the couple was already practicing artificial birth control, and could not be dissuaded to cease attempting birth regulation, the confessor might morally *teach* them of periodic abstinence.

Early Twentieth Century

In 1905, Theodoor Hendrik van de Velde, a Dutch gynecologist, showed that women only ovulate once per menstrual cycle.[153] In the 1920s, Kyusaku Ogino, a Japanese gynecologist, and Hermann Knaus, from Austria, working independently, each made the discovery that ovulation occurs about fourteen days before the next menstrual period.[154] Ogino used his discovery to develop a formula for use in aiding infertile women to time intercourse to achieve pregnancy.

In 1930, John Smulders, a Roman Catholic physician from the Netherlands, used Knaus and Ogino's discoveries to create a method for *avoiding* pregnancy. Smulders published his work with the Dutch Roman Catholic medical association, and this was the official rhythm method promoted over the next several decades. While maintaining procreation as the primary function of intercourse, the December 1930 encyclical *Casti Connubii* by Pope Pius XI gave the highest form of recognition to a secondary-unitive-purpose of sexual intercourse. This encyclical stated that there was no moral stain associated with having marital intercourse at times when *"new life cannot be brought forth."* Although this referred primarily to conditions such as current pregnancy and menopause, the Sacred Penitentiary in yet another ruling in 1932,[155] and the majority of Catholic theologians also interpreted it to allow moral use—for couples with "upright motives"—of the newly created rhythm method.[156]

In 1932, a Catholic physician published a book titled *The Rhythm of Sterility and Fertility in Women* describing the method, and the 1930s also saw the first U.S. Rhythm Clinic (founded by John Rock) to teach the method to Catholic couples. It was during this decade that Rev. Wilhelm Hillebrand, a Catholic priest in Germany, developed a system for avoiding pregnancy based on basal body temperature.

Later Twentieth Century to Present

The 1950s also saw another major advance in fertility awareness knowledge: Dr. John Billings discovered the relationship between cervical mucus and fertility while working for the Melbourne Catholic Family Welfare Bureau. Dr. Billings and several other physicians studied this sign for a number of years, and by the late 1960s had performed clinical trials and begun to set up teaching centers around the world.[157]

Humanæ Vitæ, published in 1968 by Pope Paul VI, addressed a pastoral directive to scientists: "It is supremely desirable … that medical science should by the study of natural rhythms succeed in determining a sufficiently secure basis for the chaste limitation of offspring." This is interpreted as favoring the then-new, more reliable symptoms-based fertility awareness methods over the rhythm method. Just a few years later, in 1971, the first organization to teach a symptothermal method (one that used both mucus and temperature observations) was started. Now called Couple to Couple League International, this organization was founded by John and Sheila Kippley, lay Catholics, along with Dr. Konald Prem. During the following decade, other now-large Catholic organizations were formed: Family of the Americas (1977), teaching the Billings method, and the Pope Paul VI Institute (1985), teaching a new mucus-only system called the Creighton Model.

Methods: How Do They Work? Are They Effective?

There are three main types of NFP: the symptoms-based methods, the calendar-based methods, and the breastfeeding or lactational amenorrhea method. Symptoms-based methods rely on biological signs of fertility, while calendar-based methods estimate the likelihood of fertility based on the length of past menstrual cycles. The Ovulation Method and the Sympto-thermo method are 98 to 99% effective to avoid pregnancy if used according to the rules. They are also highly effective in achieving pregnancy.

NFP is based on five scientific principles:[158]

1. A woman ovulates only one time per fertility cycle.

2. Cervical mucus is the most accurate, definitive sign of woman's fertility. It must be present for conception to take place.

3. A woman can detect this cervical mucus without any devices.

4. The ovum can live a maximum of 12 to 24 hours once released.

5. Sperm can survive in a woman's body a maximum of 3 to 5 days when the most fertile mucus is present.

Symptom-based

The three primary signs of a woman's fertility:

1. *Basal body temperature* is the lowest temperature attained by the body during rest (usually during sleep). It is generally measured immediately after awakening and before any physical activity has been undertaken, although the temperature measured at that time is somewhat higher than the true basal body temperature. In women, ovulation causes an increase of one-half to one degree Fahrenheit (one-quarter to one-half degree Celsius) in basal body temperature (BBT); monitoring of BBTs is one way of estimating the day of ovulation. The tendency of a woman to have lower temperatures before ovulation, and higher temperatures afterwards, is known as a biphasic pattern. Charting of this pattern may be used as a component of fertility awareness.

2. *Cervical mucus*: This will be covered in the videos.

3. *Fertility monitors* is a computerized device used for fertility awareness. Some brands are marketed only to assist in pregnancy achievement, while other brands are advertised for both pregnancy achievement and as birth control. A fertility monitor may analyze hormone levels in urine, basal body temperature, electrical resistance of saliva and vaginal fluids, or a combination of these methods.

From these symptoms, a woman can learn to assess her fertility without use of a computerized device. Some systems use only cervical mucus to determine fertility.

Two well-known mucus-only methods are:

1. *The Billings ovulation method* (*www.billings-centre.ab.ca, www.boma-usa.org*).

    John Billings developed this method in order for women to monitor their fertility, by identifying when they are fertile and when they are infertile during each menstrual cycle. Users pay attention to the sensation at their vulva, and the appearance of any vaginal discharge. This information can be used to achieve or avoid pregnancy during regular or irregular cycles, breastfeeding, and peri-menopause. Described by the BOM organization as "Natural Fertility Regulation," this method may be used as a form of fertility awareness or natural family planning, as well as a way to monitor gynecological health. (*This will be the system presented in the two videos.*)

2. *The Creighton Model Fertility Care System:* (*www.creightonmodel.com, www.popepaulvi.com*).

> This system is a form of natural family planning which involves identifying the fertile period during a woman's menstrual cycle. The Creighton Model was developed by Thomas Hilgers, the founder and director of the *Pope Paul VI Institute*. Hilgers describes the Creighton Model as being based on "a standardized modification of the Billings ovulation method," which was developed by John and Evelyn Billings in the 1960s. The CrMS is used in conjunction with NaProTechnology (Natural Procreative Technology: *www.naprotechnology.com*), which aims to restore fertility naturally, by identifying and then correcting the underlying causes of the couples' infertility. (*This will be discussed more in depth in Presentation Ten.*)

The Sympto-Thermal Method

It involves observing and charting regular changes in a woman's cervical mucus and body temperature as well as other physical signs. These signs provide a cross-check by which couples can reliably determine the woman's fertile and infertile times.

> National organization:
>
> The Couple to Couple League International, Inc.
> P.O. Box 111184 Cincinnati, OH
> 45211–1184
>
> Phone Numbers:
> (513) 471–2000 | (800) 745–8252 | FAX: (513) 557–2449
>
> Local organization
> Couple to Couple League Chicago
>
> Web page: *www.naturalfamilyplanningchicago.com*

Catholic doctrine holds that God created sexual intercourse to be both unitive and procreative. The Church considers deliberately altering fertility or the marital act with the intention of preventing procreation to be sinful. Thus, artificial birth control methods are forbidden, as are acts intended to end in orgasm outside the context of intercourse (e.g., masturbation or oral sex). At the same time, abstinence is considered morally acceptable.[159]

Having sex at an infertile time in a woman's life (such as pregnancy or post-menopause) is also considered acceptable, since the infertile condition is considered to be created by God, rather than as an act by the couple.[160] Similarly, under Catholic theology, it may be morally acceptable to abstain during the fertile part of the woman's menstrual cycle.[161] Increasing the postpartum infertile period through particular breastfeeding practices—the lactational amenorrhea method—is also considered a natural and morally unobjectionable way to space a family's children.

The Catholic Church acknowledges a potential benefit of spacing children[162] and use of NFP for this reason is encouraged. *Humanæ Vitæ* cites "physical, economic, psychological and social conditions" as possibly compelling reasons to avoid pregnancy.[163] Couples are warned, however, against using NFP for selfish, immoral, or insincere reasons. At times God will be asking you to have another child. At others, you will need to postpone having another child. Why might God ask you to postpone? Perhaps one of you has lost his/her job. Maybe there is a serious illness, or your last child was only born three months ago. God's plan is specific to you in that it takes into account the circumstances of your life. Keep in mind that God delights in children, and therefore reasons for which he would ask you to postpone would be serious and nontrivial. Therefore, the Church does not teach that couples must have as many children as they are biologically able to beget. The real question is not "how many children must we have" but "how many children would God like to give us?" The Catholic Church extols the benefits children bring to their parents, their siblings, and society in general, and encourage couples to be open to God's gift of life as their circumstances make practical.

HOW IS NFP DIFFERENT FROM CONTRACEPTION?[164]

Physically Different:

- Hormonal methods of contraception (pill, Depo-Provera injection, Lunelle, Ortho Evra patch, NuvaRing) work in three ways: suppression of ovulation (blocking hormones which cause development of follicle); impede sperm migration (thickening of cervical mucus; and/or inhibit implantation/abortifacient) by making endometruim lining thin and hostile to new embryo. IUD—usually works as abortifacient.

- Contraception looks at fertility as a disease to be treated or an unwanted condition to be suppressed. It alters or inhibits the natural fertility process or outcome with artificial hormones or barriers. So it basically alters the sex act.

- NFP does not interfere with the natural fertility process, nor does it alter the sexual act. It allows the natural fertility cycle to play itself out each month, and the couple work in harmony with it. Also, it is immediately reversible.

- Contraceptive methods all have physical side effects such as blood clot formation, cervical cancer, liver tumors, and bone density changes.

- NFP has no side effects whatsoever.

Emotionally Different:

- Contraception says "I'm not waiting for you to get to the infertile period in your cycle. I want sex now." Sex on demand. Women can feel like sexual objects—always available, but not always interested.

- "I don't want the natural consequences of this act—arming for battle—"It's your turn."

- NFP users say: "I respect and love you so much that I'm willing to wait for you." No "burn out" from always being available, never having to set aside a time of repose.

Spiritually Different:

- Contraception says: "I love you and accept you, but not your fertility." It puts conditions on a love that by its very nature should be unconditional. Our fertility is part of our identity. We reject that part of the person. At the moment of closest union a couple is putting up barriers.

- NFP says: "I love you completely and unconditionally, and I embrace your fertility."

- We as Catholics believe that marriage is a Sacrament, which mirrors Christ's love for the Church, which is unconditional. Sexual union is a renewal of the marriage covenant.

- Sexual union actually starts to lose its unitive meaning as well as its procreative meaning when contraception is used.

- When a couple uses NFP to postpone children, they are not changing the meaning of sexual union; they are not blocking God out of their embrace. If he truly wanted to, he could create a life at the infertile time. Since God usually obeys his own laws, he very seldom does this. Contraception changes the meaning of sexual union by rejecting its procreative power and withholding its unitive power.

Arguments against NFP[165]

- *NFP is no different than contraception, the objective is the same.*

  Contraception demands sex on its own terms, whenever the mood strikes. There is no sacrifice on the part of the couple. An NFP user couple may very much want to have sexual relations, but they give it up for a greater good in the marriage. It requires sacrificial love.

- *NFP is not spontaneous. It's not natural to abstain.*

  How much spontaneity is there with a condom, diaphragm? Women can feel used being always available. What they mean is, it's not easy. Nothing worthwhile in life is easy.

- *NFP doesn't work.*

  It has been scientifically proven to be 98—99% effective to postpone or avoid pregnancy in several worldwide studies. It has involved 50 years of research and counting.

- *NFP can be abused, used for the wrong reasons.*

  To some degree this is true, but there is a built-in mechanism to prevent this. Every month a couple has to ask themselves why they are doing this. If they don't have a good reason, they will probably not abstain in the fertile time.

Achieving a Pregnancy with NFP—The Other Part of the Gift[166]

NFP can be used to consciously conceive a child. A couple actively cooperates with God in bringing a new life into the world. This can be a truly "awesome" experience.

God wants us to be conscious co-creators with him. No longer is a couple in a fog. Not about when a pregnancy might have happened. A baby can never be considered an "accident" or a "mistake." A baby is never "unplanned" as is the case with a couple using contraception. As one couple said after they conceived while using NFP, "We cannot imagine life without our little girl Grace." NFP is one of the greatest discoveries of the twenty-first century. It can prevent so much physical, emotional and spiritual harm; prevent so many marital problems and so many divorces. It is really worth learning and practicing in your marriage.

WATCH THE FOLLOWING FOUR VIDEOS ON THE *OVULATION METHOD*

(This can be done anytime throughout the month)

- Session One (12 minutes) *Natural Family Planning: Fertility Awareness*

- Session Two (10 minutes) *Natural Family Planning: How to space births or postpone pregnancy for a serious reason*

- Session Three (6 minutes) *Starting to Chart Your Symptoms*
  A sample chart is available at *www.ovulationmethod.org*.

- Natural Family Planning (36 minutes) by Janet Smith on *Contraception and Natural Family Planning*

HOW ARE WE TO LIVE GOD'S PLAN FOR LIFE AND LOVE IN OUR OWN PARTICULAR FAMILY SITUATION?

Why shouldn't we continue to use contraception if it doesn't bother our conscience?

Reality Check #1: Mark and Jenny

Mark and Jenny had attended a Catholic Marriage Preparation Course at their parish. Although contraception was mentioned, they were told that a couple had to make their own decision. Their parents had used contraception, their Catholic friends had used contraception, and they used contraception. They already have three children, and their marriage has its set of pressures and problems. They are both working, and still buckling under economic stress. It does not bother their conscience to be using contraception when they think it helps reduce the stress in their sex life. Why would they consider Natural Family Planning now if they want to avoid pregnancy anyway? What's the problem?

What does the Pastoral Letter on Marriage have to say?

We recognize that couples face many challenges to building and sustaining a strong marriage. Conditions in contemporary society do not always support marriage. For example, many couples struggle to balance home and work responsibilities; others bear serious economic and social burdens.

Some challenges, however, are fundamental in the sense that they are directed at the very meaning and purpose of marriage. (*Marriage: Love and Life*, 17)

"By using contraception" married couples "may think that they are avoiding problems or easing tensions, that they are exerting control over their lives."[167] At the same time they may think that they are doing nothing harmful to their marriages. In reality, the deliberate separation of the procreative and unitive meanings of marriage has the potential to damage or destroy the marriage. Also, it results in many other negative consequences, both personal and social. (*Marriage: Love and Life*, 19)

Openness to procreation in the marital act involves acknowledg[ing] that one is not the master of the sources of life.[168] Using the technology of contraception is an attempt at such mastery. By contrast, couples using methods of NFP do nothing to alter the conjugal act. Rather, they abstain from conjugal relations during the portion of the woman's menstrual cycle when conception is most likely. This practice fosters in couples an attitude of respect and wonder in the face of human life, which is sacred. It also fosters profound respect for one's spouse, which is necessary for the mutual enjoyment of authentic intimacy. (*Marriage: Love and Life*, 21)

So why would Mark and Jenny use Natural Family Planning at this stressful time of their marriage?

Jenny and Mark should follow God's plan and avoid the fear-based contraceptive mentality. In this way, they would complete their love, improve their marriage, and increase the respect between them, especially in the area of sexual relations. By following the teachings of the Church, Jenny and Mark would express and celebrate the fundamental meaning and purpose of marriage. By contrast, by deliberately closing sexual intercourse to life through contraception, they change the meaning of the marriage act. Instead of honoring God and the way he created us, the contraceptive act leaves God out and places oneself over him. Most importantly, during stressful times, Mark and Jenny more than ever need God's grace in their marriage. Contraception, is a serious sin which sets ourselves in direct opposition to God, whose love and grace we need for growth in virtue, and for our earthly and eternal happiness.

Why shouldn't couples get sterilized?

Reality Check #2 Jason and Stephanie:

Jason and Stephanie have six children. They started out very open to life and are now exhausted. Stephanie stays home with the children, and Jason works two jobs. They can barely afford the Catholic School tuition, let alone vacations. They think they have done their part by having the children they have. They never learned Natural Family Planning because they thought they did not need to, since they wanted a large family. They are considering having Jason get a vasectomy.

What does the Pastoral Letter on Marriage have to say?

Sometimes one hears it said that as long as the marriage as a whole is open to children, each individual act of intercourse need not be. In fact, however, a marriage is only as open to procreation as each act of intercourse is, because the whole meaning of marriage is present and signified in each marital act. (*Marriage: Love and Life*, 18)

What does the Church teach about voluntary sterilization?

The Church teaches that we must take care of our bodies and our souls, and may not do intentional harm to ourselves. Direct voluntary sterilization is designed to destroy the normal functioning of a healthy organ in order to prevent the conception of children. This is considered an act of mutilation and is considered morally wrong. Regarding unlawful ways of regulating births, Pope Paul VI asserted, *"Equally to be condemned … is direct sterilization, whether of the man or of the woman, whether permanent or temporary."*[169] The Catechism also states, *"Except when performed for strictly therapeutic medical reasons, directly intended amputations, mutilations, and sterilizations performed on innocent persons are against the moral law."*[170]

So what should Jason and Stephanie do now?

They should take a course in Natural Family Planning from one of the many organizations that teach it. The Diocesan Marriage and Family Office can refer them to teachers of the different methods.

Please see the two articles in the appendix on **Just Cause and Natural Family Planning** that answers common questions, such as, when should we space births? How many children should we have? What are serious reasons for avoiding pregnancy, are the reasons temporary or permanent? And why contraception and sterilization are always outside God's plan for life and love?

What if one of us has already undergone deliberate sterilization, not for health reasons, but rather for contraceptive purposes?

Excerpt from *Married Couples Who Intentionally Chose Sterilization for Contraceptive Purposes and Lasting Repentance* by Monsignor Charles M. Mangan:

> However, imagine a married couple who have done something permanent in order to prevent conception. The husband has undergone a vasectomy or the wife a tubal ligation. There immediately appears to be a substantial and ongoing problem. How can this couple show their genuine sorrow since the effect of the direct sterilization continues unabated? May they ever be really reconciled to their Creator, thereby shunning their sin and the prevailing ethos of the Culture of Death and assume their place in the Christian community as those who give good example to others and testify to the Truth, notwithstanding the not insignificant cost?
>
> This essay offers guidance for married couples who deliberately selected sterilization to prevent conception. Although the teaching of the Catholic Church is the foundation for this article, the remarks herein are not limited to Catholic married couples who chose to be sterilized so as not to conceive but are germane to persons of all faiths and to those of no faith, because the doctrine of the Catholic Church is based on Sacred Scripture, the Apostolic Tradition and the Natural Law—the trio of sources expressing the One Truth that sustains and applies to everyone without exception.
>
> It is hoped that all married couples who intentionally chose to be sterilized so as not to conceive but who seek forgiveness and a new beginning in Christ and those married couples in the same category but who have never thought much about the vital importance of rejecting the sin of direct sterilization and the subsequent urgent need of conversion will benefit from these brief reflections.

For more about the Church's teaching on sterilization, please see this entire article, *Married Couples Who Intentionally Chose Sterilization for Contraceptive Purposes and Lasting Repentance,* in the appendix.

What if we are infertile and want to have children?

Reality Check #3 Maria and Garret:

Maria and Garret desperately want to have children. They have tried for eight years and have seen three fertility specialists to assist them with conception. Time is running out, and the most recent doctor offered to refer them to an *in vitro* specialist. It sounds better to them than adoption. After all, the reason they got married was to have a family. Should they be deprived of this if there is technical help available?

What does the Pastoral Letter on Marriage have to say?

> It is true that some marriages will not result in procreation due to infertility, even though the couple is capable of the natural act by which procreation takes place. Indeed, this situation often comes as a surprise and can be a source of deep disappointment, anxiety and even great suffering for husband and wife. When such a tragedy affects a marriage, a couple may be tempted to think that their union is not complete or truly blessed. This not true. (*Marriage: Love and Life*, 14–15)

It is a reality that more and more couples are having difficulty achieving pregnancy. You may be one of those couples or know couples who are unable to have children. You might also know couples who have been told by their doctors that they cannot have children and have had children miraculously. So do not give up hope.

The first place to start if you are having difficulty is to pray. At various points in the Bible, we read of couples who were unable to conceive, but after prayer, were granted their miracle baby or babies. Read about Abraham and Sarah or Zachariah and Elizabeth. Sometimes however, God does not always grant that prayer in the same way that the couple wishes. Know that he still loves you very much and trust that he may have other plans for you.

> Couples who still suffer from infertility after exhausting legitimate medical procedures should unite themselves with the Lord's cross, the source of all spiritual fecundity. They give expression to their generosity by adopting abandoned children or undertaking demanding service to others. Their marriage can nevertheless have a full meaning, in both human and Christian terms. Their marriage can radiate a fruitfulness of love, of hospitality, and sacrifice.[171]

Susan Jordon writes of her experience of infertility:

> I certainly empathize with women struggling to have children, since cancer and other illnesses have denied me the joy of motherhood. I am blessed today with wonderful nieces and nephews spanning two generations. But I have sought comfort from my faith, family and friends. I also gleaned meaningful insights from an important teaching that "children are a gift, not a right." In working through my own painful experience of infertility, I have come to embrace my Catholic faith more deeply, to be open to God's invitation to be of service to others through my unique charisms, perhaps even understand more profoundly the meaning of sacrifice in one's journey to holiness and salvation.[172]

Even if the couple is unable to have children, the conjugal love act in no way loses its meaning, because the couples' loving communion and desire for life is what makes it ultimately life-giving and fruitful.

"Von Hildebrand spoke of procreation as the *primary purpose* of marriage and marital intercourse, but of loving communion as their *primary meaning*."[173]

> The intrinsic meaning and value of marriage consists in its being the deepest and closest love union. In its mutual self-donation and in its constitution of a matchless union, the conjugal act has the meaning of a unique fulfillment of spousal love. *But to that high good, which has a meaning and value in itself, has been entrusted procreation.* But let it be stated again emphatically: to stress the meaning and value of marriage as the most intimate, indissoluble union of love does not contradict the doctrine that procreation is the primary end of marriage.

> The conjugal act does not in any way lose its full meaning and value when one knows that a conception is out of the question, as when age, or an operation for the sake of health, or pregnancy excludes it. The knowledge that a conception is not possible does not in the least way taint the conjugal act with irreverence. In such cases, if the act is an expression of a deep love, anchored in Christ, it will rank even higher in its quality and purity than one that leads to a conception in a marriage in which the love is less deep and not formed by Christ. And even when for good and valid reasons conception should be avoided, the marital act in no way loses its *raison d'être*[174], because it's meaning and value is the actualization of the mutual self-donation of the spouses. The intention of avoiding conception does not imply irreverence as long as one does not actively interfere in order to cut the link between the conjugal act and a possible conception.[175]

Keep in mind the option of adoption. You may not get the miracle you want, but you can be the miracle for a child who needs to be adopted. There are many children who do not have parents, who need to be loved. This may include infants, but also somewhat older children. They are probably praying for a miracle: to have parents who will love them. Perhaps you can be the answer to their prayers. Do you know of any couples who have adopted?

David and Vanessa from Chicago, IL write of their experience of infertility and adoption:

> David and I have been married almost seven years. Even while we were dating, we always talked about having a large family—five, six, seven children … as many children as God would give us! Early in our marriage, we were trained in Natural Family Planning (NFP) and began using the method immediately.
>
> We began using the method to conceive a baby and after several months without being able to conceive, we began to wonder if maybe something was wrong. After meeting with several doctors, we learned that we were infertile and we would never be able to have biological children together. However, the doctors suggested several reproductive technologies including sperm donation and in vitro fertilization in order for us to conceive a child. These methods are not consistent with the Church's infallible moral teaching as they all share a common characteristic—the baby is created outside of the procreative marital act. We felt no desire to create a child outside of God's perfect design and as a result, we quickly declined all of these suggestions. We truly felt that it was God's will that we would not conceive a child together. This did not mean it was easy for us because we did not understand how God could answer our desire for a large family with infertility, but we knew it was morally wrong to pursue these other methods.
>
> Knowing that the Lord knows our hearts and wills and what is good for our marriage, we prayed and trusted that He would form our family in His timing and in His way. As the Lord's Prayer clearly states, "Thy will be done," not *our* will be done. We believed that by submitting to God's will and being obedient to His Church's Teaching, He would truly provide for us and bless us abundantly. We consider our infertility a tremendous blessing because we know that it came from the Hand of God from the beginning. It is part of His perfect plan for our marriage; therefore, we must remain faithful and accept it, ask for His grace to live it, and remain obedient to His will.
>
> It took us several years to be ready to begin the adoption process. We had heard that the process was lengthy and challenging and that some couples wait years for their child. While it was a difficult process emotionally and at times we felt that we were being scrutinized, we knew that this was the way we were going to build our family, so we persevered. We formed a strong relationship with our social worker and we felt well-supported and prepared by our adoption agency. We were able to complete the paperwork and the required classes in about seven months and were placed on the "waiting family list" in March 2008. With just one month on the list, we received the life-changing phone call that we had been chosen by a birthmother! We would have the baby that we so desired! At that point, we owned three items—a bottle, a set of receiving blankets, and a car seat. It was amazing to see how our family and friends came together to bring everything that we needed to welcome a new baby into our home. Nicholas Benedict came home to us on May 1, 2008, and we could not be happier!
>
> Life is more exciting, fun, busy, and rich now that Nicholas is part of our family. We decided that I would "retire" from my accounting career and become a stay-at-home mom. I don't miss the

stress of the working world one bit and I'm so happy to spend each day with Nicholas. Our marriage has become stronger since we've become parents and we can hardly remember what life was like before Nicholas came home. We have now been through the adoption process again and we're awaiting our second child!

We were amazed at how God knew our hearts and formed our family better than we could have planned it ourselves.

To those couples who might learn that they are infertile, support each other and above all, pray! Especially pray the Holy Rosary! Trust that God has more for your life than you could ever ask for or imagine … it may not be what you envisioned for yourself, but surprisingly enough, it will be better!

What does the Pastoral Letter on Marriage have to say?

The procreative capacity of man and woman should not be treated as just another means of technology, as also happens with *in vitro* fertilization (IVF) or cloning. When that happens, human life itself is degraded because it becomes, more and more, something produced or manufactured in various ways, ways that will only multiply as science advances. Children begin to be seen less as gifts received in a person communion of mutual self-giving, and increasingly as a lifestyle choice, a commodity to which all consumers are entitled. There is a true issue of the dignity of human life at stake here. (*Marriage: Love and Life*, 20)

WHAT ABOUT ARTIFICIAL REPRODUCTIVE TECHNOLOGIES?

A child is not something *owed* to one, but is a *gift*. The "supreme gift of marriage" is a human person. A child may not be considered a piece of property, an idea to which an alleged "right to a child" would lead. In this area, only the child possesses genuine rights: the right "to be the fruit of the specific act of the conjugal love of his parents," and "the right to be respected as a person from the moment of his conception."[176] (CCC 2378)

Research aimed at reducing human sterility is to be encouraged, on condition that it is placed "at the service of the human person, of his inalienable rights, and his true and integral good according to the design and will of God."[177] (CCC 2375)

While the Church strongly encourages science to aid couples trying to achieve pregnancy, the ends never justify the means. Some reproductive technologies, while achieving the goal of giving couples children, nevertheless contradict the meaning of love and life.

Children are Begotten not Made

"A child does not come from outside as something added on to the mutual love of the spouses, but springs from the very heart of that mutual giving, as its fruit and fulfillment."[178]

Each new life, each human being, even if he or she is born with physical defects, is to be the fruit of an act of love between husband and wife. This is what it means to "beget" children. The union of husband and wife not only share in God's love, but also in his creation of a new life. Therefore, technology that separates the conception of children from the one-flesh union of spouses also denies the link to God. It is an attempt to "make" a human being though technology rather than "beget" a human being by cooperating with God.

TECHNOLOGIES THAT CONTRADICT THE MEANING OF LOVE AND LIFE

IVF (In Vitro Fertilization) & AI (Artificial Insemination)

1. Heterologous artificial insemination and fertilization

2. Homologous artificial insemination and fertilization

   Techniques that entail the dissociation of husband and wife, by the intrusion of a person other than the couple (donation of sperm or ovum, surrogate uterus), are gravely immoral. These techniques (heterologous artificial insemination and fertilization) infringe the child's right to be born of a father and mother known to him and bound to each other by marriage. They betray the spouses' "right to become a father and a mother only through each other."[179] (CCC 2376)

   Techniques involving only the married couple (homologous artificial insemination and fertilization) are perhaps less reprehensible, yet remain morally unacceptable. They dissociate the sexual act from the procreative act. (CCC 2377)

IVF (In Vitro Fertilization) is immoral and is an intense burden on women physically, emotionally, and spiritually:

- The manufacturing of human life in a laboratory usually results in a large number of embryos, which leads to selective abortion of some embryos and the destruction of human life.

- In multiple gestation pregnancies, women have increased risk of gestational diabetes, bleeding, and pre-eclampsia (dangerously high blood pressure). Infants born as multiples are almost always premature and have higher rates of low birth weight, cerebral palsy, developmental delays, birth defects, and death.

- Financial burden: One cycle of IVF can cost $10,000. Fertility drugs, such as Clomid, however, are moral to use and can cost a few hundred dollars. These drugs, nevertheless, may also result in multiple embryos.

The Church does not say that children conceived through IVF or other immoral means have less moral worth than other children. This also applies to children who are physically or emotionally challenged. Every human life is a precious gift from God. Many parents have been deceived by doctors who try and pressure desperate and vulnerable couples into IVF. Couples, however, who know the immorality of IVF and still choose to do it, commit grave sin.

   The act [IVF or AI] which brings the child into existence is no longer an act by which two persons give themselves to one another, but one that "entrusts the life and identity of the embryo into the power of doctors and biologists and establishes the domination of technology over the origin and destiny of the human person.

   Such a relationship of domination is in itself contrary to the dignity and equality that must be common to parents and children."[180] Under the moral aspect procreation is deprived of its proper perfection when it is not willed as the fruit of the conjugal act, that is to say, of the specific act of the spouses' union … Only respect for the link between the meanings of the conjugal act and respect for the unity of the human being make possible procreation in conformity with the dignity of the person.[181] (CCC 2377)

RESOURCES ON INFERTILITY

Pope Paul VI Institute—Dr. Thomas Hilgers and Fertility Care Practitioners Internationally renowned expert on infertility and reproductive health issues. *www.fertilitycare.org* or *www.naprotechnology.com*

Respect Life Office of the Archdiocese of Chicago Consultations, information or moral questions regarding fertility treatments. (312) 534–5355 *www.respectlifechicago.org*

National Catholic Bioethics Center Consultations with bioethicists by phone on infertility issues and treatments. (215) 877-2660 *www.ncbcenter.org*

Dr. Kristi Graham–Christian counseling addressing the emotional and psychological impact of infertility. Offices in downtown Chicago and Wheaton. (630) 653–1717 *www.meierclinics.com*

Catholic Infertility Online Support Group for women seeking support or information on infertility and the teachings of the Catholic Church. *health.groups.yahoo.com/group/catholic-fertility*

Jean Blair Packard and Thomas W. Hilgers, *In Their Own Words: Women Healed* (Omaha, NE: Pope Paul VI Institute Press, 2004). This book contains testimonies of women cured of infertility, multiple miscarriages, premature births, premenstrual syndrome, and postpartum depression through NaProTechnology treatment.

"Trading on the Female Body," a video produced by the organization Hands Off Our Ovaries that highlights the risks to women's health of egg harvesting, a procedure that is part of IVF. *www.handsoffourovaries.com*

Prenatal Partners for Life and Be Not Afraid organizations providing support to parents who have received a difficult prenatal diagnosis. *www.prenatalpartnersforlife.org* and *www.benotafraid.net*

"Assisted Reproductive Technologies are Anti-Woman," article by Marie Anderson, M. D., FACOG and John Bruchalski, M. D. *www.usccb.org/prolife/programs/rlp/04anderson.shtml*

Related Vatican Documents

Dignitas Personæ: Instruction on the Dignity of a Person on Certain Bioethical Questions, by Sacred Congregation for the Doctrine of the Faith, 2008.

The Dignity of Human Procreation and Reproductive Technologies, by Pontifical Academy for Life, 2004.

Evangelium Vitæ: Encyclical letter to the Bishops, Priests, and Deacons, Men and Women religious, lay Faithful, and all People of Good Will on the Value and Inviolability of Human Life, by John Paul II, 1995.

Donum Vitæ: Instruction on Respect for Human Life in Its Origin and on the Dignity of Procreation, by Sacred Congregation for the Doctrine of the Faith, 1987.

Humanæ Vitæ: Encyclical letter to the Patriarchs, Archbishops, Bishops and other Local Ordinaries in Peace and Communion with the Apostolic See, to the Clergy and Faithful of the Whole Catholic World, and to All Men of Good Will, on the Regulation of Birth, by Paul VI, 1965.

The Workout

1. What has our family planning journey been like? What good have we done? What mistakes have we made? How has this affected our marriage? What are our regrets? Do we have anything we need to repent of, or do reparation for?

2. Can each of us explain the difference between using Natural Family Planning and using contraception? Who in our lives might we be able to explain this to?

3. How do we feel about offering our sexual life to God? How can this help us grow closer to each other and become one in Christ?

4. How have our lives been fruitful for God?

5. If we are experiencing infertility, have we discussed the option of adoption?

LET US PRAY

God our Father, you taught us to be generous with love and life.
Mary, you always said "yes" to God.
Jesus, fill us with your grace that we may be as fruitful as we are made to be.

Hail Mary, full of grace, the Lord is with you.
Blessed are you among women, and blessed is the fruit of your womb, Jesus.
Holy Mary, Mother of God, pray for us sinners now and at the hour of our death. Amen.

Group Workout

Unit Three: Week Three
God's Plan for Life and Love: Life in Christ

- Moral life: A virtual workout with the Holy Spirit

- Complementarity leads into unitive

- The unitive end of marriage: unity for the sake of mission

- The procreative end of marriage: planning your family God's way

- Natural Family Planning and the harms of contraception

WEEKLY GROUP MEETING: THIRD WEEK

1. **Prayer (10 minutes including table reflection)—**

St. Francis Prayer for Peace
Lord, make me an instrument of your peace;
Where there is hatred let me sow love,
Where there is injury, pardon;
Where there is doubt, faith;
Where there is despair, hope;
Where there is darkness, light;
Where there is sadness, joy.

O Divine Master, grant that I may not so much seek to be consoled as to console;
To be understood as to understand;
To be loved, as to love,
For it is in giving that we receive,
It is in pardoning that we are pardoned,
And it is in dying that we are born to eternal life.

Icebreakers 1: Write and share with your table-group what part of the prayer stood out to you and why.

Icebreaker 2: Share any successes in your resolutions from this unit OR how these first two weeks have helped your marriage.

2. (15 minutes) Read the life of Saint Gianna Beretta Molla. Have a couple read it aloud to the group, alternating paragraphs.

Saint Gianna Beretta Molla— A Model for Mothers[182]

"A woman of exceptional love, an outstanding wife and mother, she gave witness in her daily life to the demanding values of the Gospel". In his homily on the occasion of her beatification, April 24, 1994, Pope John Paul II proposed Gianna Beretta Molla as a model for all mothers: "By holding up this woman as an exemplar of Christian perfection, we would like to extol all those high-spirited mothers of families who give themselves completely to their family, who suffer in giving birth, who are prepared for every labor and every kind of sacrifice, so that the best they have can be given to others".

In canonizing Gianna Beretta Molla this spring (2004), the Church officially recognized the extraordinary sanctity of a woman who chose to live an ordinary life—as a professional and, later, as a wife and mother. Though she had once considered entering a religious order, instead she practiced medicine (receiving her medical degree in 1949, and her specialty in pediatrics in 1952). She devoted herself to caring for her patients, and her selflessness and dedication as a physician endeared her to the people. But it was not only her practice of medicine that influenced them. She regarded her profession as a mission through which she could aid and nurture both bodies and souls. The young doctor's devotion to her Catholic faith was well known in her community, and especially her instruction of young Catholic girls in their faith.

Gianna meditated long and prayerfully on God's will for her. "What is a vocation?", she wrote: "It is a gift from God—it comes from God Himself! Our concern, then, should be to know the will of God. We should enter onto the path that God wills for us, not by 'forcing the door', but when God wills and as God wills" (in *Blessed Gianna Beretta Molla: A Woman's Life*. Boston: Pauline Books, 2002, p 71, 72). Gianna believed she was called to marriage and family life, but she waited patiently for God's will to be revealed.

Gianna Beretta did not marry until she was thirty-three years old—to an engineer ten years her senior, Pietro Molla, whose sister had earlier been a patient of the young Dr. Beretta. Letters Gianna wrote during their year-long courtship reveal her deep commitment to this new vocation. The couple married in September 1955. Several days before their wedding, Gianna wrote to Pietro, reflecting on their vocation to marriage: "With God's help and blessing, we will do all we can to make our new family a little cenacle where Jesus will reign over all our affections, desires and actions … We will be working with God in His creation; in this way we can give Him children who will love Him and serve Him".

Gianna's faith and her communion with Christ were profound, and from this grace she drew deeper understanding of the dedication and self-giving love that is fundamental to Christian marriage and family life.

After her marriage and even after she had children Gianna continued her medical practice, extending her gifts beyond her immediate family to the children of others. Three children, a son and two daughters, were born between 1956 and 1959, and Gianna had two miscarriages before conceiving another baby in 1961. Pietro and Gianna referred to their children as their "treasures".

In his own account of these years, Pietro Molla says that he did not object to Gianna's continuing her medical practice, because she was so deeply attached to her patients, though after she became pregnant with their fourth child, Pietro and Gianna had agreed that she would stop working outside the home after the baby was born.

Early in the pregnancy it was discovered that Gianna had a fibroma, a benign tumor, on her uterine wall. Surgery that would involve aborting the baby was suggested, but the Mollas instantly and firmly rejected this idea, and chose surgery that would remove only the tumor. Because of her medical knowledge, Gianna understood more fully than most the risks involved in this delicate surgery—both to her and to her unborn child. She insisted that the baby be protected at all costs.

The surgery successfully removed the fibroma, and the pregnancy continued, apparently normally, and the family made plans for the future in joy and hope. But all was not well, and a few days before the baby was born, Gianna realized it would be a difficult—possibly life-threatening delivery. She asked her husband to promise that if it were necessary to choose between saving her and saving the baby, he should choose the baby. "I insist", she said.

On Good Friday, Gianna entered the hospital. And a lovely, healthy baby daughter, Gianna Emanuela, was born the next day, April 21, 1962. But the mother had developed a fatal infection—septic peritonitis. (Modern antibiotics most likely would have saved her.) The inflammation caused immense suffering during her final week on earth. In the midst of her terrible pain, Gianna called to her own mother, Maria, who had died in 1942—and she prayed. As she lay dying, she repeated, "Jesus, I love you", over and over.

Her agony ended on April 28—at home. She was 39. The tiny infant, Gianna Emanuela, was exactly one week old.

The bereft Pietro was left to raise four very young children without their mother: Pierluigi, the eldest, was not yet six; Mariolina, four; Laura, nearly three; and of course the new baby. In this book are Pietro's own reflections on the difficult years that followed, and how the example of his wife's serene and joyous faith helped sustain him through his grief at Gianna's death; when their little daughter, Mariolina, died only two years later; and through all the ordinary difficulties of raising a family alone— with the added extraordinary challenges of raising children whose absent mother had already become a revered public figure.

Almost immediately upon her death a devotion to Gianna arose among those whose lives she had so deeply touched, and who knew her heroic devotion to her faith and her family.

Her "cause" was introduced formally in 1970. She was beatified April 24, 1994; and canonized on May 21, 2004—forty-two years after her death.

That her husband, now 91, and three children attended her canonization ceremony is one of several historic "firsts" connected with her canonization. (Pierluigi, an engineer, is married; Laura is a political scientist; Gianna Emanuela is a physician who specializes in Alzheimer's disease.)

Gianna Beretta Molla is the first married laywoman to be declared a saint (though there are many sainted widows). She is also the first canonized woman physician—a professional woman who was also a "working mom" four decades ago, when this was unusual.

Her witness of abiding faith in Christ, and her example of generous, loving, self-donation—wherever and however she was called to serve the Lord—provide particular inspiration for women of our time and in our culture, where conflicting demands and confusing signals are a daily part of our lives.

There is another aspect of this new saint's life that is worth pondering—and this book affords a glimpse of it. That is, the role of her family—the example of her parents—in her formation as a committed, active young Catholic. Her family was outstanding for its deep Christian faith, expressed not only in worship, in private prayer and family devotions, but in generously extending their gift of faith to others.

Her family's example of unselfish love set the direction of young Gianna's life. It gave her the firm foundation upon which, through the grace of God and her trusting acceptance of His will for her, she confidently built her life—a life that would shelter, nurture, guide, and inspire countless others. Gianna's plans for raising her own children in the Faith were influenced by her own experiences growing up. Her understanding of motherhood came from her own mother. Even though her own children could not know her tender motherly presence while they were growing up, she interceded for them. At the very end of her life, as Gianna suffered mortal pain, she sought her mother's prayers. As we—especially mothers of young families—may now seek hers.

Saint Gianna, pray for us.

Helen Hull Hitchcock
Feast of Saint Joachim and Saint Anne
July 26, 2004
Ignatius Press

Women for Faith and Family
Introduction by Helen Hull Hitchcock:

> Pope John Paul II made the following remarks during the Mass celebrating the canonization of St. Gianna Beretta Molla on May 16, 2004.
>
> Gianna Beretta Molla was a simple, but more than ever, significant messenger of divine love. In a letter to her future husband a few days before their marriage, she wrote: "*Love is the most beautiful sentiment the Lord has put into the soul of men and women*".
>
> Following the example of Christ, who "*having loved his own ... loved them to the end*" (Jn 13:1), this holy mother of a family remained heroically faithful to the commitment she made on the day of her marriage. The extreme sacrifice she sealed with her life testifies that only those who have the courage to give of themselves totally to God and to others are able to fulfil themselves.
>
> Through the example of Gianna Beretta Molla, may our age rediscover the pure, chaste and fruitful beauty of conjugal love, lived as a response to the divine call!

Reflect on lives of the saints:

What struck me about the life of this couple; about Gianna's life? What can we take from their lives to help strengthen our own marriage?

3. Process/discussion on the material read for homework in Unit Three.

    a.   What is the "hidden agenda" behind the commandments?

_____

_____

    b.   How does the law help a person practice self-control?

_____

_____

    c.   What really is sin? What does sin cost us?

_____

_____

    d.   Is it possible to forgive adultery? What does Jesus say about forgiveness?

_____

_____

    e.   What is a "married single"?

_____

_____

    f.   What is the secret to melting someone's heart?

_____

_____

    g.   What five virtues bring unity to marriage? What is a virtue?

_____

_____

    h.   What breaks unity in marriage?

_____

_____

    i.   What is the "supreme" gift of marriage?

_____

_____

j. Are contraception and sterilization really so bad, now that they are so widely accepted?

_____

_____

k. What is this "thing" called Natural Family Planning?

_____

_____

Group Activity: (25 minutes) Write a Love Song

A. Assign each group of four couples one of the topics of the unit.

B. Using a well-known tune from a popular love song or nursery rhyme tune, have each group write a real love song about marriage and family using at least two quotes from one of this unit's lessons.

C. Have each team sing their song for the group (optional)

4. Video: *Forever One.*

5. Sharing real life examples on the Unit Three topics. Practical applications. (15 minutes)

Table Talk in small groups.

a. Having reviewed the section of the bishop's Pastoral Letter on divorce pp. 24–26, discuss how vices and virtues play a role in setting the stage for divorce or lasting marriage. Discuss what are some practical things we can do to change patterns or habits of vice into habits of virtue?

b. In his encyclical, *Humanæ Vitæ,* of 1968, Pope Paul VI warned that three things could happen if we accepted contraception. 1) That man would lose respect for a woman's physical and psychological equilibrium and treat her as a "mere instrument of selfish enjoyment." 2) That artificial birth regulations would "place a dangerous weapon in the hands of those public authorities who take no heed of moral exigencies." 3) That contraception would mislead human beings into thinking that they have unlimited dominion over their bodies, turning the human person into the object of his own intrusive power. Discuss how all of these have come true in the world today.

c. After reviewing the bishop's Pastoral Letter (pp. 17–21), explain what they mean when they say, "In reality, the deliberate separation of the procreative and unitive meaning of marriage has the potential to damage or destroy the marriage." Then discuss what we can do to promote the acceptance of NFP better in our parish.

d. What are some of the great gifts and virtues (not just pleasures) that children bring to marriage.

6. **Private couple time/ Couple resolution. (15 minutes)**

   a. Couples discuss in private: Out of this unit's lessons and today's discussion, which area should we examine more closely to help our marriage? Consider the exercises from the unit—which were most challenging? How might God be asking us to "stretch" this workout with a new resolution this week? What would be a good resolution for us to strengthen our marriage this week?

   b. Our personal resolution for this unit. (Please write it in the space below.)

   _____

   _____

7. **Large group sharing on practical applications. (10 minutes)**

   What can we take away with us today to improve our marriages?

   Leaders can offer open discussion, or else have couples write their answers down, turn them in, and read some of them aloud to the group.

   Warm Up before Unit Three: prepare our minds and hearts.

   a. Please review the Learning Goals for each of the four exercises in Unit Four.

   b. Next group workout you should be able to answer the following questions.
      i. What is a good alternative to nagging?
      ii. What are the ten ground rules for fighting in marriage?
      iii. What if I don't "feel" the love, is it still love?
      iv. Is mediocre love enough to sustain marriage?
      v. How can any of the seven "deadly" sins kill a marriage?
      vi. Which one virtue do you need the most for a successful marriage?
      vii. How can the Corporal and Spiritual Works of Mercy increase our love for God and neighbor? How can they help our marriage?
      viii. Isn't our marriage just between us? What does the Church and society have to do with our relationship?
      ix. What can our families do to be holy? Why would we want to be holy?
      x. What do the bishops suggest for couples in crisis?
      xi. Name four reasons why a family needs a father.
      xii. What does it mean to pray? What are some methods of prayer? How can we begin to increase our prayer life as a family? As an individual?

8. Closing Prayer. (5 minutes) Suggested Prayer:

The Angelus

V.   The Angel of the Lord declared to Mary:

R.   And she conceived of the Holy Spirit.

Hail Mary, full of grace, the Lord is with thee; blessed art thou among women and blessed is the fruit of thy womb, Jesus. Holy Mary, Mother of God, pray for us sinners, now and at the hour of our death. Amen.

V.   Behold the handmaid of the Lord:

R.   Be it done unto me according to Thy word.

Hail Mary …

V.   And the Word was made Flesh:

R.   And dwelt among us.

Hail Mary …

V.   Pray for us, O Holy Mother of God,

R.   That we may be made worthy of the promises of Christ.

Let us pray:

Pour forth, we beseech Thee, O Lord, Thy grace into our hearts; that we, to whom the incarnation of Christ, Thy Son, was made known by the message of an angel, may by His Passion and Cross be brought to the glory of His Resurrection, through the same Christ Our Lord. Amen.

9. Social Time.

Communication and Communion

Unit Four: Week One Exercise

What does the Pastoral Letter on Marriage have to say?

On their wedding day, the couple says a definitive "yes" to their vocation of marriage. Then the real work of marriage begins. For the remainder of their married lives, the couple is challenged to grow, through grace, into what they already are: that is, an image of Christ's love for his Church.[183] (*Marriage: Love and Life*, 45)

PERFECTION: ARE WE THERE YET, DEAR?

Perfection, well probably not, so there is always room for improvement.

- Are we actually living in union, in marital communion?
- Is our love greater and deeper than it was on our wedding day?
- Is our love more than a feeling? Is it a commitment to the good of the other?
- Is our love just like that love of Christ for his Church?
- How close are we? How loving are we in our thoughts, words, and actions?
- What do we communicate to our spouse on a regular basis?
- Are we comparing our relationship to the TV shows and commercials instead of measuring our loving union with Christ's love?

What does the Pastoral Letter on Marriage have to say?

"Become what you are!"[184] might be a great exhortation to newly married couples, especially given the strong tendency nowadays to reduce the love of the marriage bond to only a feeling, perhaps the romantic love of courtship and honeymoon. When that feeling dries up, it may seem to them that they have nothing left and that they have failed.

It is at these very times, however, that their vocation as spouses calls them to go further, to "become what they are," members of a marital communion defined by the unbreakable spousal love of Christ for his Church. While husbands and wives can cling to the unconditional promise that they made at their wedding as a source of grace, this will require persistent effort. Maintaining the common courtesies—preserving in fidelity, kindness, communication, and mutual assistance—can become a deep expression of conjugal charity. It means growing in a love that is far deeper than a romantic feeling. (*Marriage: Love and Life*, 46)

WHY GOOD COMMUNICATION IS NECESSARY

Communication comes from the Latin *communicare*.

- ❧ To share … to make common.

- ❧ To make union with.

- ❧ Remember that at Mass we enter into communion with Christ!

As we presented before, your marriage here on earth is a Sacrament, meaning a sign and participation in the marriage of Christ and his Church. Just as entering into communion with Christ at Mass strengthens our relationship with him, so too does your communication with each other.

BASICS OF COMMUNICATION

If receiving Christ in the Eucharist is a form of communication, then communication is more than just words. It involves the body, i.e., body language, gestures, and actions. If communication is to "make union with," then body language (or better yet, "the language of the body") as well as words, gestures, and actions are part of it. Good communication is a union of all forms to share the same message. Words and actions should all harmoniously "speak" the same thing.

TEN COMMANDMENTS OF COMMUNICATION[185]

10. *Keep confidences confidential*

    The best way to shut down the all-important communication process is to reveal family secrets. Some of us may feel that we are only confiding in "best friends." But once you are married, you have only one "best friend," your spouse. Do not complain, especially to relatives. Bear in mind, too, that the right kind of friend will strengthen your marriage by causing you to feel satisfied rather than dissatisfied.

9. *Use sex for the purpose intended by God*

    At its best, marital intercourse can be an extremely beautiful way of saying, "I love you." At its worst, it is likely to convey just the opposite meaning. One hears much these days about "having sex." What a contradiction in terms! If the procreative act is anything, it is the supreme act of giving; and, because it transmits the tenderest of messages in the tenderest of ways, it can be one of the most effective forms of communication. The message will be distorted, however, if not altogether lost, if it involves manipulation or if too much emphasis is placed on the physical.

8. *Learn the ground rules for fighting*

   Every couple has arguments. It has undoubtedly already happened in your courtship, and will happen at different times in your marriage. The important thing is that you argue charitably, meaning "lovingly." Just because you are arguing doesn't mean that you do not love one another. However, you should make certain that there are careful boundaries to your arguments so that your relationship is not wounded as a result.

   Therefore, both of you should know the rules for marital arguments.

   - There can be no name calling (no matter how angry you are).
   - Absolutely no pushing, shoving, or other physical contact—even if you don't think it is a big deal, your spouse might.
   - Do not bring up all the things your spouse "has done wrong" from the past. Stay focused on the issue at hand.
   - Avoid raising your voice and yelling.
   - No "transferred aggression" to objects in the house.

   Avoiding the Don'ts of Fair Fighting

   - Don't look for total victory or unconditional surrender.
   - Don't intentionally prolong the argument.
   - Don't nag or withdraw.
   - Don't bring out the heavy artillery. (Don't go for your spouse's vulnerabilities or sore spots. Also, don't bring up past sins or old fights.)
   - Don't use threats of divorce. This can be very harmful to the marriage.

   Remember your marriage vows—"for better or worse."

   The point is to keep focused on the specific disagreement and to remember that you are trying to work it out with the person you love so much that you married him/her. While you may need some time to cool-off and think about the matter, *always* talk out your differences before you go to bed.

   "Be angry but do not sin; do not let the sun set on your anger, and do not leave room for the devil."[186]

7. *Express gratitude*

   [This will be discussed in the next section: The "*Five Love Languages.*"]

6. *Avoid nagging*

   Instead of asking directly for certain favors when your wife or husband is distracted, you might consider writing a little "love note" that can be left in plain view for action when convenient. If you need something badly enough and one or two gentle reminders do not suffice, it may be time to sit down and calmly explain the urgency of the problem from your point of view. Occasionally, though, even this will not work, and you may simply have to accept what you cannot change, offering it up as a share in the Lord's suffering.

5. *Accept criticism gratefully and learn to apologize*

Learning to take criticism is good, but better still is asking for it on occasion and being quick to apologize. The phrase "I'm sorry" is a wonderful all-purpose solvent capable of cutting through the gummiest mounds of double-talk and misunderstanding.

4. *Be patient and discreet in drawing the other person out*

Some spouses may want to be left alone for a spell before they open up, especially after a long days work. There may be times, too, when your partner will be talked out. At moments like this, you might decide to take a quiet walk together simply to show that you care. Whatever you do, never "dump" on your spouse the moment he/she arrives home from work. Allow time for the new arrival to wash up, have a snack, and look over the mail. Later on, there will be enough time to catch up on the latest in your respective spheres.

3. *Learn to listen*

[This will be covered in the next section: The *"Five Love Languages."*]

2. *Take nothing for granted*

Marital relations rarely stand still. If they do not thrive, they languish. It is important, therefore, to ask questions while keeping a hot line open to your spouse at all times. In business, the boss is always checking to make sure the secretary understands what needs to be done; the attitude is one of "give me a buzz if there's a problem." So too, lifelong collaborators should be saying that same thing at every juncture, anxious to know how they are doing. There may be virtue in the "strong, silent type," but such virtue lies more in the strength than in the silence. If one party is reticent by nature, the other should not give up. The ideal couple will converse about all aspects of life, including matters of delicacy, for unless both parties can deal verbally with issues across the board, it will be hard for either of them to meet the full range of the other's needs and expectations. One might add that children, too, should have their forum. Often, parental willingness to hold a family conference for the airing of proper concerns will do wonders to restore peace and harmony.

1. *Make time for each other*

The Five Love Languages

BY GARY CHAPMAN[187]

*W*hile all forms of communication are important … each person has a primary love language.

This form of communication satisfies a person's emotional need for love. It is the way the person hears that his spouse loves him/her. There are five basic forms of communication, or love languages.

To nourish your married love, you need to speak love to your spouse in your spouse's primary love language.

A husband and wife may each have a different primary love language than the other.

THE FIVE LOVE LANGUAGES
by Gary Chapman

1. Words of Affirmation
   • A verbal affirmation of your spouse
   • Compliments and thanks

   The first love language is "words of affirmation." The language is spoken when you verbally affirm your spouse. It is usually done out loud, but can also be done through letters. It involves both complimenting your spouse (for example: on how she or he looks, on the quality of his or her cooking, or on how warm and caring he or she is) and thanking your spouse for what he or she does for you (e.g., bathing the kids, fixing the car, etc).

2. Quality Time
   • Giving your spouse your undivided attention
   • Listening to your spouse
   • Doing an activity together

   The second love language is "quality time." You speak this language when you either give your spouse your undivided attention, do an activity together, or both. It is a way of telling your spouse that he or she is so important that you are stopping everything else to focus your attention on him or her. If you are giving your spouse your attention, it is best to begin by simply listening. It not only indicates that you care what your spouse is thinking, but also that you are his or her companion in all the areas of his or her life. Listen to one another and solve problem together. Similarly, doing an activity together is a way of sharing in your spouse's life. Examples include the following: going for a walk together, playing tennis, cooking dinner together, dancing together, exercising together, praying together, etc.

3. Receiving Gifts
   - Giving your spouse a gift as a sign that you were thinking of him or her.
   - Does not need to cost much or any money and do not forget that your marriage is more important than money.

The third love language is "receiving gifts." Some people feel loved when their spouse gives them gifts. It is a sign that their spouse was thinking of him or her. If you give your spouse a gift, it also represents that you are giving him or her your life. For this kind of love language, it is helpful to recall the adage "It is the thought that counts." The gifts do not need to cost much or any money. The gift can be a handmade card, a flower picked from the field, or some other items that you made or went out of your way to find. At the same time, once in a while it would be helpful to purchase a gift, especially if it is something you know your spouse would really appreciate, like chocolate. While a couple *must be* fiscally responsible, the marriage is more important than the money.

4. Acts of Service
   - Doing things (cooking a meal, painting the bedroom, washing the car, doing the laundry, cleaning the house, doing the grocery shopping, changing the oil on the car, etc.) for your spouse that you know *he or she will like.*

The fourth love language is "acts of service." As the name describes, it entails doing things for your spouse that you know he or she will like. You may want to consider surprising your spouse by doing a chore that he or she normally does, or doing something that he or she used to have to remind you to do. When you do some act of service for your spouse, it indicates you love him or her in that you put his/her needs first before your agenda. It also brings joy in that it completes a task or project that your spouse wanted done. Acts of service are truly gifts of time and generosity to your spouse.

Consider the fact that your acts of virtue are attractive to your spouse. Virtue draws him or her toward you. When your spouse sees you working diligently, cheerfully, and generously, he or she will appreciate what you are doing and will be moved by your generosity. When, out of thoughtfulness, you "go that extra mile" and do something for your spouse that would deeply please him or her, or if you relieve him or her of a burdensome chore, you help to grow a bond between the two of you, built on self-giving love. This is the kind of love that remains in the memory and helps a couple through the rough spots of life.

By carefully observing your spouse and his or her reactions to things, you can get to know what your spouse really wants and needs, sometimes without even having to ask him or her. However, if you are uncertain what type of service your spouse would like, it may be best to simply ask, and then be ready to perform cheerfully that act of service, even if it includes a sacrifice on your part.

5. Physical Touch
   - Communicating your love by holding hands, a hug, the one-flesh union, etc.

The fifth and final love language is "physical touch." This is more than simply the one-flesh union. It is true that spouses communicate love by means of the language of the body in sexual intercourse. For some spouses, however, the emotional need for love needs to be communicated in terms of holding hands, a hug, a caress, or a massage. Physical touch indicates not only your affection but also your contact with and consideration of your spouse.

Remember, being united as one flesh does not mean the selfish pursuit of pleasure, such as putting one's own interests before the other. But rather it demands patience, kindness, and a selfless desire to serve the other, not to dominate or subjugate the other for personal gain or satisfaction. Only self-sacrificial, forgiving, and patient love can lead to a healthy and holy marriage.

Chances are that if you give yourself unreservedly with one eye trained on the hereafter, your marriage will not only survive but prosper. Storms there will be, along with periods of aridity. You may be faced with a rash of catastrophes when God seems to be looking the other way. But there is no reason to panic. If you can't resolve an issue, see a mutual friend or counselor (or your parish priest), who is sound in the faith. Above all, remember that love is not a feeling that comes and goes depending upon one's mood. It is a lifelong commitment which, like fine wine, improves with age. Someone once remarked that "love is what you've been through together," and how true. Perseverance is nine-tenths of the battle and, given such an attitude, communication crises, if and when they occur, will only bring you closer together. In the end, you will be more secure as a couple, and better off as a team, for having braved the winds of adversity.[188]

$\mathcal{T}$HE $\mathcal{W}$ORKOUT

1. What is your spouse's love language? What is your love language? What can you do to speak to him or her in the language he or she best understands?

2. In what areas of our life together do we communicate clearly? What area of communication often ends in a disagreement?

3. What can we do to grow in understanding of one another's needs and desires?

4. How do we resolve conflicts? Do I humble myself often enough? Do I find our conflicts to be an opportunity for spiritual growth?

5. Do we have regular family meetings or couple meetings to air our concerns or organize and harmonize our life together? Are these discussions filled with kindness toward one another? If not, what can we do to begin this habit? Make a plan now.

LET US PRAY

God our Father, our love for each other is strong but sometimes we are weak.
Let the goodness of your grace be our strength.
Help us to love each other as you love us,
especially when we have hurt one another through our words and actions.
Let nothing come between us and your love for us. Amen.[189]

GROWTH IN VIRTUE

Unit Four: Week Two Exercise

LEARNING GOALS

- ❧ To learn about virtuous habits of doing good, and how to acquire them.

- ❧ Be able to identify the seven capital sins and how they may be affecting our marriages.

- ❧ To make a plan to become one another's helpmates for growth in virtue.

What does the Pastoral Letter on Marriage have to say?

There is another way to look at growth in marriage: namely, as growth in virtue. As a couple grows in virtue, they grow in holiness. In other words, the couple acquires, by prayer and discipline, those interior qualities that open them to God's love and allow them to share in his love more deeply. Couples instinctively understand this when they speak about their marriage being a means of leading each other to heaven.

Love in the Sacrament of Matrimony includes all the virtues, and each specific virtue is a manifestation of love. A holy marriage, one that is a communion of persons and a sign of God's love, is made up of many virtues that are acquired by human effort.

Rooted in the theological virtues, a couple must also grow in the principal moral virtues. These include prudent, justice, fortitude and temperance. All the other virtues are grouped around these four. Practicing the moral virtues draws us ever more deeply into God's love through the Holy Spirit, with the result that we habitually manifest his love in our daily lives. (*Marriage: Love and Life*, 47–48)

COMMUNICATION AND THE VIRTUOUS LIFE

"It is the greatest good for a man to discuss virtue every day and those other things about which you hear me conversing and testing myself and others, for the unexamined life is not worth living."[190]

If you are not in the state of sanctifying grace, that is, in right relationship with God, your actions will show it, especially in the way you communicate with your spouse. Most Christian couples who truly know what it means to love and are living lives of holiness rooted in Christ, are genuinely charitable, kind, generous, patient, etc., and these virtues are all expressions of the state of the soul.

Holiness is contagious only if a person recognizes his or her sinfulness and strives to continually root out vices with the help of God's grace so as to grow in virtue. Virtue is a firm disposition of the soul to choose the good. The virtuous life is the means by which we become saints.

"Through love of God we conceive virtues, and through love of our neighbor, they are brought to the birth."[191] "Now is the time to prepare yourself for [marriage] and family life. You cannot follow this path if you do not know how to love. To love means to want to perfect yourself and your beloved; to overcome your selfishness and give yourself completely."[192]

Striving to grow in virtue, with the help of God's grace, will strengthen your communication and "love language" in marriage so that, as a couple, you will increase in holiness and be one step closer to Heaven.

KNOW THE SIN AND THE CORRESPONDING "HEAVENLY" VIRTUE[193]

The Catholic Encyclopedia states that *"Sin is nothing else than a morally bad act (St. Thomas, De malo, 7:3), an act not in accord with reason informed by the Divine law."* God has given us free will, reason, and a sense of responsibility. We are to use these gifts to live by his law. Sinning is what we do when we use our gifts of reason and free will in deviation from God's law.

The concept of the seven capital virtues has been an aspect of Catholic Faith for several centuries, having gained recognition and popularity in the Middle Ages. This list of seven virtues is a set of virtues which are to counter the temptation to succumb to the seven capital sins. For this reason, they are sometimes also called the seven contrary virtues; they represent the opposite of the seven capital sins.

What are the Seven Capital Sins and their corresponding "Heavenly" Virtues?

- *PRIDE* is an unrestrained and improper appreciation of our own worth. This is listed first because it is widely considered the most serious of the seven sins; pride often leads to the committing of other capital sins. Pride is manifest in vanity and narcissism about appearance, intelligence, status, etc. Dante described pride as "love of self perverted to hatred and contempt for one's neighbor."

  HUMILITY is the virtue that counters pride. As pride leads to other sin, true humility clears a path for holiness. Pride is a sin based on undue and inappropriate appreciation of self-worth. Conversely, the virtue of humility is about modest behavior, selflessness, and the giving of respect.

- *GREED,* which is also known as avarice or covetousness, is the immoderate desire for earthly goods, as well as situations such as power. It is a sin of excess. The object of greed need not be evil, but the issue lies in the way one regards the object, placing inappropriate value on it. Greed can further inspire such sinful actions as hoarding of materials or objects, theft, robbery, trickery, and manipulation.

GENEROSITY is the virtue that counters greed. The virtue of generosity is focused not merely on the appropriate concern regarding earthly things, but also on generosity and a willingness to give freely and without request for commendation.

☙ *GLUTTONY,* which comes from the Latin *gluttire*—to gulp down or swallow, refers to the sin of overindulgence and overconsumption of food and drink. The manners in which gluttony can be committed are eating too soon, eating too expensively, eating too much, eating too eagerly, eating too daintily, and eating wildly.

St. Alphonsus Liguori explained that "it is not a fault to feel pleasure in eating: for it is, generally speaking, impossible to eat without experiencing the delight which food naturally produces. But it is a defect to eat, like beasts, through the sole motive of sensual gratification, and without any reasonable object."[194]

TEMPERANCE or abstinence counters the sin of gluttony. To be gluttonous is to overindulge. Conversely, the virtue of temperance is centered on self-control and moderation.

☙ *LUST* refers to impure desire of a sexual nature. Sexuality is a gift from God, and not inherently impure in itself. However, lust refers to the impure thoughts and actions that misuse that gift, deviating from God's law and intentions for us. Indulging in the sin of lust can include (but is not limited to) fornication, pornography, masturbation, adultery, bestiality, rape, and incest and can lead to such things as sexual addiction. (More on this vice in presentations six and seven).

CHASTITY is the counter-virtue to the sin of lust. Chastity embraces moral wholesomeness and purity, and in both thought and action treats God's gift of sexuality with due reverence and respect. (More on this virtue in presentations six and seven).

☙ *SLOTH* is often described simply as the sin of laziness. However, while this is part of the manifestation of sloth, the central problem with sloth as a capital sin is spiritual laziness. The sin of sloth means being lazy and lax about living the Faith and practicing virtue.

The Catholic Encyclopedia explains: "In general [sloth] means disinclination to labor or exertion. As a capital or deadly vice, St. Thomas calls it sadness in the face of some spiritual good which one has to achieve … St. Thomas completes his definition of sloth by saying that it is torpor in the presence of spiritual good which is Divine good. In other words, a man is then formally distressed at the prospect of what he must do for God to bring about or keep intact his friendship with God. In this sense sloth is directly opposed to charity."

DILIGENCE or persistence is the virtue which acts as a counter to the sin of sloth. Sloth, as a capital sin, refers to laziness in matters of Faith. Diligence in spiritual matters combats laziness. This virtue manifests itself in appropriately zealous attitudes toward living and sharing the Faith.

☙ *ANGER OR WRATH*—The Catholic Encyclopedia explains, "[Anger is] the desire of vengeance. Its ethical rating depends upon the quality of the vengeance and the quantity of the passion. When these are in conformity with the prescriptions of balanced reason, anger is not a sin. It is rather a praiseworthy thing and justifiable with a proper zeal. It becomes sinful when it is sought to wreak vengeance upon one who has not deserved it, or to a greater extent than it has been deserved, or in conflict with the dispositions of law, or from an improper motive. The sin is then in a general sense mortal as being opposed to justice and charity."

Anger can be just. But due to the common usage of the word "anger," this capital vice is often referred to as "wrath" or "rage," emphasizing the unbalanced and improper motives which result in anger being a mortal sin.

MEEKNESS or patience is the virtue that counters the sin of unjust anger, also called "wrath" or "rage." Where the sin of wrath is about quick temper and unnecessary vengeance, the virtue of meekness focuses on patiently seeking appropriate resolution to conflicts, and on the ability to forgive and show mercy.

❧ *ENVY* or jealousy is more than merely one person wanting what someone else has; the sin of envy means one feels unjustified sorrow and distress about the good fortune of someone else. The law of love leads us to rejoice in the good fortune of our neighbor—jealousy is a contradiction to this. Envy is named among the capital sins because of the other sins to which it leads.

KINDNESS or brotherly love or love for neighbor, is the virtue that counters the sin of envy. Envy, in contradiction to God's law of love, is manifest in a person's sorrow and distress over the good fortune of another person. Conversely, kindness and brotherly love is manifest in the unprejudiced, compassionate, and charitable concern for others.

"The heart itself is but a small vessel, yet dragons are there, and there are also lions; there are poisonous beasts and all the treasures of evil. But there too is God, the angels, the life and the kingdom, the light and the apostles, the heavenly cities and the treasures of grace—all things are there."[195]

Recommended Book: Donald DeMarco, *The Many Faces of Virtue* (Steubenville, OH: Emmaus Road Publishing, 2000).

THE VIRTUES OF A CATHOLIC MAN[196]

❧ A Catholic man has some sense of what or whom he would die for if necessary.

❧ A Catholic man passes his faith to his children and sees to their religious education.

❧ A Catholic man informs himself about his faith, reads Scripture, selects Catholic literature, and studies the *Catechism of the Catholic Church*.

❧ A Catholic man insures that there are sacred symbols in his household, such as, crucifix(es), Bible, use of sacramentals such as Advent wreath, Christmas crèche, holy water, etc.

❧ A Catholic man leads prayer in his household at significant domestic events, such as birth, Baptisms, graduation, marriage, illness, death, and other special meals and events with use of a passage from Scripture or other Catholic sources.

❧ A Catholic man practices patience with his wife and children.

❧ A Catholic man invests himself in some project or apostolate at the parish or diocesan level.

❧ A Catholic man is faithful to his wife, his children, his Church, and his friends, indeed in all his commitments.

THE VIRTUES OF A CATHOLIC WOMAN[197]

- A Catholic woman is an instrument of God's love, allowing his love to flow through her as she gives life to others. She is especially self-disciplined when her feelings might oppose love.

- A Catholic woman is grateful for the talents and gifts of Catholic men, always seeking to appreciate and complement, not criticize the opposite sex.

- A Catholic woman exemplifies truth and beauty through the way that she acts, dresses, and keeps her home orderly.

- A Catholic woman is prudent and discreet in her speech, avoiding any unkind words that might reveal the faults of others, or hurt others.

- A Catholic woman is patient and gentle while teaching and encouraging others to grow in character.

- A Catholic woman is generous with her time; always faithful, humble, and sincere in her duties toward God, family, and society. She is diligent, reliable, and thoroughly practical in her work.

$\mathcal{T}$HE $\mathcal{W}$ORKOUT

1. Have we ever learned about or discussed that virtues are a manifestation of love? How does a person's refusal to grow in virtue harm a marriage? How does growth in virtue improve a marriage?

2. What virtues come naturally to my spouse? What virtues come naturally to me?

3. What virtues present a challenge to a person of my temperament? What am I doing to fight against my vices? How can we help each other grow in virtue?

4. Each of you select one virtue on the list that you would like to grow in. Together, formulate a plan to become one another's "coach" in giving each other encouragement to grow in it. Make a plan that includes specific daily opportunities to change that vice into a virtue, creating a new habit.

   For example:

   - To grow in humility and root out pride, I will choose to not correct you for interrupting me. I will turn my thoughts to God, thank him for you, and listen to what you have to say.

   - To grow in spiritual diligence and root out laziness, I will gather the children after dinner each evening and pray one decade of the rosary with them.

   - To grow in temperance and root out gluttony, we will cut out buying processed and junk food for snacks, or stop snacking altogether.

   - To grow in meekness and root out anger, I will practice forgiving you more quickly, instead of configuring a way to even things out.

LET US PRAY

God, your glory is proclaimed in body and spirit,
in the love we have for one another—great, strong, and wonderful.
Sometimes this love is our comfort, and sometimes it is overwhelming.
Help us to be gentle in learning to love each other and grow in virtue.
In our prayer together, remind us always that our purpose in life
is to help each other get to Heaven, for we believe that with your grace, anything is possible.
We ask this through Jesus Christ, our Lord and King. Amen.[198]

"Do Unto Others As You Would Have Them Do Unto You"

Unit Four: Week Three Exercise

LEARNING GOALS

- To explore ways that families can evangelize.

- To consider how families can spread Christ's love to other families and society.

- To review the Corporal and Spiritual Works of Mercy in light of family activities.

What does the Pastoral Letter on Marriage have to say?

Marriage is not merely a private institution, however. It is the foundation for the family, where children learn the values and virtues that will make good Christians as well as good citizens. The importance of marriage for children and for the upbringing of the next generation, highlights the importance of marriage for all society. (*Marriage: Love and Life*, 7–8)

Even when their childbearing years have passed, a couple should continue to be life-affirming. They can do this by staying involved in the lives of young people, and especially their grandchildren, as spiritual mentors, teachers and wisdom figures. They can also continue to be nurturing through the exercise of care for those who are needy, disabled, or pushed to the margins of society, and by their support for or participation in works of charity and justice. (*Marriage: Love and Life*, 15)

Marriage is not just for the couple. It is for all of society. Marriage is made by God to reflect his love to the world, just like a mirror reflects our faces. What does the love of God look like? We see it in the actions of Jesus. Jesus healed, comforted, admonished, instructed, fed, and spent time with his family and friends.

Is our family a holy family? Do we even want to be a holy family? That is what God wants. Is it not enough to go to Mass on Sundays? What does it mean to be a holy family?

The *Catechism of the Catholic Church* teaches us that

> The family is the *original cell of social life*. It is the natural society in which husband and wife are called to give themselves in love and in the gift of life. Authority, stability, and a life of relationships within the family constitute the foundations for freedom, security, and fraternity within society. (CCC 2207)

> The Christian family has an evangelizing and missionary task. (CCC 2205)

What does the Pastoral Letter on Marriage have to say?

> In contemplating the Jewish family of Joseph, Mary, and Jesus, people today can understand how this Holy Family is indeed the model and source of inspiration for all Christian families.

> From the earliest days of the Church, entire families and households found salvation in Jesus … As the first Christian families were islands of faith in their time, so Catholic families today are called to be beacons of faith, "centers of living, radiant faith."[199] (*Marriage: Love and Life*, 38–39)

Little by little, our family can become more like Christ and the Holy Family. People see this first by the example of our married love, our affection for one another, and our speaking kindly of our spouse when in other circles. The society sees our Christian love when we are generous and open to life, particularly when we have more children than the standard two or three. We grow closer to Christ through our prayers and by carrying our crosses in life with his joy. We become more holy as we become present to one another in our families, looking one another in the eye and listening, and looking to meet their needs, just as Jesus Christ did to each individual he met.

As we grow in virtues, our families grow in holiness. When we are patient with our children, diligent in our work, humble at success, and generous with our time and talents, we display the love of Christ to all those around us. When we write thank you notes, and teach our children to do so, we grow and share the virtue of gratitude. When we refuse to buy things we really do not need, or refuse excess in any area such as entertainment, we begin to live the simple life that the Holy Family lived. When we keep Sundays holy and refuse to participate in things that day that do not lead us to God, we display our unwavering love for our Creator. All these things help to make us more like the Holy Family.

What does the Pastoral Letter on Marriage have to say?

> A marriage that is truly in Christ, a marriage upon which his school of gratitude and openness has left its mark of joy and warmth, is a sign of the Kingdom that is coming. It is a blessing to the couple, to their children and to everyone who knows them. It offers a sign of hope and a loving witness to human dignity in a world where hope often seems absent and human dignity is often degraded. It is a sign of the Kingdom because the love of Christ moves the married couple to ever greater heights of love. (*Marriage: Love and Life*, 56)

The first way that married couples evangelize is by their love. Real Christian love for one another stands out in a world of cruelty, irritation, complaints, and disrespect. The second way that married couples evangelize is by teaching the Good News of the Gospel to their children, both in example and in word. The third way that families evangelize is by reaching out of their own circle to share the mystery of Christ's love with their extended family and society as a whole.

Married couples with their eyes open to loving others do not have to look too far to find people who are needy. Sometimes our own spouse feels neglected when more attention is paid to work or the children. Sometimes there is a needy child in our family who is starving for love and attention. There may be elderly grandparents or aunts and uncles who are lonely, or neighbors who crave a visit. It is our right, duty, and privilege as Christians to respond to these needs around us. We can be missionaries without even leaving the country.

Acts of compassion toward those who are in need are called works of mercy. Mercy and compassion are essential components of Christian love. We pray in the Lord's Prayer, "Thy kingdom come, thy will be done on earth as it is in Heaven." Thus, Jesus Christ is counting on the Christian families to act in his name, and build his Kingdom of justice and love here on earth. The Church has identified these duties as the Corporal Works of Mercy and the Spiritual Works of Mercy. People who perform these works of mercy acknowledge the whole person, body and soul, and seek to meet the needs of others.

Corporal Works of Mercy	Spiritual Works of Mercy
To feed the hungry	To instruct the ignorant
To give drink to the thirsty	To counsel the doubtful
To clothe the naked	To admonish sinners
To give shelter to the homeless	To bear wrongs patiently
To visit the sick	To forgive offenses willingly
To visit the imprisoned	To comfort the afflicted
To bury the dead	To pray for the living and the dead

Just as we exercise our bodies by lifting increasing weights or lengthening our cardio walk or run, we must exercise our souls to grow in love and generosity. Are we "stretching" ourselves to do works of mercy, as much as our kids stretch themselves physically in their gymnastics class?

A mother and father see that they are already living these Corporal Works of Mercy daily for their own children and others. They work to feed, clothe, and shelter their children, care for them when they are sick, and send cards to others or visit the sick. They may bring their children to wakes and funerals to help them show consolation to the bereaved, and to fulfill our duty to respect the bodily remains of the person. They may bring their used clothes to the homeless shelter or go to the nursing home. They may bring food to the church food pantry a couple times a year. They may give to the missions during Lent. Ask yourselves these questions: Is this enough? Are we as generous as we can be? Are we doing all that we can do? Do we truly realize that we are serving "Christ" who lives within each of these persons?

How often do we see the Spiritual Works of Mercy as important? These seem to be counter cultural. Today, it seems that we are politically correct if we ignore the sins of others rather than rock the boat by admonishing them. It might seem more acceptable to allow ourselves or other people to remain ignorant of the true teachings of the Church, because these teachings might not be popular. We might be more judgmental than helpful with others. We might refuse to forgive, or might carry grudges that create bitterness in the extended family. The Spiritual Works of Mercy are not always easy to do, but it is what Jesus did. Jesus seemed to comfort the afflicted and afflict the comfortable. How are we like him? How can our family be more like him?

Mother Teresa Shows Families How to Be Holy

INTERVIEW WITH AUTHOR DONNA-MARIE COOPER O'BOYLE BY GENEVIEVE POLLOCK

NEW YORK, MARCH 18, 2010 (Zenit.org).—Mother Teresa encouraged working with the poor not only in the slums of India, but primarily in our own families, says the author of a new book about the nun. Donna-Marie Cooper O'Boyle is the author of the recently published "Mother Teresa and Me: Ten Years of Friendship" (Circle Press). She spoke with ZENIT about her experiences with Mother Teresa, now recognized as Blessed Teresa of Calcutta, and the ways in which the nun taught the Missionaries of Charity, the congregation she founded, and others to love Christ in the poor.

Mother Teresa encouraged O'Boyle, a wife and mother, to live her vocation well and to help other families thrive. O'Boyle has written for several newspapers and magazines, and maintains various personal blogs, including a new saints' Web site for youth. In this interview with ZENIT, she spoke about the holiness of Mother Teresa, and the ways in which her teachings can be implemented in families today.

ZENIT: In one point in your book, you talk about Mother Teresa's unshakeable faith coupled with a feisty attitude; in another part you mention that she was called extraordinarily ordinary. Yet you also say that you have no doubt about Mother Teresa's eventual canonization. What makes you so certain? How does the normality of your relationship affect your belief that she is a saint?

O'Boyle: My relationship with Mother Teresa was certainly normal but I feel that it was extraordinary as well because I never had a doubt that I was visiting and corresponding with a living saint.

I saw great holiness in everything about Mother Teresa—in her speech, her posture, her demeanor, the "glow" about her that radiated Christ's love, peace, and joy.

I knew that she truly lived the Gospel of Matthew: "Whatever you do to the least of these that are in my family, you do to me."

She lived her life, her every moment to satiate the thirst of Christ for souls.

She prayed that Jesus would live through her while she also served the Jesus living in all she met, which of course was from that same Gospel message (Mt 25:31–46): "You did it to me." Since her life echoed the crux of that passage I just knew that she was an absolute living saint who brought countless souls to God.

I also knew about her deep prayer life centered on the Eucharist as well as her intimate devotion to our Blessed Mother.

And even with all of this holiness, she wasn't an abstract saint from hundreds of years ago and no stranger to the realities of modern life. She met each person right where they were coming from and ministered to them at their unique level and state of life.

ZENIT: You describe how Mother Teresa saw Jesus in the face of each poor person, and this was the reason behind all of the work that she did and taught her Missionaries of Charity to do. How did she teach people to see others in this way? Many of us have a hard time seeing Jesus in our own family members, let alone the social outcasts of the world. Is there something she told you that helped you to understand her secret?

O'Boyle: Yes, the answer is very simple: Jesus taught us all how to see him in others in the Gospel of Matthew.

He taught us that everything we do to others we do to Jesus. Mother Teresa believed this concept wholeheartedly and served Our Lord in everyone.

Mother Teresa often said that it is far easier to serve or love Jesus in strangers and outcasts than it is to serve him in our own families, easier to give a dish of rice to a poor person on the other side of the world or to a complete stranger than to give that "dish of rice" to someone who is starving for love right under our own roof.

In very simple ways, she taught others to do the same as she did. She would simply raise up her hand and holding up each finger she would say, "You-did-it-to- me," in this manner teaching us that we can even be reminded of our duty to love Jesus in others every time we look upon our hands.

ZENIT: So many of us are surrounded by those "creature comforts" that Mother Teresa rejected for herself and her missionaries. Yet, especially when the economy is tough, we could all use her example of trust in Divine providence. Could you say more about the way she lived this virtue, and how modern families can live it as well?

O'Boyle: Blessed Mother Teresa would not own or use anything that she considered to be unnecessary or extravagant in her daily life and would not allow the Missionary of Charity Sisters to either.

She believed that they shouldn't own or use anything that the poor didn't own themselves.

They don't use the things that we might consider to be staple items, such as carpeting, hot water, and fans or air conditioning.

She wanted the sisters to truly understand the plight of the poor and also felt that to be free of belongings would also allow the soul to be free to cling to Our Lord for everything, as well as help one to develop a deeper and more genuine love for God.

Modern day families might consider how they can live with a little less.

If we had less material objects to worry about, we might find that we have more time to tend to essential things and to be more present to one another.

Families today can pray together for an increase in faith, hope, and love. They can pray to offer their lives to God in full surrender, accepting God's holy will in their lives, asking him for all of their needs.

As Mother Teresa and her nuns have felt a deep freedom in giving their lives completely over to God and accepting whatever he gives them, families can strive to emulate that virtuous way of living as well.

ZENIT: Mother Teresa told you that your first apostolate should be to your family, husband and children, and she also placed importance on your writing for mothers, women and families. Why do you think she emphasized this?

O'Boyle: Mother Teresa often said, "Love begins at home."

That's where God puts us—right in the middle of our family's life, right in the heart of the home. She instructed others to focus on the ones that are in our midst, starting with our families and then to reach out to others in need.

She knew that we shouldn't run off to do charity work when we may have family members at home needing our presence.

Yes, Mother Teresa encouraged me to write for women and families because she was acutely aware of the breakdown of the family in our day and the fact that we need to help and encourage the family—the vital cell of society.

We need to steer mothers and women in the right direction so that families will be protected from further breakdown.

Mothers and women in general can use much encouragement in a world that tears down the family, promotes killing our own unborn children through abortion and abortifacients, and euthanizing the elderly. We must pray and help the family.

ZENIT: You often brought your children, even at a young age, while following Mother Teresa in different venues around the country. How did you see your children affected by their nearness to holy people? Did they ever protest these religious events?

O'Boyle: I always felt that I should bring my children as near to holiness as possible as I raised them.

I brought my children to daily Mass whenever I could, visits to the Blessed Sacrament, and near to any living "saint" I knew!

They never protested. It was their way of life. We must train our children in lives of holiness and prayer so that it will become as natural as breathing to them.

ZENIT: Mother Teresa said that we need to take care of the poor in our own homes first, but it seems easier sometimes to send a monetary donation to Haiti. How would she suggest that we go about taking those steps toward reaching out to the "poor" around us?

O'Boyle: "Love begins at home," she would say.

It is much easier to write out a check or even venture out to do charity work in some far-off land but it would be wrong to neglect our own families in the process.

To reach out to the "poor" around us we only need to open our eyes and hearts to see where there is a need.

Do we have a child that requires more of us, a spouse who feels neglected? Is there someone who is cranky but is really starving for our love? Do we have elderly parents who are lonely and crave a visit or some attention?

We have to trust Our Lord that he knows what he is doing in putting us together with our family members and neighbors. We all help to work out one another's sanctification too.

I believe that it starts first thing in the morning in the words of the Morning Offering, giving everything over to Our Lord so that he will sanctify all of our prayers, works, joys, and sufferings of the day.

We must also respond with love to each person we meet along the way, particularly the ones who contradict us, antagonize us and annoy us!

God calls us to holiness in the here and now of our lives right in the nitty-gritty details.

THE WORKOUT

1. Review the Corporal Works of Mercy. List those you already practice. List those you are not practicing. Discuss opportunities to perform these, in light of the practicality of your family situation, and discuss opportunities that can help you to grow in generosity. Make a plan to add one or two this year to your family life.

2. Review the Spiritual Works of Mercy. List those you already practice in your family and outside your family. Which of these can be better done for your own family? Which would help your extended family? Which would help your circle of friends and children's friends? Decide together the first three steps you should take this year to live the Spiritual Works of Mercy in your family life.

LET US PRAY

Lord Jesus, I give you my hands, to do your work.
I give you my feet, to go your way.
I give you my eyes, to see as you do.
I give you my tongue, to speak your words.
I give you my mind, that you may think in me.
I give you my spirit, that you may pray in me.
Above all, I give you my heart, that you may love in me.
I give you my whole self, that you may grow in me,
so that it is you, Lord Jesus, who lives and works
and prays in me. Amen.

One in Christ: One in Prayer

Unit Four: Week Four Exercise

LEARNING GOALS

- ❧ To see how couple prayer is an essential part of marriage.

- ❧ To learn the value of an intimate relationship with God.

- ❧ To explore ways to pray as a couple.

What does the Pastoral Letter on Marriage have to say?

By symbolizing and sharing in Christ's purifying and sanctifying love for his Church, married couples are called to an ever deeper holiness of life, just as Christ calls his Church to an ever deeper holiness of life. (*Marriage: Love and Life*, 53)

As the Church is a community of faith, hope, and love, so the Christian family, as the domestic church, is called to be a community of faith, hope, and love. Through this faith, hope, and love, Jesus, by the power of his Holy Spirit, abides within each Christian family as he does within the whole Church, and pours out the love of his Father within it.

Not only do parents present their children for Baptism, but, having done so, they become the first evangelizers and teachers of the faith.[200] They evangelize by teaching their children to pray and by praying with them. (*Marriage: Love and Life*, 40)

- ❧ Have you ever been vacuuming the floors with an electric vacuum plugged into an outlet, and tried to reach a spot farther away than the cord reaches, only to realize that the vacuum has been unplugged?

- ❧ Have you ever been trimming the hedge or bushes in the yard and not noticed the cord was in the way until you cut through it, created the fireworks, and destroyed your ability to complete the project?

Just as we need to stay connected to the source of power for our tools and appliances to work, we need to stay connected to God through prayer for our marriage to work.

> I am the vine, you are the branches. Whoever remains in me and I in him will bear much fruit, because without me you can do nothing. (Jn 15:5)

Note that Jesus did not say, "Without me you can do a little bit" or "half as much." Jesus said, "Without me, you can do NOTHING." Our efforts to live without Christ will be fruitless. Why not stay plugged into the source of power?

There is no activity more intimate than praying as a couple. Praying together is an awesome opportunity to become "One in Christ" spiritually, just as couples' holy acts of conjugal love bring them one in Christ physically and emotionally. Prayer reinforces your relationship with God. Prayer is one of the most powerful defenses against divorce. More true than not is the saying, "a family that prays together stays together." Praying for your spouse and with your spouse is essential for a good marriage, because our lives are filled with imperfections that need God's assistance and mercy.

Prayer is not a mysterious practice reserved only for priests and religious. Prayer is simply communicating with God—listening and talking to him. Individuals and families can pray from the heart, freely, spontaneously, and in their own words. If couple prayer is a difficult area for you, it is time to learn a little more about it and to practice and exercise it, just as you would for a sports team or band group. Both husbands and wives learn and grow in prayer. If we never speak to our spouse or never listen to anything he or she might have to say, our marriage relationship will quickly deteriorate. It is the same way with God. Prayer—communicating with God—helps us grow closer and more intimately connected with God.

Prayer is lifting up our hearts and minds to God. When a couple prays daily in unity, they begin to see their vocation to serve God with their marriage. Daily prayer also keeps a couple focused on God and helps the husband and wife grow in humility. Couple prayer should always be focused on God and not on the manipulation of the spouse. (God, please help my spouse _____!) Prayer invites God into our hearts and minds. In prayer we not only praise God and seek his assistance, but we also offer our lives to him.

The only requirement for prayer is a humble heart. This includes an acknowledgement of who is God, with all his greatness, and who we are as human beings with our frailties and efforts to please him. This sets the tone for a humble conversation with our Creator.

Couples who are new to prayer often begin with vocal prayer. It can include reading from a prayer book or Bible, praying memorized prayers (such as reciting the Rosary) or bringing to God your adoration, contrition, thanksgiving, and petitions. Catholic couples can also read the upcoming Scripture readings for Sunday's Mass and reflect on them as a couple or as a family.

Some couples meditate together on some truths of the Faith in a quiet place and time for ten or fifteen minutes a day. This meditation begins with a prayer to the Holy Spirit, and then the couple reflects together on the daily Gospel, a psalm, a holy picture, or spiritual writings. They spend some quiet time thinking about God and what truth he is trying to teach. This can be followed by sharing with the spouse the thoughts that came to mind in light of the Holy Spirit. Together, they make a resolution based on what God is revealing through this Word or work of his.

Eucharistic adoration is another unifying form of prayer for couples. Why not a weekly or monthly date with Jesus in the Blessed Sacrament chapel? It is a perfect way to end a dinner out or to begin a weekend on Saturday morning before the kid's activities and sports.

What does the Pastoral Letter on Marriage have to say?

Conflicts, quarrels, and misunderstandings can be found in all marriages. They reflect the impact of Original Sin, which "disrupted the original communion of man and woman."[201] They also reflect modern stresses upon marriage: the conflict between work and home, economic hardships, and social expectations.

Nevertheless, God's plan for marriage persists, and he continues to offer mercy and healing grace. We bishops urge couples in crisis to turn to the Lord for help. (*Marriage: Love and Life*, 25)

Some people wait until they are desperate to pray. They consider God's help "the last resort." Whether you need help with your finances, your job, your children, or your marriage, you should first ask God to bless the efforts you make. Although we should seek him first, we have seen many people in the Bible pray in desperate situations. When King David was running from Saul who was trying to kill him, he cried out to God, "I raise my eyes toward the mountains. From where will my help come? My help comes from the LORD, the maker of heaven and earth." (Ps 121:1–2). When the Apostles were confused and anxious the night before his Death, Jesus Christ taught them how to pray under stress, "*Do not let your hearts be troubled.* You have faith in God; have faith also in me." (Jn 14:1)

Many couples discover a deep intimacy in praying together. Couples have observed that, "Hearing my future spouse pray with me is very powerful."

This is a popular reading used at weddings.

Tobiah arose from bed and said to his wife, "My love, get up. Let us pray and beg our Lord to have mercy on us and to grant us deliverance." She got up, and they started to pray and beg that deliverance might be theirs. He began with these words: "Blessed are you, O God of our fathers; praised be your name forever and ever. Let the heavens and all your creation praise you forever. You made Adam and you gave him his wife Eve to be his help and support; and from these two the human race descended. You said, 'It is not good for the man to be alone; let us make him a partner like himself.' Now, Lord, you know that I take this wife of mine not because of lust, but for a noble purpose. Call down your mercy on me and on her, and allow us to live together to a happy old age." They said together, "Amen, amen," and went to bed for the night. (Tb 8:4–9)

One subscriber to *Magnificat* Magazine relates her own exerience:

My husband and I write to you during our honeymoon from the terrace of an Italian-style villa in California's wine country. We have just prayed the *Magnificat* Prayer for the Morning and the Meditation of the Day. Praying together has been one of the most important and intimate elements of our sixteen-month courtship. Over our first days and weeks together, I invited my now husband to pray with me. Looking back, he says *Magnificat* led him to rediscover a desire for and a delight in, prayer, which he had lost through a highly secularized young adulthood. We are now both big fans of *Magnificat*! Thank you for making possible a daily rhythm of prayer for courting and married couples like us.

For more information about the *Magnificat* prayer booklet, visit their Web site at *www.magnificat.com*.

WHAT IS CHRISTIAN PRAYER?

The following text is taken from the *Catechism of the Catholic Church.*

"For me, prayer is a surge of the heart; it is a simple look turned toward heaven, it is a cry of recognition and of love, embracing both trial and joy."[202]

"Prayer is the raising of one's mind and heart to God or the requesting of good things from God."[203] But when we pray, do we speak from the height of our pride and will, or "out of the depths" of a humble and contrite heart?[204] He who humbles himself will be exalted;[205] *humility* is the foundation of prayer. Only when we humbly acknowledge that "we do not know how to pray as we ought,"[206] are we ready to receive freely the gift of prayer. "Man is a beggar before God."[207] (CCC 2559)

Where does prayer come from? Whether prayer is expressed in words or gestures, it is the whole man who prays. But in naming the source of prayer, Scripture speaks sometimes of the soul or the spirit, but most often of the heart (more than a thousand times). According to Scripture, it is the *heart* that prays. If our heart is far from God, the words of prayer are in vain. (CCC 2562)

The heart is the dwelling-place where I am, where I live; according to the Semitic or Biblical expression, the heart is the place "to which I withdraw." The heart is our hidden center, beyond the grasp of our reason and of others; only the Spirit of God can fathom the human heart and know it fully. The heart is the place of decision, deeper than our psychic drives. It is the place of truth, where we choose life or death. It is the place of encounter, because as image of God we live in relation: it is the place of covenant. (CCC 2563)

Christian prayer is a covenant relationship between God and man in Christ. It is the action of God and of man, springing forth from both the Holy Spirit and ourselves, wholly directed to the Father, in union with the human will of the Son of God made man. (CCC 2564)

Prayer is the life of the new heart. It ought to animate us at every moment. But we tend to forget him who is our life and our all. This is why the Fathers of the spiritual life in the Deuteronomic and prophetic traditions insist that prayer is a remembrance of God often awakened by the memory of the heart: "We must remember God more often than we draw breath."[208] But we cannot pray "at all times" if we do not pray at specific times, consciously willing it. These are the special times of Christian prayer, both in intensity and duration. (CCC 2697)

Expressions of Prayers

I. Vocal Prayer

Through his Word, God speaks to man. By words, mental or vocal, our prayer takes flesh. Yet it is most important that the heart should be present to him to whom we are speaking in prayer: "Whether or not our prayer is heard depends not on the number of words, but on the fervor of our souls."[209] (CCC 2700)

II. Meditation

Meditation is above all a quest. The mind seeks to understand the why and how of the Christian life, in order to adhere and respond to what the Lord is asking. The required attentiveness is difficult to sustain. We are usually helped by books, and Christians do not want for them: the

Sacred Scriptures, particularly the Gospels, holy icons, liturgical texts of the day or season, writings of the spiritual fathers, works of spirituality, the great book of creation, and that of history—the page on which the "today" of God is written. (CCC 2705)

To meditate on what we read helps us to make it our own by confronting it with ourselves. Here, another book is opened: the book of life. We pass from thoughts to reality. To the extent that we are humble and faithful, we discover in meditation the movements that stir the heart and we are able to discern them. It is a question of acting truthfully in order to come into the light: "Lord, what do you want me to do?" (CCC 2706)

There are as many and varied methods of meditation as there are spiritual masters. Christians owe it to themselves to develop the desire to meditate regularly, lest they come to resemble the three first kinds of soil in the parable of the sower.[210] But a method is only a guide; the important thing is to advance, with the Holy Spirit, along the one way of prayer: Christ Jesus. (CCC 2707)

Meditation engages thought, imagination, emotion, and desire. This mobilization of faculties is necessary in order to deepen our convictions of faith, prompt the conversion of our heart, and strengthen our will to follow Christ. Christian prayer tries above all to meditate on the mysteries of Christ, as in *lectio divina* or the rosary. This form of prayerful reflection is of great value, but Christian prayer should go further: to the knowledge of the love of the Lord Jesus, to union with him. (CCC 2708)

III. Contemplative Prayer

What is contemplative prayer? St. Teresa answers: "Contemplative prayer [*oración mental*] in my opinion is nothing else than a close sharing between friends; it means taking time frequently to be alone with him who we know loves us."[211] Contemplative prayer seeks him "whom my soul loves."[212] It is Jesus, and in him, the Father. We seek him, because to desire him is always the beginning of love, and we seek him in that pure faith which causes us to be born of him and to live in him. In this inner prayer we can still meditate, but our attention is fixed on the Lord himself. (CCC 2709)

The choice of the *time and duration of the prayer* arises from a determined will, revealing the secrets of the heart. One does not undertake contemplative prayer only when one has the time: one makes time for the Lord, with the firm determination not to give up, no matter what trials and dryness one may encounter. One cannot always meditate, but one can always enter into inner prayer, independently of the conditions of health, work, or emotional state. The heart is the place of this quest and encounter, in poverty and in faith. (CCC 2710)

Entering into contemplative prayer is like entering into the Eucharistic liturgy: we "gather up" the heart, recollect our whole being under the prompting of the Holy Spirit, abide in the dwelling place of the Lord which we are, awaken our faith in order to enter into the presence of him who awaits us. We let our masks fall and turn our hearts back to the Lord who loves us, so as to hand ourselves over to him as an offering to be purified and transformed. (CCC 2711)

Contemplative prayer is the prayer of the child of God, of the forgiven sinner who agrees to welcome the love by which he is loved and who wants to respond to it by loving even more.[213] But he knows that the love he is returning is poured out by the Spirit in his heart, for everything is grace from God. Contemplative prayer is the poor and humble surrender to the loving will of the Father in ever deeper union with his beloved Son. (CCC 2712)

Contemplative prayer is the simplest expression of the mystery of prayer. It is a *gift*, a grace; it can be accepted only in humility and poverty. Contemplative prayer is a *covenant* relationship established by God within our hearts.[214] Contemplative prayer is a *communion* in which the Holy Trinity conforms man, the image of God, "to his likeness." (CCC 2713)

These are some questions that many of us ask frequently:

- Why pray? Is God really listening?

- Does God really answer our prayers?

- Am I really listening to God?

THIS STORY MAY HELP US UNDERSTAND WHAT IT MEANS TO PRAY AND WHY WE PERSEVERE IN PRAYER:

On September 5, 1997, after 8:00 pm, Mother Teresa complained of severe back pain. Soon she was having trouble breathing. The sisters called for doctors and a priest. Unexpectedly, the electricity failed and the whole house was in darkness.

Foreseeing an emergency, the sisters had secured two independent electric supplies. But both lines went out at the same time. They said that this had never happened before. It was 9:30 pm. While Calcutta was in darkness, the earthly life of the one who had brought so much light into the world was passing into the next world in complete darkness.[215]

There she was in Calcutta literally dying in darkness. Considering the life of Blessed Teresa of Calcutta and how she frequently experienced spiritual darkness in prayer, this was probably not a coincidence.

She prayed for several hours a day, and when she would pray, she often times felt nothing, or darkness as she described it. She would pray and then go out to serve with "her inseparable traveling companion," as she called Jesus, to serve Christ in others no matter who they were or what they needed. We could ask why did God not give Mother Teresa, who prayed over five hours a day, a sense of consolation or affirmation in prayer, especially as she did so much for those people who were unwanted and unloved in society? Could you imagine praying that intensely and only experiencing emptiness and darkness? We may be asking ourselves at times, why does God not answer my prayers? Why do I feel so empty after I pray?

Mother Teresa once said, "What a wonderful gift from God to be able to offer him the emptiness I feel. I am so happy to give him this gift." Her "everything" was exactly what the saints prayed for: God's will to be done. Her "everything" was to be nothing, in a sense, to be stripped totally of self-will and selfishness and to be filled with his gracious will.

The closer we move toward God, the more we persevere in prayer, the more God recedes beyond the horizon. He is not abandoning us or playing games with us, but rather, he is saying to us, "Come closer. Come closer … Forget yourself and surrender your will to me."

In prayer, God desires that our desires be perfectly conformed to his will. Often times in prayer, however, we are too busy telling him what we want or desire. God knows our desires and he does want what is best for us. Our desires and wants may not be what is necessary for our salvation. In our nothingness, God is trying to show us that we need him always, for with him we receive everything that is good, holy, pure, and true.

Think about the times that we have prayed like never before for the recovery of a sick relative or friend, and the person dies. The question arises again, more intensely and personally than before, "Does God answer my prayer?" Jesus did say, " Ask and it will be given to you; seek and you will find; knock and the door will be opened to you." (Mt 7:7)

If we lost our job or home or were unable to pay the bills and we ask God to help and nothing seems to happen, what are we to think? Does God answer our prayers?

When C.S. Lewis' wife was in remission from cancer, his pastor said to him, "I know how hard you have been praying and now God is answering your prayer." C.S. Lewis responded, "That's not why I pray, I pray because I can't help myself … I pray because I'm helpless … I pray because the need flows out of me all the time, waking and sleeping … My prayer doesn't change God, it changes me."

His statement is profound. God does not change nor do we pray to change God's will. Prayer changes us. It conforms us, sometimes in the most painful way, to God's divine will. The experiences of darkness, of pain and suffering, and of dryness and emptiness challenge us to move closer to God with faith and hope in order to understand his providence. Many times it may not seem to make sense, but if we persevere in prayer, God comforts and guides us in ways beyond our imagining.

Mother Teresa would have agreed with St. Augustine, who came to the conclusion that we come to know God's will, not through feelings or emotions, but rather through a strong and unwavering faith as the psalmist proclaims: "Blessed are they who hope (trust) in the Lord."

Most of the time, all we can do is cling to the assurance of faith. God's providence for us takes us far beyond our own terms. God takes us beyond life and death.

People speak of "finding comfort in God's will," but this does not mean "comfort" in the ordinary sense of ease and good feeling. It means comfort in the original sense of the word: *strength* (the word comes from the Latin *fortis*, which means strong).

God answers our prayer by giving us a kind of strength we never knew we had—or rather, a kind of strength we did not have until the moment we needed it.

Our Lord Jesus teaches us that God will never refuse us anything, if it be in accordance with his will, for he said, "Ask and it will be given to you; seek and you will find; knock and the door will be opened to you." (Mt 7:7)

Before Mother Teresa's death, a sister entered the room where she was praying before the Tabernacle and heard her saying over and over again, *"Jesus, I never refuse you anything. Jesus, I never refuse you anything."*

Our Lord teaches us through this holy woman, and many of the Saints, not to refuse God anything, but to trust in Him alone, and to offer our lives to Him without reserve. The key to true happiness in prayer is surrender as Blessed Teresa said so well, "*True love is surrender and the more we love, the more we surrender.*"

Recommended Books on Prayer:

- Fr. Thomas Dubay, S.M., *Deep Conversion/Deep Prayer* (San Francisco: Ignatius Press, 2006); available at *www.ignatius.com*.

- Francis Fernandez Carvajal, *Lukewarmness: The Devil in Disguise* (Makati City, Philippines: Sinag Tala, 2005); available at *www.theologicalforum.org*.

- Francis Fernandez, *In Conversation with God: Meditations for Each Day of the Year* (7 Volume Set) [Box set] [Paperback] (New York: Scepter Press, 1993); available at *www.scepterpublishers.org*.

The Workout

1. What typifies our couple prayer? Our family prayer?

2. What can we do to improve our couple prayer life? Our family prayer life?

3. How have we seen God answer our prayers?

4. What can we do to grow in our dependence on and trust in God?

5. Make a three-step plan to improve your prayer life this week.

LET US PRAY

Dear Heavenly Father,

Thank you for the gift of love and the blessing of our marriage.
Thank you for life and the fruit we have borne together.
We praise you for the joy you've poured into our hearts through this love.
We thank you for the joy and happiness of our home.

We ask you to bless our marriage, so that we may grow in love for each other and love for you.
Help us to remain forever attached to you, so that we may have the grace to keep
our vows to each other and to you, Lord.

We will need your strength daily Lord, as we live together with the goal of following and serving you.
Develop within us the character of your Son, Jesus,
that we might love each other with the love he demonstrated—
with patience, respect, understanding, honesty, forgiveness, and kindness.
Help us to grow in our loving friendship,
so that we may listen to and encourage one another on the journey.

Lord, be our refuge in the storms of life, and stay with us always.
Be our strength when we are weak.
Guide us through the difficult moments of life and comfort us in our grief.
May our lives together bring glory to you, our Savior, and testify of your love.
We ask this through Christ our Lord. Amen.

GROUP WORKOUT

Unit Four: Week Four:
Living Out the Communion of Love

- ◈ Growth toward perfection: virtues and gifts of the Holy Spirit.

- ◈ Covenantal communication: the language of true love, love languages, and the Ten Commandments of communication and marriage.

- ◈ Living out our vocation and being a sign of hope : Corporal and Spiritual Works of Mercy.

- ◈ Prayer.

WEEKLY GROUP MEETING: FOURTH WEEK

1. **Prayer (10 minutes including table reflection)—Litany of Humility**

O Jesus, meek and humble of heart,	*Hear me.*
From the desire of being esteemed,	*Deliver me, Jesus.*
From the desire of being loved,	*Deliver me, Jesus.*
From the desire of being extolled,	*Deliver me, Jesus.*
From the desire of being honored,	*Deliver me, Jesus.*
From the desire of being praised,	*Deliver me, Jesus.*
From the desire of being preferred to others,	*Deliver me, Jesus.*
From the desire of being consulted,	*Deliver me, Jesus.*
From the desire of being approved,	*Deliver me, Jesus.*
From the fear of being humiliated,	*Deliver me, Jesus.*
From the fear of being despised,	*Deliver me, Jesus.*
From the fear of suffering rebukes,	*Deliver me, Jesus.*
From the fear of being calumniated,	*Deliver me, Jesus.*
From the fear of being forgotten,	*Deliver me, Jesus.*
From the fear of being ridiculed,	*Deliver me, Jesus.*
From the fear of being wronged,	*Deliver me, Jesus.*
From the fear of being suspected,	*Deliver me, Jesus.*

That others may be loved more than I,	*Jesus, grant me the grace to desire it.*
That others may be esteemed more than I,	*Jesus, grant me the grace to desire it.*
That, in the opinion of the world, others may increase, and I may decrease,	*Jesus, grant me the grace to desire it.*
That others may be chosen and I set aside,	*Jesus, grant me the grace to desire it.*
That others may be praised and I unnoticed,	*Jesus, grant me the grace to desire it.*
That others may be preferred to me in everything,	*Jesus, grant me the grace to desire it.*
That others may become holier than I, provided that I may become as holy as I should.	*Jesus, grant me the grace to desire it.*

— Rafael Cardinal Merry del Val (1865–1930), Secretary of state for Pope Saint Pius X

Icebreaker1: Write and share with your table-group what part of the prayer stood out to you and why.

Icebreaker 2: Share any successes in resolutions from this unit OR how these units have helped your marriage.

2. **(15 minutes) Read the life of a father and deacon of the Church who talks about the meaning of spiritual fatherhood.**

The Meaning and Necessity of Spiritual Fatherhood

DEACON HAROLD BURKE-SIVERS, MTS

*N*ine years ago, my life changed forever. When my wife Colleen and I were married, we made a permanent decision to love; to give ourselves to each other freely and completely. In doing this, we entered into a profound and intimate relationship; we became a one-flesh covenant in communion with Christ through the gift of sacramental grace.

The Real Power of Love

The life-giving bond that Colleen and I share is so powerful and so real that we had to give that love names: Claire, Angela, Benjamin, and Sophia. Children are the result of the central act of sacrifice and worship between a husband and wife, namely, the union of their bodies in the conjugal act, which mirrors the total gift of self by the Eucharistic Christ to his Church. Together, the married couple forms a lifelong, self-donating, and indissoluble union of love: a "communion of persons intended to bear witness on earth and to image the intimate communion of persons within the Trinity" (William E. May, *Marriage: The Rock on Which the Family is Built*, 65).

163

Marriage and, indeed, all the sacraments, tell us something about who God is. Marriage, in fact, reflects the reality that the Father, Son, and Holy Spirit are of one divine nature, essence, and substance, for Scripture tell us: "God created man in His image; in the divine image He created him; male and female He created them" (Gn 1: 27), and again "'this at last is bone of my bones and flesh of my flesh; she shall be called Woman, because she was taken out of Man.' Therefore a man leaves his father and his mother and cleaves to his wife, and they become one flesh" (Gn 2: 23–24).

In creating husbands and wives, God has made two things very clear: first, that the one-flesh union between a husband and wife reflects His own divine image and likeness, and second, the fact that husbands and wives are truly equal does not mean they are the same person or have the same role in the marriage.

We can understand the role of husbands and fathers within marriage by correctly interpreting chapter five of St. Paul's Letter to the Ephesians, particularly verses 22–24: "Wives, be subject to your husbands, as to the Lord. For the husband is the head of the wife as Christ is the head of the church, his body … As the church is subject to Christ, so let wives also be subject in everything to their husbands."

St. Paul is saying that wives should put themselves under the mission of their husbands. What is the mission of the husband? Verse 25: to "love your wives as Christ loved the Church." How did Christ love the Church? He gave himself up for her; he died for her. Jesus tells us, "I came into the world not to be served but to serve" and to lay down my life for my bride. "The husband's headship in the family derives from the fact that he is the chief servant" (Christopher West, audio tape, "Sacramentality of Marriage").

Fathers Who Follow Christ to the Cross

Our role as husbands and fathers necessarily means that we must sacrifice everything: our bodies, our desires and wills, our hopes and dreams; everything we have and everything we are for the sake of our wives and children. Living our fatherhood by the example of Christ on the Cross is what separates the boys from the men: what separates the men who are merely "daddies" from the real men who are truly fathers.

Our spiritual fatherhood is truly authentic when it is "centered in Jesus Christ and through him to the Trinity" (Jordan Aumann, *Spiritual Theology*, 17). Jesus, in the Gospel of John, confirms this authentic spirituality when he said to His disciples "I am the way, the truth and the life. No one comes to the Father except through me" (Jn 14:6). To be authentically spiritual, then, means that we must enter into the life of Christ and, through God's grace and the Holy Spirit, transform our hearts, minds, and wills to that of Christ's.

It is only through Christ that we can receive salvation and any spirituality that is truly genuine must be Christocentric and Trinitarian at its very core. *Lumen Gentium*, the Vatican II document on the Church, states it this way: "The followers of Christ … have been made sons of God in the baptism of faith and partakers of the divine nature, and so are truly sanctified" (*Lumen Gentium*, 40).

Hence, it is only through an authentic spirituality of fatherhood, a spirituality that imitates Christ; that meditates on God's Word and responds to that Word in faith and, through the Holy Spirit, makes us share in the Triune life, that we can foster and nurture growth in holiness. The more we act under God's spirit, the more we seek to know and to do God's holy will in our lives, the more we implore the assistance and grace of the Holy Spirit, the more we grow in holiness. The Lord Jesus is the quintessential model of holiness and by following His perfect example, we grow in our love of God, our families, and ourselves.

The Most Blessed Sacrament is the source of spiritual fatherhood because the Eucharist is Jesus Christ. It is not a symbol or representation of Christ, but the reality of God with whom we are in intimate relationship: a relationship which "draws the faithful and sets them aflame with Christ's insistent love" (*Sacrosanctum Concilium,* 10).

The Eucharist, therefore, is the fountain where we receive the strength, power, and grace to seek the Lord in faith, hope, and love. The Eucharist is the beginning of spiritual fatherhood and "is for the soul the most certain means of remaining united to Jesus" (Abbot Columba Marmion, O.S.B., *Christ the Life of the Soul: Spiritual Conferences,* 261). It is a deepening of the relationship which began in Baptism and realizes a level of intimacy which is inherently supernatural and mysterious, yet inexhaustive. In the reception of the Eucharist, we literally become one with God in a way that is purposeful and real. It is the "fount" from which flows the definition of who we are as men in terms of our relationship with Christ. By receiving the Body and Blood of Christ in the Eucharist, we become more of who we already are in Christ "who maintains and increases the Divine life in us" (Marmion, 263).

Strengthened by the Eucharist, fathers should personify and exude faith, that is, they should exhibit a clear awareness that the work of the Church is, first and foremost, God's work. Therefore, we should foster ongoing growth in faith and personal formation, which must include daily prayer, so that our spirituality is firmly grounded in the Trinity and the Catholic faith.

Taking the Faith to the Entire Family

Spiritual fathers must be aware of the influence of secular thought and culture, with its disordered values, ideologies, and disintegrated view of the human person, and its profound influence within and upon our children today. Many of our teenagers and young adults are struggling to hold on to the Catholic belief in absolute and objective truth. Many, because they have been poorly catechized in the faith, plummet down the slippery precipice of subjective and relativistic "truth"; of societal norms that place themselves as the center of all reality and truth.

This view is in direct contrast to the life and mission of Jesus Christ and is, therefore, the antithesis of the life and mission of the Church. Solid faith formation within the family must occur and operate within the context of faith and Church, so that, as the domestic church, we are continually molded into the image of Christ for the purpose of salvation. Pride of place must be given to a systematic approach to disseminating the teachings of the Catholic Church—firmly rooted in the foundational truths of the Trinity, the Incarnation, and grace as revealed to us in Sacred Scripture, passed down through Sacred Tradition, and protected by the Magisterium—that makes Jesus Christ come alive in the hearts of our youth (cf. Lk 24:32).

To this end, the chief servant of the family must nurture an atmosphere of inclusion in all aspects of family and parish life so that even the young persons, "who by Baptism are incorporated into Christ and integrated into the People of God, are made sharers in their particular way in the priestly, prophetic, and kingly office of Christ, and have their own part to play in the mission of the whole Christian people in the Church and in the World" (CCC 897). The youth should participate fully in the evangelizing and sanctifying activity of the domestic church as well as the corporal and spiritual works of mercy, the renewal of the social order in the spirit of the gospel, and the pastoral ministry of the parish.

In addition, the sacramental dimension of family life must be encouraged in young people. The home must embody a spirituality that enhances and promotes devotion and active participation in the Eucharist where "grace is channeled into us and the sanctification of men in Christ and the glorification of God, to which all other activities of the Church are directed as toward their goal, are most powerfully achieved" (*Sacrosanctum Concilium*, 10). This must be accompanied by a deeper appreciation and understanding of the reality of sin and the need for frequent reception of the Sacrament of Penance.

All of this must be fostered in the home, the domestic Church and foundation of the parish community, where education in the fundamental truths of the faith are nurtured, fostered, and ensconced through family prayer, e.g., rosaries, Eucharistic Adoration, weekly attendance at Mass, recitation of the Liturgy of the Hours, and Scripture study. Families, led by truly spiritual fathers, are a special witness to God's loving plan in the world and the breeding ground for future generations of Catholic men and women. Hence, the domestic Church, while always remaining faithful to the Magisterium, must work together as an evangelizing society to produce "shining witnesses and models of holiness" in the world (*Lumen Gentium*, 39).

The qualities of fatherhood must include practical aspects as well. We should be empathetic, careful, and attentive listeners. As chief servants of the domestic church, we must develop the skills to become excellent managers of our time and family resources that must be exercised "in accord with the knowledge, competence, and preeminence which [we] possess … [and] with consideration for the common good and the dignity of persons" (CCC 907).

To do this effectively, the spiritual father must see clearly with the eyes of Jesus Christ, through the lenses of faith, hope, and love. This vision, in turn, must give spiritual strength to the faithful, concreteness to the domestic church, and extend charitably to the broader community. We must live our lives "in harmony with [our] faith so that [we] can become the light of the world. We need that undeviating honesty which can attract all men to the love of truth and goodness, and finally to the Church and to Christ" (*Apostolicam Actuositatem*, 13).

The spirituality of fatherhood must be rooted in Jesus Christ, the pillar of our salvation, through whom we can begin to understand the depths of the Heavenly Father's loving kindness. If we follow Christ's example and allow ourselves to be open to the Father, who is rich in mercy, we can "evoke in the soul a movement of conversion, in order to redeem it and set it on course toward reconciliation" (Pope John Paul II, *Reconciliatio et Pænitentia*, 20). Our response to God's love and mercy must be that of the prodigal son: recognition of our sinfulness, humility before the Father, and the conversion of our hearts, minds, and wills.

We must lead our families under Christ's call to service, because it is only by imitating the self-sacrificing Christ that we can ever hope to be role models and heroes worthy of the whole family's gratitude and honor.

(Deacon Harold Burke-Sivers, MTS, is a permanent deacon in the Archdiocese of Portland, Oregon and is the Director of Public Safety for the University of Portland. He is the founder of *Aurem Cordis*, a Christian evangelization and apologetics organization dedicated to disseminating and promoting Catholic values, principles, and teaching in complete faithfulness and total submission to Holy Scripture, Sacred Tradition, and the Magisterium. He has been a guest on "EWTN Live" and "Catholic Answers Live" and hosts a weekly radio program on KBVM, the Catholic radio station in Portland. Deacon Harold is currently writing a book on Catholic spirituality for men. He, his wife Colleen, and their four children reside in Portland.)

Go to *http://www.dads.org/*

Reflect on the life of this family and his perspective on fatherhood:

What struck me about his testimony? How can I apply this to our marriage?

3. Process/discussion on the material read for homework in Unit Four

   a. What is a good alternative to nagging?

      _____

      _____

   b. What are the ten ground rules for fighting in marriage?

      _____

      _____

   c. What if I don't "feel" the love, is it still love?

      _____

      _____

   d. Is mediocre love enough to sustain marriage?

      _____

      _____

   e. How can any of the seven "deadly" sins kill a marriage?

      _____

      _____

   f. Which one virtue do you need the most for a successful marriage?

      _____

      _____

   g. How can the Corporal and Spiritual Works of Mercy increase our love for God and neighbor? How can they help our marriage?

      _____

      _____

h. Isn't our marriage just between us? What does the Church and society have to do with our relationship?

_____

_____

i. What can our families do to be holy? Why would we want to be holy?

_____

_____

j. What do the bishops suggest for couples in crisis?

_____

_____

k. Name four reasons why a family needs a father.

_____

_____

l. What does it mean to pray? What are some methods of prayer? How can we begin to increase our prayer life as a family? As an individual?

_____

_____

Group Activity: (25 minutes) Group Role Play "Talent Search for Virtues"

Virtue and Vice Activity

A. Assign one of the sets of virtues and vices from this unit to each group of 2 or 4 couples.

B. Teams write a script and have two people role play a typical marriage conversation depicted in two ways, one exemplifying the vice, and the other exemplifying the person taking the higher road of virtue.

C. Have each team present their role play skit to the group.

4. **Video: *On Prayer.***

5. **Sharing real life examples on the Unit Four topics. Practical applications. (15 minutes)**

Table Talk in small groups.

a. Share any successes you have in couple prayer. When, how, etc? Share any successes you have in family prayer.

b. Discuss each of the Love Languages and offer some examples of how you can love your spouse with their love language.

c. Discuss types of apostolic activities that are available for families in your area. What are some opportunities for evangelization that are not available now, but we could organize?

6. **Private couple time/ Couple resolution. (15 minutes)**

Couples discuss in private: Out of this unit's lessons and today's discussion, which area should we examine more closely to help our marriage? Considering the exercises from the unit, which were most challenging? How might God be asking us to "stretch" this workout with a new resolution this week? What would be a good resolution for us to strengthen our marriage this week?

7. **Large Group sharing on practical applications. (10 minutes)**

What can we take away with us today to improve our marriages?

Leaders can offer open discussion, or else have couples write their answers down, turn them in and read some of them aloud to the group.

8. **Closing Prayer. (5 minutes) Suggested Prayer: Unit Four Exercise Four Prayer.**

9. **Social Time.**

Closing Workout Ceremony

Renew your vows—Rekindle your love

Marriage Renewal Party

Registration

Social Time

Gospel Reflection and Renewal of Vows

Dinner

*Renew*lywed Game

Couple's Conference

Dancing

"For this reason a man shall leave
his father and mother and cleave to his wife
and they shall become two in one flesh."
Gen 2:24

THE 10 COMMANDMENTS OF MARRIAGE

I. Thou shalt learn the true meaning of married love. Love has to be sacrificial, never selfish, caring, unbreakable, respectful, and where Jesus is ever present.

II. Thou shalt forget your dreams of a perfect marriage and work on a good marriage. Accept the limitations of your spouse. The successful marriage works around that. Be patient with defects in your spouse and concentrate on his/her good qualities.

III. Thou shalt discover the particular needs of your spouse and try to fulfill those needs with joy. There cannot be a 50/50 split rule in giving to your spouse. Give as much as you can to the one you love.

IV. Thou shalt show praise and appreciation to your spouse rather than look for it for yourself. Praise your spouse in front of others and defend your spouse in front of others.

V. Thou shalt forget the desire to control or dominate your spouse.

VI. Thou shalt always greet your spouse with joy and affection. Your spouse is your number one concern.

VII. Thou shalt abandon ALL hope of changing your spouse through nagging or complaining. Patience and grace with prayer, sacrifice, and penance is needed to change a spouse.

VIII. Remember the importance of unimportant details. That is how you should express love and concern to your spouse.

IX. Know how to say, "I'm sorry" AND, mean it. Know how to accept forgiveness graciously.

X. Pray TOGETHER every day. Accept your spouse's level of spirituality.

SAMPLE SCHEDULE

3:00 pm	Registration
	Hors d'œuvres
3:45 pm	Gospel Reflection and Renewal of Vows
4:45 pm	Marital Questionnaire (Confession available)
5:30 pm	Dinner
6:45 pm	*Renew*lywed Game
7:30 pm	Couples' Conference: Easy to Say but Hard to Obey!
8:00 pm	Dance

QUESTIONNAIRE #1
Marital Conscience Exam
(Please reflect privately and discuss together)

GOD AS A PARTNER IN OUR MARRIAGE

1. Have I been open to God as an essential partner in our marriage? Do I ask Him to help me be a better spouse? Do I pray for the graces of the Sacrament of Matrimony to strengthen me or do I assume I can handle everything myself?

2. Do I pray for my spouse? If so, what do I pray for? For God to make my spouse see things my way, or do I honestly place my spouse's needs and intentions before the Lord?

3. Do I pray that God will help me and my spouse be faithful, not just in action but in heart and mind as well? Do I pray for a big heart and the grace to love my spouse well?

4. Have I tried to build a shared spiritual life with my spouse? Am I willing to talk about God and spiritual things with him/her? Do I pray with my spouse or am I merely an onlooker letting my spouse "be spiritual" for both of us?

RENEWAL OF MARRIAGE VOWS
(Please stand for the vows)

Priest:

My dear friends, you have come together in this place so that the Lord may seal and strengthen your love in the presence of the Church's minister and this community. Christ abundantly blesses this love. He has already consecrated you in Baptism and now enriches and strengthens you by a special sacrament so that you may assume the duties of marriage in mutual and lasting fidelity. And so I ask you to join your right hands and renew your consent before God and His Church.

Husband and wife join hands and profess their vows:

Husband:

I, _____, take you, _____, for my lawful wedded wife, to have and to hold from this day forward, for richer or poorer, in sickness and in health, forsaking all others, I pledge myself to you. I thank God for blessing me with your precious gift of love to perfect His plan for my life. I enter our marriage freely and happily realizing the obligations and responsibilities involved in making this commitment. Before all the people present here today, and before God (who can look into my heart and know the truth), I vow my loyalty and fidelity to you, my beloved _____. I will protect you and be your partner. _____, I will love you and cherish you forever.

Wife:
I, _____, take you, _____, for my lawful wedded husband, to have and to hold from this day forward, for richer or poorer, in sickness and in health, forsaking all others, I pledge myself to you. I thank God for blessing me with your precious gift of love to perfect His plan for my life. I enter our marriage freely and happily, realizing the obligations and responsibilities involved in making this commitment. Before God and all the people present here today, I vow to you my love and fidelity. I commit myself to making Christ the guiding light in our marriage so that we may grow closer to one another through Him. I promise to honor and respect you as head of our home. I ask God to grant me the grace necessary to fulfill this vow. _____, I will love you and cherish you forever.

Blessing and Exchanging of Rings
(Remove and exchange wedding rings)

Husband: (placing ring on wife's finger, repeat after the priest):
Take this ring as a sign of my love and fidelity. In the name of the Father, and of the Son and of the Holy Spirit.

Wife: (placing ring on husband's finger, repeat after the priest):
Take this ring as a sign of my love and fidelity. In the name of the Father, and of the Son and of the Holy Spirit.

SELF-GIVING TO MY SPOUSE

1. Have I put a "price" on the gift of myself? Do I mentally keep track of who is giving more in our relationship, so that I hold back until the "score" evens out? Do I keep giving, but internally resent the fact that I am always the one who gives more effort, or who apologizes first, etc.?

2. Have I stopped really listening to my spouse? Do I assume that after this many years of marriage I know everything about him or her? Have I scheduled my life to allow us time for unhurried one-on-one conversations that are not about the kids, schedules, or money?

3. Have I made it a priority to find time for romance and to bring energy into our love life? Or does my work or commitment to the children always seem to prevent us from deepening our intimacy?

4. Do I treat my spouse with respect and honesty, even when we disagree? Have I fallen into a pattern of name-calling, insults, or habitually assuming the worst when we argue?

5. Can I quickly list ten positive attributes of my spouse-attributes that I value in our marriage? What are they? Do ten negative qualities more easily come to mind? Have I adopted an interior critical attitude towards my spouse that makes it easy to focus on failings and overlook gifts he or she brings to the marriage?

6. What are my principal faults as a husband/wife? Have I stopped working on them figuring that it's time my spouse simply accepted them?

BUILDING A SHARED VISION

1. What do we envision the concrete circumstances of our life will be like in ten years? (In terms of kind of jobs, number of working hours, number of kids and amount of family time, where we will live, responsibilities for ageing parents, financial circumstances, etc.)

2. What are the personal goals each one of us has over the next ten years with respect to spiritual growth, jobs, additional education, personal interests or hobby, family satisfaction ("I will be happy if our family is like…")?

3. What do we want our marriage to be like in ten years in terms of love, commitments, emotional support, sexual relationship, shared interest?

4. In order to arrive at these goals (for our relationship, our personal satisfaction, and our concrete circumstances), what do we need to change over the next year? The next five years? What ate the obstacles present now which will hinder us from building the life we desire together? What good habits or traditions should we hold on to in the coming year?

5. What are the concrete ways we can meet the challenges that we anticipate over the next ten years?

SUGGESTED READING

William Harley, Jr.
His Needs, Her Needs: Building an Affair-Proff Marriage

Judith Allerstein and Sandra Blakeslee
The Good Marriage: How and Why Love Lasts

Gregory Popcak
A Catholic Guide to Lifelong Marriage

Matthew Kelly
Seven Levels of Intimacy

Christopher West
Good News about Sex and Marriage

Sam Torode
Body and Gift

Fr. Walter Schu, LC
The Splendor of Love: John Paul II's Vision for Marriage and Family

Jeff Cavins, Matthew Pinto, Patti Armstrong
Amazing Grace for Married Couples

QUESTIONNAIRE #2
A Family Mission Statement

What is the purpose of our family? _____
_____
_____

What kind of family do we want to be? _____
_____
_____

What kind of things do we want to accomplish? _____
_____
_____

What kind of spirit do we want in our home? _____
_____
_____

How do we want to treat one another and speak to one another? _____
_____
_____

What things are truly important to us as a family? _____
_____
_____

What role does Christ play in our family? _____
_____
_____

What are our family's highest priorities? _____
_____
_____

What are the unique gifts, talents, and abilities of each family member? _____
_____
_____

What are our responsibilities as family members? _____
_____
_____

What are the principles and guidelines we want to follow? _____
_____
_____

Who are our heroes? _____
_____
_____

What is it about them we like and would want to emulate? _____
_____
_____

What families inspire us and why do we admire them? _____
_____
_____

How can we contribute to a society and to the Church as a family? _____
_____
_____

What will we do to communicate our faith with others? _____
_____
_____

Adapted from Steven R. Covey, *Seven Habits of Highly Effective Families*

COMMUNICATION AND CONFLICT RESOLUTION

1. What aspects of my life do I most enjoy talking over with my spouse? When does he or she make me feel most loved? How?

2. Are there some subjects we no longer speak about because they are too touchy? Or because we have brought "peaceful coexistence" at the price of open, constructive dialogue?

3. Are there certain areas of our life that continually provoke disagreement, arguments or resentment? What are they? Even when we do disagree, do we make an effort to respect and understand each other's needs and opinions.

4. What are the obstacles to effective communication that characterize our relationship; stonewalling, defensiveness, blame-laying, criticism or contempt? Are there times when I suspect my spouse would rather just give in instead of telling me what he/she really thinks to avoid continuing an argument?

5. What has made each of us happiest over the past year? What has brought each of us the greatest sadness over the past year?

Appendix
Post-Workout Drills

The Sanctity of Marriage and the Family

Husband and wife, by the covenant of marriage, are no longer two, but one flesh. By their intimate union of persons and actions they give mutual help and service to each other, experience the meaning of their unity, and gain an ever deeper understanding of it day by day. This intimate union in the mutual self-giving of two persons, as well as the good of the children, demands full fidelity from both spouses, and an indissoluble unity between them. Christ the Lord has abundantly blessed this richly complex love, which springs from the divine source of love and is founded on the model of his union with the Church.

In earlier times God met his people in a covenant of love and fidelity. So now the Savior of mankind, the bridegroom of the Church, meets Christian husbands and wives in the sacrament of matrimony. Further, He remains with them in order that, as He loved the Church and gave Himself up for her, so husband and wife may, in mutual self-giving, love each other with perpetual fidelity. True married love is caught up into God's love; it is guided and enriched by the redeeming power of Christ and the saving action of the church, in order that the spouses may be effectively led to God, and receive help and strength in the sublime responsibility of parenthood.

Christian spouses are therefore strengthened, and as it were consecrated, by a special sacrament for the duties and the dignity of their state. By the power of this sacrament they fulfill their obligations to each other and to their family, and are filled with the spirit of Christ. This spirit pervades their whole lives with faith, hope, and love. Thus they promote their own perfection and each other's sanctification, and so contribute together to the greater glory of God.

Hence with parents leading the way by example and family prayer, their children, indeed all within the family circle, will find it easier to make progress in natural virtues, in salvation, and in holiness. Husband and wife, raised to the dignity and responsibility of parenthood, will be zealous in fulfilling their task as educators, especially in the sphere of religious education, a task that is primarily their own. Children as active members of the family, contribute in their own way to the holiness of their parents. With the love of grateful hearts, the loving respect and trust, children will return the generosity of their parents, and will stand by them as true sons and daughters when their parents meet with hardship and the loneliness of old age.[1]

LEARNING TO SPIRITUALLY SEE AGAIN

FR. THOMAS G. ASCHENBRENER

Conversion story of French Atheist and Communist Andre Fossard:

> It happened one day when I was waiting for a friend. Standing outside of a small chapel, I decided to wander in and take a look. Upon entering into the small chapel I noticed a beautiful chapel brightly lit, and the altar was draped in white with many plants and candles. Above the altar was a large crucifix, and on the altar was a monstrance exposing the Blessed Sacrament. Suddenly, my eyes became fixed on the host and the words *spiritual life* were spoken to me by someone who was seeing something which I had not yet seen.

> What I was beginning to experience was a different world, whose brilliance and density made our world seem like the apparition of an unfulfilled dream. What I saw was reality; this was truth, the manifestation of God: a manifestation which is an all-embracing presence, a presence which became a person; the Living God. This overwhelming invasion brought with it a sense of joy: now I wondered how I had ever been able to breathe and to live without this presence.

Just imagine, in an instant, Andre was able to see spiritually; he was able to see God in the Eucharist.

Helen Keller once said: "*I can see, and that is why I can be happy, in what you call the dark, but which to me is golden. I can see a God-made world, not a manmade world. It gives me a deep comforting sense that "things seen are temporal and things unseen are eternal." "It is a terrible thing to see and have no vision,* {spiritual vision that is.}"

Very often God smashes into our little world when we least expect it. He breaks into our lives to show us our blindness and the ugliness of sin that keeps us from him.

For many of us, spiritual healing happens overtime, not overnight, and this can be very painful, especially when something is being revealed to us by God, which we are not ready to see. We may want to continue to conceal our sins, or we just do not want to recognize and own up to them. Consequently, we impede our growth in the interior life.

St. Augustine once said: "*When I first came to know you, you drew me to yourself so that I might see that there were things for me to see, but that I myself was not ready to see them.*"

Many people prefer to remain comfortably blind in their sin because of the instantaneous pleasure they get from sin. But in the end, they are miserable. Christianity is not about comfort and complacency; it is about repentance and conversion and this can be painful. A saint once said that Jesus came to afflict the comfortable and comfort the afflicted.

From my experience before and during my priesthood, hitting rock bottom was the only way to wake people up from their spiritual blindness. With the help of God's grace, many of the people I worked with were able to confront their alcoholism, drug addictions, sexual addictions, problems with family or friends, greed (stealing money from work), etc. They were able to see that instead of filling the void in their life with God, they had allowed sin to consume them with miserable consequences.

Once they opened themselves up to God's grace, they were able to joyfully proclaim, *"Now I see. Now I see that I am nothing without God; I can do nothing good without him."*

St. Augustine said, "You overcame the weakness of my blurred vision, sending most strongly the beams of your light … You were with me, Lord, but I was outside and it was there that I searched for you … Created things kept me from you … You called, you shouted through my deafness. You flashed, you shone, and you dispelled my blindness … You touched me now I burn for your peace."

Many of the Church Fathers saw physical blindness as a type or figure of spiritual blindness: an inability in the interior/spiritual life to foster intimacy with God. We could say it is when the state of soul is neither hot nor cold. This spiritual paralysis is known as lukewarmness.

"Lukewarmness has nothing to do with an absence of spiritual dryness. It derives from a prolonged carelessness towards the interior life. It is usually preceded by a series of small infidelities and when these are allowed to accumulate, they gradually weaken our relationship with God."

We can see this in our lack of contrition and impatience in our dealings with God and neighbor. The life of prayer loses its focus, and eventually the soul becomes paralyzed and blind. Why? Because we increasingly tolerate venial sins and become comfortable with them. Many times we even try to justify them by our tiredness, exhaustion, or laziness. In our weakness, we begin to feel a sense of entitlement; we begin to deceive ourselves into thinking that we deserve to indulge a bit in sloth, lust, drink, anger, or envy after a long days work. Unfortunately, this path leads us to think that as long as we avoid the serious or deadly sins, we are assured of our salvation. But we know this is the Devil's great lie!

St. Augustine said, "While it is quite normal that everyone will sin in small matters, no one should treat these sins casually. How true it is that many small offenses can add up to something quite sizable …"

These minor faults are always fertile ground for the growth of lukewarmness and they can eventually dispose the soul towards mortal sin.

St. Thomas said: "We are placed in between the things of this world and spiritual goods … The more we cling to one, the more we recede from the other and vice versa." For example, the more we cling to anger and gossiping the more we recede from forgiveness, mercy, and charity. The more we cling to generosity and patience, the more we recede from greed, and irritation, or annoyance. The more we recede from impurity and lust, the more we cling to chastity and purity of heart.

Many people are experiencing despair, hopelessness, and depression, because they carelessly allow themselves to gravitate toward vices that give deceptive and instantaneous "happiness." Our soul can be likened to a garden. The vices grow like weeds, while the virtues grow like fruit trees and beautiful flowers. We need to be vigilant in eradicating the weeds and cultivating the fruits and flowers.

Like any garden, it takes work to root out the weeds so that the garden can flourish and bear an abundance of fruit. That is why Jesus said, "I am the vine and you are the branches … whoever remains in me and I in Him will bear much fruit." (Jn 15:5) It is interesting to note that in the natural world of vineyards, the best and finest wine is produced in the worst soil. Figurative speaking, we can say then that the roots of the grapevine have to suffer and struggle in order to bear the choicest wine. It is the same with virtues and prayer life. The interior or spiritual life demands that we care for our souls with the utmost vigilance, because in the end, we cannot enter into the Kingdom of Heaven with a garden full of weeds.

If we are not in the state of sanctifying grace, that is, in right relationship with God, or if we remain blind and complacent to our sins, our actions will reveal this spiritual apathy toward others. We begin to lead people astray—the blind leading the blind. Instead of helping others become saints, we distract them from God and his personal call to each of them.

St. Catherine of Siena once said, "Through love of God we conceive virtues, and through love of our neighbor, they are brought to the birth."

Jesus comes to meet us in our need, to save us, and to restore us to spiritual health. We cannot continue to let our carelessness, tepidity, lack of patience, or discouragement, continue to paralyze our souls, blinding us to God and his grace.

The remedy for spiritual blindness is the Sacrament of Penance and the Eucharist. If we allow God's grace to penetrate the depths of our soul, "Jesus will do just what his name implies, 'He who saves us from our sins.'" Consequently we will experience an abundance of grace and new life, which will transform the way we think, speak, and act. His grace can be so much more efficacious in souls, if we are properly disposed and have removed the weeds of vice. The roots of sin can be deep, and it will take constant vigilance, prayer, patience, self-denial, and mortification to root them out completely. In the end, however, we will experience peace of soul and a presence that will leave us burning with a deep desire for him alone.

Healing Marriages of Control and Trust Issues

Interview with Catholic Psychiatrist Richard Fitzgibbons by Genevieve Pollock

WEST CONSHOHOCKEN, Pennsylvania, JAN. 28, 2010 (Zenit.org). More marriages and families these days are affected by control and trust issues, says Richard Fitzgibbons, but through the sacraments and practice of virtue these problems can be overcome.

This was the theme of a recent webinar in a series sponsored by the Institute for Marital Healing, which offers resources for couples, counselors and clergy on the topics of parenting, manhood, family life and marriage.

Fitzgibbons, the director of the institute, has worked with thousands of couples and has spoken and written extensively on these topics. In 2008, he was also appointed as a consultant for the Holy See's Congregation for Clergy.

In this interview with ZENIT, Fitzgibbons speaks about modern causes of trust issues, the distinction between being strong and being controlling, and particular virtues that provide an antidote to these problems.

ZENIT: You mention that the most popular section on your Web site is the page about the controlling spouse or relative. Why you think there is such an interest in this topic?

Fitzgibbons: We had expected that the most frequently visited chapter would be the angry spouse or relative and were surprised initially by the response to the controlling spouse chapter.

As I thought and prayed about this interest, I came to a deeper understanding of the serious personal and cultural factors that are contributing to the tendency to dominate or not trust others that results in a need to control.

ZENIT: Could you describe briefly some of the characteristics of the controlling person?

Fitzgibbons: The worst character weakness in the person who gives in to the tendency to control, and all of us can at times, is that of treating a spouse, who is a great gift from God, with a lack of respect.

The controlling person becomes turned in and thereby fails to see the goodness in his/her spouse.

The other major weakness is that of giving in quickly to excessive anger. Controlling spouses and relatives are also irritable and often sad because it is, in fact, not possible to control anyone since we all have inherent dignity and strength as children of God.

Finally, controlling tendencies damage healthy, cheerful self-giving in marriage and reinforce selfishness, a major cause of controlling behaviors.

ZENIT: What harm can be caused by controlling spouses or relatives?

Fitzgibbons: Controlling behaviors damage the marital friendship, romantic love and betrothed love, three essential areas of marital self-giving which John Paul II describes in "Love and Responsibility."

The lack of respect leads the other spouse to feel sad, angry, mistrustful and insecure. Unless this conflict is addressed properly and corrected, serious conflicts can develop including depressive illness, anxiety disorders, substance abuse, infidelity and separation and divorce.

ZENIT: In our fast-paced society, where people are required to control or manage so many aspects of their lives—finances, health, job, family, etc.—isn't a controlling nature more of a benefit, even a necessity for survival? Do you see a positive side of this type of personality?

Fitzgibbons: Yes, confidence and strength are healthy personality traits that enable us to respond to the many challenges in the great sacrament of marriage and family life.

However, daily growth in virtues is necessary so that a spouse doesn't cross over a line with these gifts and become controlling.

The virtues that are essential to balancing the gift of strength are gentleness, humility, meekness, self-denial and faith.

A major goal in marriage is to be strong and confident, but not controlling. I encourage many strong husbands to pray to St. Peter to protect them so that they are not controlling leaders in the home.

ZENIT: You state that there are often trust issues at the heart of the controlling personality. Could you say more about this?

Fitzgibbons: A major cause of the tendency to control or dominate is the result of damage to a person's ability to trust or feel safe in childhood.

Subsequently, spouses can unconsciously be driven by fear to act in a controlling manner, that is, they only feel safe when they are in control, which, of course, they never are. Common childhood conflicts in the past were alcoholism, parental fighting and the experience of a controlling parent.

More recent causes of severe damage to childhood trust are the divorce culture, day care, and the epidemic of selfishness in parents in large part due to the contraceptive mentality. Also, insecure men engage in controlling behaviors in an attempt to bolster their male confidence. In young adults the hook-up culture is also severely damaging their ability to trust without their realizing it.

Finally, an important spiritual factor that should not be overlooked is described in the *Catechism of the Catholic Church*: "Every man experiences evil around him and within himself. This experience makes itself felt in the relationships between man and woman. Their union has always been threatened by discord, a spirit of domination, infidelity, jealousy, and conflicts that can escalate into hatred and separation" (CCC 1606).

ZENIT: How can a person begin to address these issues, and change the controlling nature? How can a loved one assist someone who may be seen as controlling?

Fitzgibbons: The first step is that this serious marital weakness needs to be uncovered.

If spouses trusted God more with their marriages, they would not fear pointing out this difficulty and asking for change.

Needed change can occur by a commitment to grow in trust in God and in one's spouse, by a forgiveness process with those who have damaged trust in childhood, by a decision to stop repeating controlling behaviors of a parent, by meditating regularly that the Lord is in control and by growth in numerous virtues including respect, faith, gentleness, humility, magnanimity and love.

The role of faith can be very effective in addressing this serious character weakness. We have seen remarkable improvement in the struggle against this harmful character weakness through the graces in the sacrament of reconciliation. We encourage controlling Catholic couples to seek healing in this powerful sacrament.

Also, controlling wives benefit from deepening their relationship with Our Lady, from turning to her as a role model and acquiring her virtues described by St. Louis de Montfort in "True Devotion to the Blessed Virgin."

Controlling husbands can benefit from meditating upon St. Joseph and asking him to help them to be gentle, protective, sensitive, cheerfully giving leaders of their marriages and families.

ZENIT: As a psychiatrist, when would you suggest seeking outside help, from a priest or a counselor, to heal the person's emotional wounds?

Fitzgibbons: I recommend going to a priest before going to a counselor because far too many mental health professionals support the present culture of selfishness.

Brad Wilcox, a young Catholic sociologist at the University of Virginia has written about the mental health field's influence upon marriage: "The psychological revolution's focus on individual fulfillment and personal growth resulted in marriage as being seen as a vehicle for a self-oriented ethic of romance, intimacy, and fulfillment."

"In this new psychological approach to married life, one's primary obligation was not to one's family but to one's self; hence, marital success was defined not by successfully meeting obligations to one's spouse and children but by a strong sense of subjective happiness in marriage—usually to be found in and through an intense, emotional relationship with one's spouse."

We believe that a sincere commitment by each spouse to grow in self-knowledge and in virtues daily can resolve the controlling spouse conflict without the need for marital therapy. However, newer marital referral sources faithful to Christ's teaching on marriage are available at the Catholic Therapists and the Catholic Psychotherapy Web sites.

Our Lady's intercession at Cana led to the Lord's first miracle to bring more joy into a young marriage. We encourage Catholic couples struggling with control and selfishness conflicts to turn to her for another miracle for their marriage.

On the Net:

Institute for Marital Healing: *www.maritalhealing.com*

Catholic Therapists: *www.catholictherapists.com*

Catholic Psychotherapy: *www.catholicpsychotherapy.com*

This article was originally published on 2010-01-28 at *www.zenit.org/article-28191?l=english* and reprinted by permission of the publisher. All rights reserved. © Innovative Media, Inc.

Married Couples Who Intentionally Chose Sterilization for Contraceptive Purposes and Lasting Repentance

Monsignor Charles M. Mangan

A common theme that has resounded for over three decades is that many—if not most—Catholic married couples in Western countries are currently demonstrating in practice their rejection of the Church's authoritative and binding teaching that proclaims that each occasion of sexual intercourse must be open to the transmission of human life. While one may dispute numbers and percentages of those Catholics involved, a fair judgment of the situation reveals that especially since the "Sexual Revolution" of the 1960s, a significant portion of Catholic married couples has used or is presently using some form of contraceptive.

As is increasingly well-known, there are some devices implanted, chemical formulæ injected, and even other products taken orally that are routinely referred to as "contraceptives" but are in fact effective after conception has occurred, thereby making these abortion-inducing agents ("abortifacients"). Sadly, a large section of the public, cutting across boundaries of race, economic status, education, and creed, are woefully ignorant about the abortifacient quality of Depo-Provera, RU-486, the Intrauterine Device, the "Morning-After Pill," Norplant, the "emergency contraceptive" and in some cases the common "Pill." Therefore, literally millions of persons throughout the world are "silently" aborting, thinking all the while that they are preventing conception when in fact they are unwittingly snuffing out the lives of preborn children.

But all is not lost. True sorrow, resolute amendment of life and deep awareness of the Truth, inspired by the Holy Spirit Who is the Lord and Giver of Life and the Master of the Truth, are possible. By yielding to God's abundant grace, a married couple who are contracepting or aborting may humbly surrender to the Truth, acknowledge their sin and sincerely repent of their error. How? By stopping the process of contracepting or aborting. Authentic repentance demands the avoidance of any and every method of contraception and those forms that parade as contraceptives but are in reality abortifacients.

However, imagine a married couple who have done something permanent in order to prevent conception. The husband has undergone a vasectomy or the wife a tubal ligation. There immediately appears to be a substantial and ongoing problem. How can this couple show their genuine sorrow since the effect of the direct sterilization continues unabated? May they ever be really reconciled to their Creator, thereby shunning their sin and the prevailing ethos of the Culture of Death and assume their place in the Christian community as those who give good example to others and testify to the Truth, notwithstanding the not insignificant cost?

This essay offers guidance for married couples who deliberately selected sterilization to prevent conception. Although the teaching of the Catholic Church is the foundation for this article, the remarks herein are not limited to Catholic married couples who chose to be sterilized so as not to conceive but are germane to persons of all faiths and to those of no faith, because the doctrine of the Catholic Church is based on Sacred Scripture, the Apostolic Tradition and the Natural Law—the trio of sources expressing the One Truth that sustains and applies to everyone without exception.

It is hoped that all married couples who intentionally chose to be sterilized so as not to conceive but who seek forgiveness and a new beginning in Christ and those married couples in the same category but who have never thought much about the vital importance of rejecting the sin of direct sterilization and the subsequent urgent need of conversion will benefit from these brief reflections.

The Nature of Sterilization

Germain G. Grisez and John F. Kippley—each a Catholic layman, husband and father—treat this issue and have provided excellent material for careful pondering.

As Grisez keenly and succinctly observes, sterilization intended as a means of birth control (often referred to as "direct," "deliberate," or "intentional" sterilization) is intrinsically evil, for it fails to promote the good of the human person because of its adamant refusal to accept the inherent procreative ("life-giving") dimension of the marital act as built into it by God. (The other inherent aspect of the marital act is the personalist [unitive] or "person-uniting" dimension.)

No benefit to the person as a whole can justify any procedure which brings about sterility and is chosen for that very purpose. In no way does sterility as such truly benefit anyone; it only facilitates sexual intercourse—the distinct act in and through which some benefit is expected—by excluding conception. Thus, the intention of choosing sterilization is contraceptive, and the sterilizing act is at best a bad means to a good ulterior end. Moreover, because sterilization involved bodily mutilation and is usually irreversible, it is, other things being equal, more seriously wrong than other methods of contraception.[1]

One here recalls the unfortunate circumstance of our era in which methods that actually kill an already conceived and developing child are cavalierly dismissed as "just another kind of birth control." Certainly, abortifacient means are more sinful than any contraception, including sterilization, because the former extinguishes a life now begun, while the latter prevents a life from being started. But, as Grisez insists, among the purely contraceptive methods, sterilization is the most morally repugnant.

Kippley explains the "types" of sin that are involved in direct sterilization. One kind is the contraceptive quality and intention of the act of sterilization, in which one deliberately wills not to conceive a child. Kippley writes: Once a person has voluntarily had himself or herself sterilized for birth control purposes, each act of sexual intercourse is seriously stained; it objectively contradicts the meaning of the marriage act for it is a permanent way of saying, "I take you for pleasure but not for the imagined worse of pregnancy."[2]

The second sin linked to intentional sterilization is that of mutilation (whether actual or attempted) of a healthy organ that has as its divinely-preordained purpose to participate and cooperate with God in the begetting of a new human life. The human body is to be loved and cherished. The "good" of human procreation as created by the Almighty is not respected when one purposely rejects the reproductive capacity of the human body and willingly alters the body with contraception in view.

Direct sterilization—indeed, all contraception—is a grave matter, that is, it is intrinsically evil. (While this assertion may seem overly audacious today, it is to be recalled that before the dawn of the twentieth century, virtually everyone thought contraception of any stripe to be patently immoral—an utter abomination against God's Eternal Law. All Christian denominations, for example, subscribed to this tenet until 1930.) Intentional sterilization in itself always fulfills the first condition required for the commission of a mortal sin—that offense which cuts one off from the Sanctifying Grace that is the very life of God Himself. Mortal sin—a repudiation of the Lord and His wise commands—may be described as the ugly chains of haughty disobedience that one prefers to the spotless garment of the Lamb. One who chooses the shackles of mortal sin will never attain the refreshing freedom earmarked for the legitimate sons and daughters of God who have been redeemed by the Precious Blood of the Savior.

Repenting Sterilization: If Possible, How?

Because the Almighty is, unquestionably, all-merciful, those married couples who have chosen direct sterilization to escape conception—regardless if the reason was one of fear, lack of trust or dissent from the Church's doctrine—can turn back to Him, ask His pardon and be restored to a life replete with His joy and peace. The Sacrament of Penance ("Confession" or "Reconciliation") is indispensable and unsurpassed for those who purposely selected sterilization; it is necessary before the reception of the Sacrament of the Most Holy Eucharist for those men and women who have knowingly (that is, were aware that intentional sterilization gravely offended God) and willingly (that is, totally) consented to the sin of direct sterilization. The supernatural rewards of the Sacrament of Penance and of the consequent eating and drinking of the Body and Blood of the Risen Lord Jesus Christ are vast and unlimited; they cannot be denied or circumscribed. The Sacraments, when received in the state of grace (that is, when one is free of mortal sin), conform one more closely to the Messiah and to His chaste Mother, Blessed Mary Ever-Virgin.

There are those who are convinced that the sin of direct sterilization presents no more difficulty than any other transgression regarding abiding repentance and true reconciliation to God. A Catholic couple in which one or both intentionally chose sterilization, so the argument goes, merely confess the sin of sterilization to the priest in the context of the Sacrament of Penance. Then, that metaphorical "bridge" spanning the abyss between one in mortal sin and the Creator has been crossed again. The wide gap has been closed; deep contentment within the soul once again reigns supreme.

Our two previously-cited authors disagree with this sentiment.

Grisez poses the quandary thus:

> People with a legalistic mentality sometimes suppose there is an easy out for Catholic couples who accept the Church's teaching on contraception, yet want no more children and do not wish to abstain during the fertile period: let one spouse be sterilized and that spouse (or both) confess the sin; then the couple can engage in intercourse whenever they please without worrying about pregnancy or feeling guilty about contraception. The trouble with this supposed solution is that a sin is not simply a technical violation which can be repaired by going to confession. The choice of sterilization, like any sin, is a self-determination, an existential self-mutilation more profound than the physical self-mutilation of sterilization; and this self-determination lasts until the person repents. Consequently, unless those who have tried to solve their problems by means of sterilization are truly contrite—"I wish I had not done that, and if I had it to do over, I would never make that choice"—confession is fruitless for them.[3]

Kippley frames the problem in this manner:

> How can a person be sorry for the sin whose fruits he enjoys? Imagine the man who thinks, "I enjoy having sex whenever I feel like it without having to be concerned about possible pregnancy. I'm glad I had the vasectomy (or my wife had a tubal ligation)." How can such spouses be sorry for their sins of sterilization? How can such spouses not be committing, at least objectively, the sin of contraceptive sterilized intercourse? How can a previous confession of the sin of sterilization forgive the current sin of contraceptive intercourse?[4]

> Repentance is possible after the sin of directly-intended sterilization. God's infinite strength does change hearts and dispose persons to the Truth who once were blind to the Transcendent. Deliberate sterilization is surely a "forgivable" sin. Those who have committed it need not be banned from Paradise and lost forever. "Like those who repent any other sin, they can be absolved and spiritually healed, so that they can live in grace again."[5]

What is Required for Real Amendment

Both Grisez and Kippley, in harmony with Catholic doctrine detailing the Lord's tender forgiveness and the corresponding genuine amendment of life after sin to which He summons His beloved children, concur that the "resolution of the sterilization dilemma" calls for real repentance and change. One must—with God's overwhelming grace—eradicate any perduring contraceptive intent. "The person who regrets having been sterilized must develop a true sorrow for a) the initial sin of sterilization and b) subsequent sins of sterilized intercourse."[6]

And sorrow for any sin necessitates genuine action and internal transformation, namely that one "rights the wrong" in part by avoiding that sin in the future and "the near occasion" that leads to that sin. Listed below are three "behaviors," which although not definitively taught by the Magisterium as requirements are recommended by theologians who teach in harmony with the Magisterium, that evidence an abiding sorrow for the sin of direct sterilization and the connected attempt to correct the evil that was caused.

1. Complete abstinence until the wife is past menopause. Some quarters would dismiss this option without delay, claiming that it is unworkable and would have disastrous implications for the married couple. Although not strictly obligatory (given what follows), it does remain a possibility.

2. A surgical reversal of the sterilization. It may appear at first glance that a surgical reversal of vasectomy and tubal ligation, which today is often an "out-patient" procedure and increasingly less expensive, is in fact the only option for the married couple who were intentionally sterilized so as to prevent conception and now wish to be "made just" in God's sight. "They purposely sterilized themselves, let them now fix precisely what they have done," is one way of putting it.

Grisez inquires whether directly sterilized married couples either ought to "abstain entirely from marital intercourse or try to have the sterilization reversed?"[7] While Church teaching does not deal explicitly with this question, general principles point to a negative answer, at least for most cases ... there usually are good reasons not to try to have the operation reversed: doing so involves costs and other burdens, the attempt often fails to restore fertility ...[8]

Kippley offers this analysis:

> If reversal surgery were as simple and inexpensive as vasectomies and tubal ligations, then it would be morally required for all as part of their repentance. This is the common teaching of respected moral theologians. However, it is also a principle of moral theology that extraordinary

burdens are not normally required as part of repentance. For example, many poor people have been seduced by public health workers into being sterilized—sometimes for no cost and sometimes even paid to be sterilized. For such couples, the cost of reversal surgery would be a very severe burden if not simply impossible, and the reversal surgery would not be morally required. In another case, reversal surgery might constitute a grave risk to health or life because of heart conditions, reaction to anesthesia, etc. Such cases would also constitute an extraordinary burden and would eliminate the moral obligation to have reversal surgery.[9]

Kippley holds that if a married couple who intentionally chose to be sterilized for the motive of contraception enjoy good health and the monetary resources that could withstand the financial strain of reversal surgery, then "there is a general moral obligation to have reversal surgery, but I would hesitate to call it a serious obligation (i.e., the grave matter of mortal sin) provided they practice periodic abstinence as noted below."[10] He further contends: "Perhaps the couple who are trying hard to do the right thing but have a general reluctance to undergo surgery might gain insight by asking this question: 'If our existing family were wiped out and we wanted children, would we have reversal surgery in the effort to achieve pregnancy?'"[11]

It seems that an honest investigation of the possibility of reversal surgery, which includes a discussion with competent medical personnel regarding the physical implications and another with a priest concerning the moral ramifications, is the very least that would be expected, given the seriousness of the matter.

Thanks to the continual advances in medical technology and praxis, the surgical reversal of sterilization is sometimes not as perplexing as it once was. A higher success rate for the reversal and the possibility of performing this surgery at more medical centers means that the reversal surgery itself is surely not as remote as before in terms of availability and a reasonable likelihood of success. One anticipates the day when the reversal procedure will be considered as commonplace as sterilization—due to its efficacy, its inexpensive cost and its universal accessibility.

3. Periodic abstinence from the marital privilege. The Church stresses that a married couple who possess a just (some theologians maintain "serious") rationale to postpone a pregnancy may limit marital intercourse to the wife's infertile days during her cycle. Kippley submits that there is a specific link between this ecclesiastical declaration rooted in the Natural Law and the plight of intentionally sterilized couples.

The current knowledge about a woman's alternating phases of fertility and infertility makes it possible for a repentant sterilized couple to restrict intercourse to those times when she is naturally infertile. In this way, they will not be taking advantage of their sterilized state, enjoying the fruits of their sin. Their behavior will be consistent with their present desire that they would not have had the sterilization in the first place …[12]

By limiting intercourse to the infertile days of the wife, the married couple who purposely chose to be sterilized in order to avoid pregnancy are conducting themselves similarly to a non-sterilized couple who are employing Natural Family Planning (N.F.P.). In both instances, the couples engage in the marital privilege during that time when pregnancy is unlikely.

Hence, if a married couple who selected sterilization as a permanent contraceptive cannot have the sterilization surgically reversed, then they show their love for God, their commitment to each other rooted in generous sacrifice, their lament for their sin, and their accompanying good will by saving the marital embrace for the infertile period, thereby acting as if indeed they were still fertile. It is then clear that this purposely sterilized but now repentant couple respect, appreciate and are grateful for the God-given fertility-dimension of intercourse and want that affectionate act of "self-donation" to be pleasing to their benevolent Creator.

Shepherds of Souls

A word to confessors and spiritual directors. May the foregoing comments be valuable in your challenging work to spread far and wide the entire Holy Gospel of Christ, even those sections that are roundly repudiated in our era.

Married couples who chose to be sterilized to prohibit conception may need assistance in concluding that what they have done is immoral. Why? Because the "modern climate" of much of society is not conducive to fostering an understanding of the nature and beauty of the human body, much less the marital privilege. True, the Natural Law ensures that one may come to the realization—even without the gift of faith—that the deliberate frustration of one of the "ends" of intercourse, namely procreation, is gravely evil; however, given the falsities in our world that counter the Truth at every turn, one need not be surprised that other voices attempt—in the end, unsuccessfully—day and night to submerge the Truth.

Kindness, clarity and a desire "to obey God rather than man" will do much for spiritual directors and confessors as they strive to adore the Living Lord and save souls, including their own.

One must be attentive when encouraging the use of N.F.P., especially to those couples that intentionally chose sterilization as a preventative against pregnancy, that N.F.P. does not come across as being "odious" or "burdensome." N.F.P. is to be a joyful exercise in heeding God's commands and sharing love with one's spouse. It is not to be seen as a continual punishment for one's sin that already has been confessed and forgiven in the Sacrament of Penance. As it always should be, N.F.P. is the vehicle by which one expresses his love for the Lord and for his spouse while simultaneously upholding God's immutable Law. And here it is to be recalled that postponing pregnancy for a significant reason and, therefore, having recourse to the infertile days of the cycle is to be the "exception." As one familiar with the contemporary scene quipped, "the option is to be for children." God expects His married sons and daughters to be generous in bringing forth new life, in such wise preparing souls for the Everlasting Kingdom.

Since the massive prevalence of intentional sterilization, not to mention other contraceptives, has never been witnessed on the grand scale that we experience in our time, we do not yet know what, if any, guilt and sorrow for the sin of direct sterilization will be manifested by the transgressors as they age and draw nearer to their Particular Judgment. Perhaps in the twenty-first century, a resurgence in comprehension of the sin of deliberate sterilization will surface specifically in the West, thereby meaning that more than ever, both men and women will seek forgiveness for their error from Emmanuel—"God-with-us." Let us pray!

Meanwhile, those charged with the care of souls should now preach and teach—both in public and private settings—the reasonableness of the Church's teaching on the procreative dimension of the marital embrace, the splendor of God's forgiveness to all when they fall and the real chance of being made whole in the Lord once again.

Conclusion

Undoubtedly, a sterilized married couple who chose the aforementioned procedure with a contraceptive purpose and who are now contrite will be forgiven by God of their sin. On what condition? That they implore His unceasing compassion, cast aside that contraceptive intent and display their love for each other in marital intercourse as God planned. To that end, the couple should, if possible, seek a reversal of the sterilization. If that cannot be accomplished, then the couple could consign the marital privilege to the normally infertile time. Then, they will illustrate their fervent desire to obey God and readily heed His life-bestowing—and life-changing—Law.

This article was published on January 25, 2004 on Catholic Online and reprinted by permission of the author Catholic Online. Copyright 2009 (*www.catholic.org*).

Contact: Mary's Field

Monsignor Charles M. Mangan

Humanæ Vitæ and Human Happiness[1]

Dr. Robert Fastiggi

As a secular discipline, anthropology investigates human origins and culture from the viewpoint of physical and social science. Theological or Christian anthropology, however, studies the human person from the vantage points of revelation, reason and salvation history.

The Whole of Man and Mission

The foundations of Christian anthropology are presented in the early chapters of Genesis, where we are told God created man in his image after his likeness (Gn 1:26); as male and female (Gn 1:27); and as material and spiritual (or body and soul). These images are expressed through the figure of God breathing "the breath of life" into the nostrils of the man formed from the clay of the ground (Gn 2:7). In Christian anthropology, the constitution of the human person as created in the divine image and likeness, as body and soul, and as male and female, is an expression of God's wisdom and love.

This Christian vision of the human person informs the anthropology of Pope Paul VI's great encyclical letter, *Humanæ Vitæ*. The subject matter of the letter is human procreation, and the Holy Father makes it clear that this subject "involves more than the limited aspects specific to such disciplines as biology, psychology, demography and or sociology. It is the whole man and the whole mission to which he is called that must be considered: both its natural, earthly aspects and its supernatural, eternal aspects" (no. 7).

The encyclical reaffirms the teaching—rooted in Scripture, Sacred Tradition and human reason—that human procreation finds its proper expression within the context of married love. All of this, the Holy Father explains, is part of the "loving design" of God who "is love" (no. 8; cf. 1 Jn 4:8). As he eloquently writes:

> Marriage, then, is far from being the effect of chance or the result of the blind evolution of natural forces. It is in reality the wise and provident institution of God the Creator, whose purpose was to effect in man His loving design. As a consequence, husband and wife, through the mutual gift of themselves, which is specific and exclusive to them alone, develop that union of two persons in which they perfect one another, cooperating with God in the generation and rearing of new lives. The marriage of those who have been baptized is, in addition, invested with the dignity of a sacramental sign of grace, for it represents the union of Christ and His Church. (No. 8)

The Anthropology of Married Love

Recognizing that married love and procreation flow from God's loving design, Paul VI provides a rich overview of "the characteristic features and exigencies" of married love (no. 9). These four features are expressions of God's plan for human life and happiness.

The first characteristic of married love is that it is **FULLY HUMAN**. It is not merely an instinct or "an emotional drive." Rather, it involves "an act of the free will," something that expresses the human dignity of husband and wife as free and rational beings. By their free gift of themselves to each other, they establish that trust, which "is meant to survive the joys and sorrows of daily life." This trust enables them "to grow, so that husband and wife become in a way one heart and one soul, and together attain their human fulfillment" (no. 9).

Married love is also **TOTAL**. It is a "very special form of friendship in which husband and wife generously share everything, allowing no unreasonable exceptions and not thinking solely of their own convenience" (no. 9). The husband and wife are caught up in a total love that moves beyond a consideration of what they each receive. This love cherishes the other for his or her own sake, and it involves a mutual giving by which each spouse becomes a "gift" to the other.

Married love is likewise "**FAITHFUL AND EXCLUSIVE** of all other, and this until death" (no. 9). Since they freely vowed themselves to each other, fidelity and exclusivity are necessary expressions of authentic marital love. This mutual fidelity is, at times, difficult, but it is always "honorable and meritorious," and a "source of profound and enduring happiness" (no. 9).

Married love, finally, is **FRUITFUL**. Citing Vatican Council II's *Gaudium et Spes*, Paul VI reaffirms that "marriage and conjugal love are by their nature ordered towards the procreation and education of children," and "children are really the supreme gift of marriage and contribute in the highest degree to their parents' welfare" (no. 9; cf. *Gaudium et Spes*, no. 50).

The Anthropology of the Conjugal Act

Since God has designed married love to be fully human, total, faithful and fruitful, clearly human procreation must likewise respect "the objective moral order established by God" (no. 10). Thus, the spouses must do what corresponds to the divine will as it relates to the conjugal act.

Experience shows that not every conjugal act results in new life, for "God has wisely ordered the laws of nature and the incidence of fertility in such a way that successive births are already spaced through the inherent operation of these laws" (no. 11). Nevertheless, both natural law and the constant doctrine of the Church teach that "each and every marital act must of necessity remain ordered per se to the procreation of human life" (no. 11).

This intrinsic ordering of the conjugal act to procreation is "a result of laws written into the actual nature of man and woman" (no. 12). From these laws, it can be seen that the conjugal act embraces the two essential meanings or purposes (*utraque … ratio*): the unitive and the procreative. Only when these two essential meanings are preserved does the marital act fully retain "its true mutual love and its ordination to the supreme responsibility of parenthood" (no. 12).

Spouses must recognize that they are ministers "of the design established by the Creator" (no. 13). They do not have unlimited control of their bodies in general, and, in a particular way, they cannot claim exclusive dominion over their "sexual faculties, for these are concerned by their very nature with the generation of life, of which God is the source" (no. 13). Therefore, married couples must avoid abortion and sterilization, as these are contrary to the moral order of God. Moreover, they must avoid "any action which either before, at the moment of, or after sexual intercourse is specifically intended to prevent procreation—whether as an end or a means" (no. 14).

Paul VI understood there might be "just reasons" *(iusta causæ)* for couples to avoid procreation at certain times of their marriage (cf. no. 16). In such cases, however, they should "take advantage of the natural cycles immanent in the reproductive system and engage in marital intercourse only during those times that are infertile" (no. 16). In this way, they do not "obstruct the natural development of the generative process" (no. 16). Rather, they abstain from sexual intercourse during the fertile times and engage in the conjugal act during infertile times "to express their mutual love and safeguard their fidelity towards each other" (no. 16).

God's Plan for Human Happiness

It is well known that many Catholics have dissented from the teaching of *Humanæ Vitæ* over the last forty years. I believe one of the reasons for this resistance is a failure to understand the theological anthropology that supports the moral teaching of the encyclical. The Church is looking after the good of the spouses in her constant teaching of the intrinsic connection between the unitive and procreative ends of the marital act. As Paul VI notes, the Church did not make the laws that govern human procreation, and it could "never be right for her to declare lawful what is in fact unlawful" since what is unlawful "is always opposed to the true good of man" (no. 18).

The wisdom of *Humanæ Vitæ* is being rediscovered now by a new generation of Catholics. Tired of the bitter fruits of the sexual revolution, many young people are looking for a deeper, more human understanding of marriage and procreation. They also are searching for God's plan for human happiness reflected in a proper Christian anthropology. Paul VI eloquently expressed a true anthropology of married love in *Humanæ Vitæ*, and his successors to the Chair of St. Peter have reaffirmed and, in some respects, deepened his insights.

Dr. Robert Fastiggi is professor of systematic theology at Sacred Heart Major Seminary, Detroit, Michigan.

The Social Footprints of Contraception

Dr. Janet E. Smith

The Church's teaching on sexuality that lies behind its teaching that contraception is intrinsically immoral is dazzlingly beautiful. Many people whose understanding has been clouded by the corruption of our culture have difficulty understanding it.

The Church understands sexuality to be an inestimable gift from God. This gift allows a man and a woman—in a personal, profound, spiritual and physical way—to express their deep desire to unite with another and to live out the essential human need to love and be loved.

Love Overflows into Life

God himself is a lover and is Love Itself. Love is a union, and the sexual union of spouses allows them to more fully actualize the love between them that unites them. Furthermore, it is natural for love to overflow. In fact, all of creation is the result of the natural overflowing of God's love. The Trinity has no need of "others." It is three perfect persons who love each other perfectly, but they "naturally" explode with love and that love "naturally" leads to new life and new possibilities for love. Thus the whole universe is fueled by love.

Spouses are meant to image the love of God; they are meant to be committed unconditional lovers whose love overflows into new life. (That new life results is not always possible because of infertility, but the spousal relationship is the kind of relationship that is designed to foster love and life.) John Paul II spoke of spouses as being "co-creators" with God who assist God in bringing forth new human souls.

Spouses because they truly appreciate the gift of fertility understand that when they are not prepared to accept the gift of a child, they should abstain from sex when a pregnancy is possible; that is, they use natural family planning (NFP). NFP is a way of respecting the great gift of fertility.

Many studies and testimonies affirm the benefits of using NFP. The U.S. Bishops issued a fine statement about the meaning of sexuality and the value of NFP in their 2006 document, *Married Love and the Gift of Life*.

Consequences of Contraception

Our culture is accustomed to thinking of sex as just a form of recreation that has no inherently profound meaning. People rarely encounter the Church's teaching in its full glory and, when they do, they don't easily understand it. One method of helping people be open to the Church's teaching is to alert them to the bad consequences that contraception has for individuals, for the culture and even the environment.

The case is quite easily made that contraception has greatly contributed to the increased incidence of abortion, unwed pregnancy, divorce, and the poverty and trauma that comes with single motherhood. After all, contraception tremendously facilitates sex between partners who have no intention of having a baby. All contraceptives have a failure rate and people fail to use contraceptives even when available. Presently, about one out of four babies conceived in the United States is aborted, nearly thirty-seven percent of babies are born to a single mother, approximately one out of two marriages contracted today is likely to end in divorce, and over eighty percent of children who experience long term poverty come from broken or unmarried families.

Who can calculate the harm done to babies born out of wedlock and to children impacted by divorce? The evidence is overwhelming that children born to parents who are married to each other and who stay married to each other have numerous advantages over children born out of wedlock or impacted by divorce. Who can calculate the harm done to individuals who are in and out of sexual relationships? The biggest selling point of natural family planning should not be that it is as effective as any form of contraception (it is), or that it has no bad health side effects (it doesn't). Rather, we should proclaim from the rooftops that NFP is so good for a marriage that those who use NFP almost never divorce. Almost everyone who uses NFP has used contraception at some point and finds that the use of NFP improves both sexual relations and marriage.

The Chemistry of Attraction

To be added to the bad consequences of contraception are the effect of hormonal contraceptives on a woman's health and on male/female relationships. The health risks of the chemical contraceptives have been known for a very long time and range from weight gain to increased incidence of breast cancer, and even death from blood clots. More and more studies are showing the bad effect that contraceptives have on relationships. In my talk "Hormones 'R Us" (mycatholicfaith.org), I report on some of the little known effects of chemical contraceptives.

We often speak of "chemistry" as being powerful between a male and a female who are strongly attracted to each other. The talk of "chemistry" is not an analogy; the attraction is truly based on chemical differences between males and females. Males and females exchange hormones, called pheromones, and these are the cause of the chemical attraction between them. These hormones are received through the olfactory nerves. Many women testify that one of the things that most attract them to a man is the way he "smells." Some studies show that males and females who are more biologically compatible—that is, those who are more likely to be able to reproduce with each other—are more attracted to each other.

But hormones also affect our judgment and responses in other ways. What is important here is that women who are on chemical contraceptives have squashed the influence of their normal fertile hormones. Chemical contraceptives work by putting a woman in a state of pseudo-pregnancy. When pregnant, women don't ovulate. Researchers who invented the chemical contraceptives realized that they could "deceive" a woman's body into "thinking" that it is pregnancy by giving it synthetic forms of the hormones that are present when a woman is pregnant. One problem with this scenario is that women respond to men differently when they are pregnant—or on a chemical contraceptive—and when they are not. And men respond to them differently.

Chemically Induced Choices

Consider the T-shirt study report in the marvelous book *The Decline of Males* by Lionel Tiger. This study involved two groups of females, one that was on contraceptives and one that was not. It also involved a group of males who had been rated for their "evolutionary" desirability. The women, who never met the men, smelled the T-shirts and on that basis identified which men they thought would make desirable mates. The non-contracepting females chose the evolutionarily desirable males, the contracepting females chose the losers!

The website nbc10.com has a fascinating video called "The Divorce Pill" that features research showing that women on the pill often choose to marry men who are not suitable spouses for them. This is of special concern since most women of child-bearing age in the United States use chemical contraceptives, especially during their years preceding marriage—precisely when they are choosing a mate. One amazing effect of chemical contraceptives is that they reduce the amount of testosterone that a female produces—and for females as well as males, testosterone is the source of sexual desire. Thus, women on chemical contraceptives find their sexual desire is reduced; when they go off the chemical contraceptives, it may never return to the level it had before that they began using chemical contraceptives.

So we have an interesting phenomenon: women are choosing their mates not under the influence of their own more reliable fertile hormones but on alien synthetic hormones. When they go off chemical contraceptives, they may find they have a higher sex drive, but they are not much interested in the men they are with!

NFP: Eco-friendly

Contraceptives not only step all over relationships, they also leave a considerable carbon footprint. Consider that NFP has a zero carbon footprint: it burns nary a fossil fuel, whereas the amount of energy needed to produce, transport, distribute and dispose of contraceptives is astronomically high. Indeed, studies have suggested that divorce has a huge carbon footprint, since divorces generally double the need for housing, etc. Moreover, the estrogens in contraceptives have a lethal effect on some elements of the environment. For instance, they have been shown to destroy the fertility of some groups of fish.

Not only is the Church's teaching on contraception based on an understanding of sexuality that is sublime, it is also eco-friendly: friendly to a woman's internal eco-system, friendly to the "ecology" of the culture and of relationships, and friendly to the environment.

Dr. Janet E. Smith is the Fr. Michael J. McGivney Chair of Life Ethics at Sacred Heart.

A Sexual Revolution

One woman's journey from pro-choice atheist to pro-life Catholic

Jennifer Fulwiler

Back in my pro-choice days, I read that in certain ancient societies it was common for parents to abandon unwanted newborns, leaving them to die of exposure. I found these stories to be as perplexing as they were horrifying. How could this happen? I could never understand how entire cultures could buy into something so obviously terrible, how something that modern society understands to be an unthinkable evil could be widely accepted among large groups of people.

Because of my deep distress at hearing of such crimes against humanity, I found it irritating when pro-lifers would refer to abortion as "killing babies." Obviously, nobody was in favor of killing babies, and to imply that those of us who were pro-choice would advocate as much was an insult to the babies throughout history who actually were killed by their "insane" societies. We were not in favor of killing anything. We simply felt that a woman had a right to stop the growth process of a fetus if she faced a crisis pregnancy. It was unfortunate, but that was the sacrifice that had to be made to prevent women from becoming victims of unwanted pregnancies.

At that time I was an atheist and had little exposure to religious social circles. As I began to search for God and open my mind to Christianity, however, I could not help but be exposed to pro-life thought more often, and I was put on the defensive about my views. One night I was discussing the topic with my husband, who was re-examining his own pro-choice stance. He made a passing remark that startled me into reconsidering this issue: "It just occurred to me that being pro-life is being pro-other-people's-life," he quipped. "Everyone is pro-their-own-life."

Growing Discomfort

His remark made me realize that my pro-choice viewpoints had put me in the position of deciding whose lives were worth living, and even who was human. Along with doctors, the government and other abortion advocates, I decided where to draw this crucial line. When I would come across Catholic Web sites or books that asserted "Life begins at conception," I would scoff, as was my habit, yet I found myself increasingly uncomfortable with my defense. I realized that my criteria for determining when human life begins were distressingly vague. I was putting the burden of proof on the fetuses to demonstrate to me that they were human, and I was a tough judge. I found myself looking the other way when I heard about things like the 3-D ultrasounds that showed fetuses touching their faces, smiling and opening their eyes at ages at which I still considered abortion acceptable. As modern technology revealed more and more evidence that fetuses were humans too, I would simply move the bar for what I considered human.

At some point I started to feel I was more determined to remain pro-choice than to analyze honestly who was and was not human. I started to see this phenomenon in others in the pro-choice community as well. As I researched issues like partial-birth abortion, I frequently became stunned to the point of feeling physically ill upon witnessing the level of evil that normal people can support. I could hardly believe my eyes when I read of reasonable, educated professionals calmly justifying infanticide by calling the victims fetuses instead of babies. It was then that I took a mental step back from the entire pro-choice movement. If this is what it meant to be pro-choice, I was not pro-choice.

Yet I still could not quite label myself pro-life.

I recognized that I too had probably told myself lies in order to maintain my support for abortion. Yet there was some tremendous pressure that kept me from objectively looking at the issue. Something deep within me screamed that not to allow women to have abortions, at least in the first trimester, would be unfair in the direst sense of the word. Even as I became religious, I mentally pushed aside thoughts that all humans might have God-given eternal souls worthy of dignity and respect. It became too tricky to figure out when we receive those souls, the most obvious answer being "at conception," as opposed to some arbitrary point during gestation. It was not until I re-evaluated the societal views of sex that had permeated the consciousness of my peer group that I was able to release that internal pressure I felt and take an unflinching look at abortion.

Sex and Creating Life

Growing up in secular middle-class America, I understood sex as something disconnected from the idea of creating life. During my entire childhood I did not know anyone who had a baby sibling; and to the extent that neighborhood parents ever talked about pregnancy, it was to say they were glad they were "done." In high school sex education class, we learned not that sex creates babies, but that unprotected sex creates babies. Even recently, before our marriage was blessed in the Catholic Church, my husband and I took a course about building good marriages. It was a video series by a nondenominational Christian group, and the segment called "Good Sex" did not mention children once. In all the talk about bonding and back rubs and intimacy and staying in shape, the closest the videos came to connecting sex to the creation of life was a brief note that couples should discuss the topic of contraception.

All my life, the message I had heard loud and clear was that sex was for pleasure and bonding, that its potential for creating life was purely tangential, almost to the point of being forgotten. This mind-set became the foundation of my views on abortion. Because I saw sex as being by default closed to the possibility of life, I thought of unplanned pregnancies as akin to being struck by lightning while walking down the street—something totally unpredictable and undeserved that happened to people living normal lives.

My pro-choice views (and I imagine those of many others) were motivated by loving concern: I just did not want women to have to suffer, to have to devalue themselves by dealing with unwanted pregnancies. Since it was an inherent part of my worldview that everyone except people with "hang-ups" eventually has sex, and that sex is, under normal circumstances, only about the relationship between the two people involved, I was lured into one of the oldest, biggest, most tempting lies in human history: the enemy is not human. Babies had become the enemy because of their tendency to pop up and ruin everything; and just as societies are tempted to dehumanize their fellow human beings on the other side of the line in wartime, so had I, and we as a society, dehumanized what we saw as the enemy of sex.

As I was reading up on the Catholic Church's understanding of sex, marriage and contraception, everything changed. I had always assumed that Catholic teachings against birth control were outdated notions, even a thinly disguised attempt to oppress the faithful. What I found, however, was that these teachings expressed a fundamentally different understanding of sex. And once I discovered this, I never saw the world the same way again.

Burdens or Blessings?

The way I had always seen it, the generally accepted view was that babies were burdens, except for a few times in life when everything might be perfect enough for a couple to see new life as a good thing. The Catholic view, I discovered, is that babies are blessings and that while it is fine to attempt to avoid pregnancy for serious reasons, if we go so far as to adopt a "contraceptive mentality"—feeling entitled to the pleasure of sex while loathing (and perhaps trying to forget all about) its life-giving properties—we not only fail to respect this most sacred of acts, but we begin to see new life as the enemy.

I came to see that our culture's widespread use and acceptance of contraception meant that the "contraceptive mentality" toward sex was now the default attitude. As a society, we had come to take it for granted that we are entitled to the pleasurable and bonding aspects of sex even when we are opposed to the new life it might produce. The option of abstaining from the act that creates babies if we see children as a burden had been removed from our cultural lexicon. Even if it would be a huge crisis to become pregnant, we had a right to have sex anyway. If this were true—if it were morally acceptable for people to have sex even when they believed that a new baby could ruin their lives—then abortion, as I saw things, had to be O.K.

Ideally I would have taken an objective look at when human life begins and based my views on that alone, but the lie was just too tempting. I did not want to hear too much about heartbeats or souls or brain activity. Terminating pregnancies simply had to be acceptable, because carrying a baby to term and becoming a parent is a huge deal, and society had made it very clear that sex was not a huge deal. As long as I accepted the premise that engaging in sex with a contraceptive mentality was morally acceptable, I could not bring myself to consider that abortion might not be acceptable. It seemed inhumane to make women deal with life-altering consequences for an act that was not supposed to have life-altering consequences.

Given my background, the Catholic idea that we are always to treat the sexual act with awe and respect, so much so that we should simply abstain if we are opposed to its life-giving potential, was a revolutionary message. Being able to consider honestly when life begins, to open my heart and mind to the wonder and dignity of even the tiniest of my fellow human beings, was not fully possible for me until I understood the nature of the act that creates these little lives in the first place.

All of these thoughts had been percolating in my brain for a while, and I found myself increasingly in agreement with pro-life positions. Then one night I became officially, unapologetically pro-life. I was reading yet another account of the Greek societies in which newborn babies were abandoned to die, wondering how normal people could do something like that, and I felt a chill rush through me as I thought: I know how they did it.

I realized in that moment that perfectly good, well-meaning people—people like me—can support gravely evil things because of the power of lies. From my own experience, I knew how the Greeks, the Romans and people in every other society could put themselves into a mental state where they could leave a newborn child to die. The very real pressures of life—"we can't afford another baby," "we can't have any more girls," "he wouldn't have had a good life"—left them susceptible to the temptation to dehumanize other human beings. Though the circumstances were different, the same process had happened with me, with the pro-choice movement and with anyone else who has ever been tempted to dehumanize inconvenient people.

I suspect that as those Greek parents handed over their infants for someone to take away, they remarked on how very unlike their other children these little creatures were: they couldn't talk, they couldn't sit up, and surely those little yawns and smiles were just involuntary reactions. I bet they referred to these babies with different words than they used to refer to the children they kept. Maybe they called them something like "fetuses."

Jennifer Fulwiler is a Web developer who lives in Austin, Tex., with her husband and three children. She converted to Catholicism from atheism in 2007 and writes about her conversion at *http://www. conversiondiary.com/*.

Marital and Family Commitment: A Personalist View

Monsignor Cormac Burke

The past several decades have seen an ongoing debate within the Church about the ends of marriage. A traditional understanding presented these ends in a clear hierarchy or order of importance: a "primary" end (procreation) and two "secondary" ends (mutual help and the remedy for concupiscence). Early on in the century a feeling began to emerge that this understanding was too exclusively centered on the procreative function of the marital relationship, while it neglected "personalist" aspects or values also characterizing this relationship, and of which modern times have become more aware: love between man and woman as the main motive for marrying, the promise of personal happiness or fulfillment that marriage seems to offer, the human values felt to underlie physical sexuality.

The Second Vatican Council incorporated these personalist values into its presentation of marriage. And, as is well known, married personalism is notable in the teaching on marriage of John Paul II. Sexuality and marriage, interpreted in a personalist light, were in fact the theme of a lengthy papal catechesis covering the first years of the present pontificate; and the same presentation has frequently recurred since. Thus it now seems beyond question that a personalist view of marriage has become firmly established in magisterial teaching.

The effect of personalist ideas is specially noticeable in the *Code of Canon Law* promulgated in 1983. In the section on marriage, the very first canon, on the nature and purpose of matrimony, says: "The matrimonial covenant, by which a man and a woman establish between themselves a partnership of the whole of life, is by its nature ordered toward the good of the spouses ["bonum coniugum"] and the procreation and education of offspring" (c. 1055).

Here, in what Pope John Paul II described as the "last document of the Second Vatican Council,"[1] we are offered a brief formula of the greatest importance, which marks a development and crystallization of the married personalism of Vatican II. Particularly to be noted is the progress from the rather vague conciliar statement about matrimony being endowed with "various" or "other" ends, besides procreation,[2] to the specific enunciation of *two* ends to marriage, the good of the spouses and the procreation/education of children.

As we can see, there is no mention here of primary or secondary ends; the presentation rather suggests two ends on equal footing. In any case, there seems to me little point in arguing which comes first because, as I see it, it is the interrelation and inseparability—and not any hierarchy—between the ends of marriage which matters most today and most needs emphasizing.[3]

An important point should be clarified here. Some writers refer to the good of the spouses as the "personalist" end of marriage, and to procreation as its "institutional" end. Such a contrast however is not accurate. *Both* ends—procreative and personalist—*are institutional* (just as both properly understood, are personalist).[4] Marriage, in other words, has two institutional ends, a point that it is easy enough to demonstrate.

The institutional ends of marriage are evidently those established in its very institution, i.e., those with which marriage was endowed by its "Institutor" or Creator—by God himself. Here it is important to note that Scripture offers two distinct accounts of the creation of man—male and female—and of the institution of marriage. One account expresses a clearly procreative finality, while the other can fairly be described as personalist. The first, in the opening chapter of Genesis, reads: "God created man in his own image, in the image of God he created him; male and female he created them. And God blessed them, and God said to them, 'Be fruitful and multiply'" (Gn 1:27–28). The second account, in the next chapter, says: "The Lord God said, 'It is not good that the man should be alone; I will make him a helper fit for him' …" (so God created woman … and, the narration continues) "therefore a man leaves his father and his mother and cleaves to his wife, and they become one flesh" (Gn 2:18–24).

In the first text, man's relative *perfection* is underlined. He is made in the image of God, and is the highest visible expression of the goodness of creation. The distinction of sexes ("male and female he created him") appears as a key to man's mission to carry on the work of creation by procreation. The idea of the goodness of this assigned mission characterizes the passage.

In the second version, it is rather man's *incompleteness* which is stressed. Man (male or female) is incomplete, if he remains on his or her own; and this is not a good thing: "non est bonum." The normal plan of God is that he will find the goodness he lacks in union with a member of the other sex; and this union should lead to the good of each and of both: to the "bonum coniugum."

If it is not good for man or woman to be without a conjugal partner, what is the good which God had in mind in instituting the plan of sexual partnership and cooperation within the marriage? What sort of help or helpmate did he intend each spouse to be for the other? Was he concerned simply about man's temporal good, thinking just of a solace for this life alone? It seems reasonable to presume that God's perspective went farther than that. After all nothing in God's plan is created for an exclusively this-worldly purpose; everything is designed for his glory and, where rational creatures are involved, for their eternal destiny.[5]

In the plan of the divine institution of matrimony, we can say that the true "good of the spouses" can be said to consist in their maturing as persons throughout their married lives so that they can attain the end for which they were created. Within the Christian dispensation, the authentic good of the spouses cannot but consist in their human and supernatural growth in Christ. Pope Pius XI, in his Encyclical *Casti Connubii*, insisted that the true purpose of marital love is "that man and wife help each other day by day in forming and perfecting themselves in the interior life, so that through their partnership in life they may advance ever more and more in virtue, and above all that they may grow in true love towards God and their neighbor."[6] Vatican II teaches that "as spouses fulfill their conjugal and family obligations … they increasingly advance *towards their own perfection, as well as towards their mutual sanctification*."[7] The supernatural aspect of this is particularly drawn out in the Vatican II Constitution on the Church: "Christian spouses help one another to attain holiness in their married life and in the accepting and rearing of their children."[8] Similarly another conciliar decree insists: "Christian spouses are for each other … cooperators of grace and witness of the faith."[9]

The Demands of Married Personalism

Some commentators reduce the "bonum coniugum" to what they call the "integration" of the spouses on the psychic, affective, physical or sexual levels. This seems inadequate from a Christian standpoint, not only because it fails to look at the spouses' "good" supernaturally, but also because it tends to resolve it into a question of natural "compatibility." One can then be easily led into holding that apparent incompatibility is an enemy of the good of the spouses, whereas pastoral experience shows that many highly "integrated" marriages are of couples whose characters are extremely diverse, and who could well have ended up "incompatible" unless they had resolved (in an evidently maturing effort) not to do so.

Similarly, to make the "good of the spouses" consist in the achieving of a comfortable or untroubled life is scarcely in harmony with a Christian understanding of the real good of the human person. In fact, any idea of the "bonum coniugum" which identifies it with some form of easy or gratifying reciprocal relationship between them is fundamentally flawed. Only passing and superficial personal contacts can be smooth and without any strains. Difficulties always make their appearance in every close interpersonal relation that is extended over a period of time. Since marriage involves man and woman in a unique relationship and commitment to be maintained over the whole of their lifetime, it is bound to be marked by difficulties between them, sometimes of a serious nature. Many happy married unions are between two persons of quite different characters who have clearly had to struggle hard to get on. One can rightly say that these marriages are the most "successful," for they have matured the spouses most.

In fact it does not seem possible to understand the "good of the spouses" in a Christian way, unless it is seen as resulting from the *commitment* aspect of the married covenant. Married commitment is by nature something demanding. The words by which the spouses express their mutual acceptance of one another, through "irrevocable personal consent,"[10] bring this out. Each pledges to accept the other "for better or for worse, for richer or for poorer, in sickness and in health … all the days of my life."[11]

It is through dedication, effort and sacrifice, especially when made for the sake of others, that people grow and mature most; that way each one comes out of himself or herself and rises above self. Loyalty to the commitment of married life—to be mutually faithful, to persevere in this fidelity until death, and to have and rear children—contributes more than anything else to the true good of the spouses, so powerfully realized in facing up to this freely accepted commitment and duty. John Paul II described this duty as calling for "a conscious effort on the part of the spouses to overcome, even at the cost of sacrifices and renunciations, the obstacles that hinder the fulfillment of their marriage."[12]

The Conjugal Instinct

St. Augustine, in the 5th century, was the first great defender of the dignity and goodness of marriage. According to his masterly analysis, marriage is good because of three essential values or properties that characterize it: the exclusiveness of the conjugal relationship, its procreative orientation, and the permanence of the marital bond. Each of these qualities he calls a *bonum*, a value or a "good thing." Elsewhere I have tried to draw attention to the modern tendency that sees the Augustinian "bona" as burdensome obligations which the married state imposes, and not principally as *values* or *benefits* which it confers.[13] This applies particularly to the "bonum" or value of indissolubility, and to that of offspring. It is important that we get back to St. Augustine's sense that these properties are natural values—"bona" or *good things*—that are in harmony with human nature, contributing powerfully to its fulfillment.

The good of fidelity or exclusiveness is clear: "You are *unique* to me." It is the first truly personalized affirmation of conjugal love; and echoes the words God addresses to each one of us in Isaiah: "Meus es tu"—"You are mine."[14]

The good of indissolubility should also be clear: the good of a stable home or haven: of knowing that this "belongingness"—shared with another—is for keeps. It is clearly a good thing for a person to know that, in marrying, he or she is exchanging with someone else the promise of mutual and faithful love to last for the whole of life. A person who marries out of love generally expects, wants and *intends* a permanent union. As Pope Pius XI wrote: "In this firmness of the marriage bond, husband and wife find a positive token of that lasting quality which the generous surrender of their persons and the intimate communion of their souls so naturally and powerfully call for, since true love knows no end."[15]

People want that, are made for that, feel that to chose such a relationship—and so to bind oneself—is the best exercise of human freedom. Chesterton used to say that the freedom he chiefly cared for was the "freedom to be bound." In Tolstoy's *Anna Karenina*, Levin, one of the protagonists, is about to get married. His friends pull his leg at the fact that he is losing his freedom. Not exactly rejecting the charge, he answers: "But the point is that I am happy to lose my freedom in this way."

Moreover people realize that it will require sacrifice to be faithful to a life-long love, and feel that the sacrifices are worth it. Pope John Paul II writes: "It is natural for the human heart to accept demands, even difficult ones, in the name of love for an ideal, and above all in the name of love for a person."[16] Something is going strangely wrong with the head or heart that rejects the permanence of the marriage relationship.

The Second Vatican Council teaches that it is "for the good of the spouses, of the children, and of society" that the marriage bond has been made unbreakable.[17] Indissolubility therefore positively favors the "bonum coniugum." The point is surely that all the effort and sacrifice involved in fidelity to the unbreakable character of the bond—in good times and in bad—serve to develop and perfect the personalities of the spouses.

Of course it is not easy for two people to live together for life, in a faithful and fruitful union. It is "easier" for each to live apart, or to unite casually or for a short time, or to avoid having children. It is easier, but not happier; nor does it contribute to their growth as persons. "Non est bonum homini esse solus," says the Book of Genesis: it is not good for a man or woman to live alone, or in temporary successive associations that tend to leave him or her more and more trapped in selfish isolation. Married commitment is not an easy endeavor; but, apart from normally being a happy one, it is one that *matures*. There is no true married personalism which ignores or fails to stress the goodness—for the spouses, and not just for the children—of the conjugal commitment.

Pope John Paul II in the Apostolic Exhortation on the Family—*Familiaris Consortio*—spoke of indissolubility in terms of something *joyful* that Christians should announce to the world: "It is necessary," he says "to reconfirm the *good* news of the definitive nature of conjugal love."[18] If this statement sounds so surprising today, surely we should read there a sign of how contemporary society has lost its understanding of the divine plan for man's authentic good. One of the special missions facing Christians today, in the work of re-evangelizing the modern world, is to spread the news that married love is too sacred and too important—also for human happiness—to be broken.

Undeniably there are many marital situations where, from a purely human point of view, it might seem justified to conclude that the good of the spouses has not been or cannot be achieved: the cases, for instance, where one of the spouses, reneging on his or her conjugal commitment, walks out on the other. Does it make any sense to talk of the "bonum coniugum" as applying to such situations?

As regards the reneging spouse, certainly the marriage would scarcely seem capable of working any longer toward his or her "good." Yet it can still work powerfully for the good of the other, if he or she remains true to the marriage bond. Moreover, if that fidelity is maintained, it may in God's providence act as a call to repentance, as a force of salvation, for the unfaithful spouse, perhaps in his or her very last moment on earth—when one's definitive "bonum" or *good* is about to be attained or lost for ever.

That the positive potential of such situations can be grasped only in the light of the Christian challenge of the Cross, does not in any way weaken the analysis. On the contrary, as the *Catechism* says, "Jesus has not weighed down the spouses with a burden that is impossible to bear, heavier than that of the Law of Moses. Having come to reestablish the initial order of creation upset by sin, he himself gives the strength and grace to live marriage in the new dimension of the Kingdom of God. Following Christ, denying themselves, taking upon themselves their own cross, the spouses can 'understand' the original sense of matrimony and live it with the help of Christ. This grace of Christian Matrimony is a fruit of the Cross of Christ, the source of all Christian life" (no. 1615).

The Personalism of the Human Procreative Power and Relationship

A deep ailment troubling the modern world is its failure to recognize the personalist character of conjugal procreativity. To speak disparagingly about "biologism," whenever stress is laid on the procreative aspect of marriage, betrays a fundamental lack of understanding of married personalism. Nothing can so uniquely express the marital relationship and the desire for marital union, as conjugal intercourse—*when it is open to its procreative potential*. True union between free persons always involves donation. It is the absolutely unique nature of what is mutually donated in the conjugal act—the gift of complementary procreativity—that makes marital intercourse so unitive. Hence derives the intrinsic *inseparability* of the unitive and the procreative aspects of the act.[19] The fundamentally anti-personalist nature of contraceptive intercourse appears here: inasmuch as it deliberately destroys that unique aspect of the conjugal act which renders it truly unitive, it marks a rejection of the marital sexuality of the other, a refusal therefore to accept him or her integrally as husband or wife.[20]

Vatican II teaches that "marriage and married love are by nature ordered to the procreation and education of children" (GS 50). The order referred to here is not merely "biological." It is not just an "institutional" order, referred to marriage as an institution. It is the very order of human love, of truly sexual and truly married love, which naturally tends to procreation.[21] If married love, in normal circumstances, does not want children, it is suffering from a disorder; it is de-natured and de-sexualized.

A marital relationship, in order to be humanly true and to tend to personal fulfillment, needs to retain a fundamental openness to offspring. A marriage which is so "closed on itself" that it does not want children is a marriage almost certain to fail, for if the spouses are not open to children—to the fruit of their sexual union—they are not really open to the richness of their love; they are not open to one another.

It is precisely this awareness of the deep personalist meaning of procreativity that renders conjugal intercourse so singularly capable of contributing to the "good" of each spouse, maturing and "realizing" each one and linking them together. Conjugality and procreativity are thus seen to have a natural complementarity. Conjugality means that man or woman is destined to become a *spouse*: to unite himself or herself to another, in an act that is unitive precisely because it is oriented to procreativity. And procreativity means that he or she is destined to become a *parent*: the union of the spouses tends of its nature to fruitfulness. Conjugality and procreativity taken together draw man out of his original solitude—which limits him as a person and is an enemy of his "self-realization," of his *bonum*.

Children strengthen the *goodness* of the bond of marriage, so that it does not give way under the strains that follow on the inevitable wane or disappearance of effortless romantic love. The bond of marriage—which God wants no man to break—is then constituted not just by the variables of personal love and sentiment between husband and wife, but more and more by their children, each child being one further strand giving strength to that bond.

In a homily in Washington, D.C., on one of his visits to the United States, Pope John Paul II reminded parents that "it is certainly less serious to deny their children certain comforts or material advantages than to deprive them of the presence of brothers and sisters, who could help them to grow in humanity and to realize the beauty of life at all its ages and in all its variety."[22] I would suggest to parents who too easily incline to family limitation, to read the Pope's reminder in the light of the Vatican II teaching that "children are the *supreme* gift of marriage and contribute to the *greatest* extent to the *good of the parents* themselves."[23] It is therefore not only their present children, but also themselves, that such parents may be depriving of a singular "good," of a unique experience of human life, the fruit of love.

It is true that the wholehearted acceptance of these "goods" takes a sustained effort; but it is also true that this effort has a deep maturing effect on the persons who face up to it, and becomes moreover an enduring source of happiness. I have made reference to one of my books on marriage, *Covenanted Happiness*. The title is meant to underline the fact that the pledge of a man and a woman to the bond or covenant of marriage, with the determination to live up to its demands, means to place oneself firmly within a life-long commitment which God wishes specially to bless with a happiness grounded in effort and generosity, that so powerfully leads on to the effortless and unlimited happiness of Heaven.

PORNOGRAPHY: WHAT'S THE PROBLEM?

MARK J. HOUCK

The startling growth of the pornography industry in the last 15 years represents a grave threat to the well-being of society. Many of the social ills and behavioral disorders plaguing our world today—teenage sexual promiscuity, crisis pregnancy, adultery, abortion, divorce, sexual abuse, sexual deviancy, rape, and incest—can be linked to the spread of pornography.[1]

The Numbers Illustrate the Scope of the Problem …

- In 2006, the world-wide pornography industry's estimated revenue was $97 *billion* (up from $57 billion in 2005).

- Porn industry revenues are larger than those of the top technology companies *combined*— Microsoft, Google, Amazon, eBay, Yahoo!, Apple, Netflix, and EarthLink.[2]

- The United States is responsible for $13. 3 billion of the industry's revenue (2006).

- U. S. sales and rental of adult videos brought in $3. 62 billion in 2006. The 957 million units sold represented the highest sales volume in history.

- There are 420 million pornographic web pages, of which 89% are U. S.-based.

- 40 million U. S. adults visit pornographic websites regularly.

- 90% of 8- to 16-year-olds have viewed porn online.

- Children aged 12–17 are the largest group of consumers of online pornography.[3]

- U. S. pornography sales via cell phones totaled $26 million in 2007, lagging behind Europe's $775 million in sales.[4]

It should be obvious from these statistics that many Christians struggle with pornography addiction. One estimate puts the number of churchgoing men who are porn users at 50%.[5] Another study found that one in six women is struggling with an addiction to porn.[6] Some priests have shared that one out of three confessions they hear today concerns this issue.

Pornography is a major problem for those in the pews because it is a major problem in the domestic church, the homes of Catholic families.[7]

From a teaching standpoint, the catechesis offered at Mass may only be as good as its reinforcement in the home. Yet the issue of pornography is seldom even given an appropriate level of attention, relative to its threat, in sermons and other instruction from the clergy.

The Dignity of the Human Person

God has revealed through Scripture that human beings are made in his image and likeness. Our human dignity and worth come from God, not from governments and not from our accomplishments or possessions. We are "like" God in that we have an immortal soul, we are called to be holy as God is holy, and we have the abilities to reason and to love.

As Catholics, we understand the beautiful reality that each unique human person is a unity of body and soul, and that our human dignity includes our sexuality.

Our sexuality is more than our gender. It is part of our person. It gives us the ability to connect and give ourselves in love to another person. Our human sexuality is an important means by which we can share in the love and creativity of God.

Only in marriage can a man and woman give their entire selves, body and soul, to their spouse. For this reason, the Church teaches that sexual intercourse finds its proper place within the Sacrament of Matrimony. This love alone—love that is free, total, faithful and fruitful—can fulfill us as human persons and satisfy the desires of our hearts.

Any action that undermines the unity of the body and soul, that treats sexuality as simply a physical activity or treats another person as an object to be used, demeans the dignity of the human person. Instead of being the expression of the self-giving love that unites husband and wife—and which in a mysterious way resembles the spiritual communion of love within the Trinity—"sex" becomes an act that isolates and dehumanizes both the user and the one used.

How Does Pornography Harm Individuals and Society?

Children, teens and young adults are being victimized by an industry that objectifies people by eliminating the human dimension of their lives. Everyone involved in the pornography industry—whether its production, distribution, sale or use—"cooperates and, to some degree, makes possible this debasement of others"[9] because sexuality "is reduced to a demeaning source of entertainment and even profit."[10]

How can we expect our young people to practice chastity when they are bombarded daily with messages that tell them to do otherwise? Young men are being taught to value women based on the airbrushed images they see in porn. This "illusion of a fantasy world" (CCC, n. 2354) violates the sexual latency of children and promotes teen/college-age promiscuity, resulting in out-of-wedlock/crisis pregnancies and the spread of STDs at epidemic levels.[11]

Within marriage, addiction to pornography can destroy intimacy. Eventually, the husband or wife who views pornography can lose the ability to relate on a personal and intimate level with the real person of his or her spouse. Being accustomed to "satisfaction on demand," he or she may no longer be able to participate in an authentic sexual relationship that involves communication and spiritual intimacy. Men or women who view pornography can become used to the "perfect" bodies they see in porn and begin to view their spouse as unattractive in comparison. A person who views porn will likely also develop an unhealthy view of sexuality, and a spouse may be unwilling to do the things demanded of them. Consequently, the spouse's refusal may sometimes result in rape or sexual abuse. How can spouses not feel rejected and betrayed when their marriage partner seeks fulfillment from the images of strangers rather than from the human being who loves them?

Pornography as Addiction

Pornography addiction is defined as "a psychological addiction to, or dependence upon, pornography, theoretically characterized by obsessive viewing, reading, and thinking about pornography and sexual themes to the detriment of other areas of one's life."[12] Although pornography addiction is not officially recognized by the *Diagnostic and Statistical Manual of Mental Disorders*, 4th Edition (DSM-IV), the statistical evidence, as well as the testimony of experts in the field of sexual addiction,[13] shows that pornography is the foremost addiction in the world today due to its pervasiveness and its growing level of acceptability in our culture. Some psychologists observe further that online pornography addiction "is stronger, and more addictive, than ordinary pornography addiction because of its wide availability, explicitness and the privacy that online viewing offers."[14]

However one chooses to define pornography addiction, it is evident that the sexual or relational behaviors of people today are causing major problems in their lives and in the Church. It is time for all of us to thoughtfully consider how best to address this problem.

Addressing Porn Addiction on a Natural Level

Pornography addiction is a multi-dimensional problem requiring a multi-faceted solution. Such addiction involves the mental, emotional, physical, relational and spiritual components of a human being.

Dr. Mark Laaser states that "many try to combat sexual addiction through only the spiritual realm by praying more, reading the Bible, or attending church. These activities are spiritual band-aids that won't adequately address the problem." In his book *Healing the Wounds of Sexual Addiction*, Dr. Laaser explains that sexual addiction is a result of trauma or wounds experienced over the course of one's life.[15] Emotional, physical or spiritual abuse during childhood, inflicted by family and the culture at large, can trigger an addiction in adulthood. Exposure to greater degrees of trauma increases the likelihood that one will develop addictions as an attempt at "self-medication" in response to the trauma. Sadly, the wounds that many suffer during childhood cut very deep. The shame and pain that result may produce a cycle of addiction requiring years of counseling/psychotherapy to overcome.[16]

However deep the wound(s) may be, there are practical measures that offer significant hope for those struggling with pornography. Here are five ways that those addicted to pornography can begin the recovery process:

- Decide to get well and resolve to stop viewing all forms of pornography—magazines, television, movies, Internet, cell phones, sexually-oriented business patronage or whatever is tempting one to act out sexually.

- Remove all sources of temptation that may prevent one from healing—magazines, television, movies, Internet, cell phone, relationships or whatever is preventing one from remaining sexually pure (Matthew 5:29–30).

- Be willing to make sacrifices in the pursuit of healing. This may involve changing current duties or habits related to employment, travel, hotel accommodations, Internet and television usage, drinking, eating, people with whom one socializes and the conversations in which one engages.

- Become familiar with the ritual or the process by which one falls into addictive behavior. This step is vital for both short- and long-term healing. Some examples of rituals are the following: overworking oneself/excessive fatigue; loneliness/opportunities for isolation; boredom with one's work/daily life; and, constantly helping/serving others without allowing one's own needs to be met.

- Find a support group or a network of "solid" people to help in one's recovery. It is imperative that men find a group of other men who relate to their struggle, who can challenge one another to grow in holiness and keep one another accountable for their actions on a daily/weekly basis. For women, finding other like-minded women for support will be a great source of comfort and can minimize feelings of isolation during the healing process.

Addressing Porn Addiction on a Supernatural Level

Thus far, we have addressed the healing of pornography addiction through natural means only. If grace truly builds on nature, as the Catholic Church teaches, then the five-step process outlined above is only the necessary primer for those seeking freedom from pornography addiction. Thanks be to God that we have Sacred Scripture, Sacred Tradition and the Magisterium as sure and certain guides on our journey of recovery from addiction.

To address a pornography addiction applying the tools given to us by our Catholic faith, I offer these next steps as a means of obtaining lasting freedom from habitual sins against purity:

- Go to confession and receive Holy Communion frequently. As the *Catechism of the Catholic Church* (CCC) states: "*Holy Communion separates us from sin* ... For this reason the Eucharist cannot unite us to Christ without at the same time cleansing us from past sins and preserving us from future sins ...*" (n. 1393). Likewise, reception of the Sacrament of Reconciliation must be a continual part of the recovery process (as often as is needed), so that the Eucharist may indeed preserve us from future mortal sins (cf. n. 1394).

- Develop a daily prayer life. This may include any of the following: frequent fasting, receiving spiritual direction, morning, evening and night prayer, praying the Divine Office, Adoration of the Blessed Sacrament, reading Sacred Scripture, and praying the Holy Rosary or other authentically Catholic devotions, meditations and readings.

- Seek education and formation in the human, cardinal and theological virtues.[17] Frequent examination of conscience will aid in the discovery of the roots of sin and allow one to begin to apply a corresponding virtue. To defeat pride, for example, practice humility; to defeat sensuality, practice temperance. Pride is the root sin of many people addicted to pornography. Philosopher Peter Kreeft advises that when striving to conquer lust, one should focus less on lust and more on pride: "Only when we are truly humble does God give us the grace to conquer lust."

- Practice patience and perseverance! It is imperative to understand that "self-mastery is a *long and exacting work*. One can never consider it acquired once and for all. It presupposes renewed effort at all stages of life. The effort required can be more intense in certain periods ..." (CCC, n. 2342). St. Augustine understood this growth process, and reminds us in his *Confessions* that often "the bridle put upon the throat must be held with moderate looseness and moderate firmness" (10, 31).

- Finally, replace the images and past behaviors that inevitably torment one during recovery with God's love. Use the near occasions of sin in daily life as grace-filled moments. In those moments of weakness, when one ordinarily might be tempted to mentally objectify and exploit someone,

STOP! Take advantage of that moment and choose to use it for a good end. Pray for that woman or man whom one may be inclined to objectify, in reparation for the damage that one may have caused that person. These images and thoughts do not have to be times when we fall. Rather, allow them to be portals into God's amazing transcendent grace, which can carry the repentant addict past sins and can draw him or her to a deeper level of intimacy with God.

Addressing Porn Addiction on a Pastoral Level

As shepherds of God's Church, bishops, priests and deacons must know their flock (Jn 10:14) and must address the issue of pornography with the faithful. It is important for all spiritual fathers to lead their sons and daughters towards freedom and healing. How does one accomplish this goal on a pastoral level?

First, educate the community of believers about the problem. Priests must equip themselves with the knowledge to speak confidently and passionately about the issue of pornography. Two excellent resources for clergy are the pastoral letters on this topic by Bishop Paul S. Loverde of the Diocese of Arlington, Virginia and by Bishop Robert W. Finn of the Diocese of Kansas City–St. Joseph, Missouri.[19]

Second, be willing to summon men to this effort from the pulpit. Remember, the Church is only as strong as its men! If our Church is being undermined by the multi-billion dollar pornography industry, it is only because the men of the Church are not defending Her. Encourage and invite the men of the parish to form a weekly men's group. Pastors can facilitate this process by putting these men in touch with the growing Catholic men's movement in the United States.[20]

Third, encourage the parents of young people in the parish to take measures to protect their children from pornography, especially on the Internet. Parents need to take every precaution to safeguard their children and home from the dangers of pornography, for example, by purchasing filter programs.[21] Parents need to be informed about online predators who attempt to lure unsuspecting victims, like their own children, into future porn addiction.

> *Children deserve to grow up with a healthy understanding of sexuality and its proper place in human relationships. They should be spared the degrading manifestations and the crude manipulation of sexuality so prevalent today. They have a right to be educated in authentic moral values rooted in the dignity of the human person … What does it mean to speak of child protection when pornography and violence can be viewed in so many homes through media widely available today? We need to reassess urgently the values underpinning society, so that a sound moral formation can be offered to young people and adults alike. All have a part to play in this task—not only parents, religious leaders, teachers and catechists, but the media and entertainment industries as well. Indeed, every member of society can contribute to this moral renewal and benefit from it.*
>
> — Pope Benedict XVI, Address to Bishops, April 16, 2008

A Final Word on the Issue of Pornography

Ultimately, the problem of eliminating pornography addiction among Catholics and other Christians is not solely the responsibility of men or of the clergy. All who desire to protect the common good and defend Christ's Church must do their part. We need to remember that pornography addiction is an intimacy disorder and that those who are struggling with it are extremely wounded people.

The sexual revolution continues to destroy millions of lives. The Body of Christ has certainly suffered. Many marriages have been destroyed, and women and children have paid the highest price. As we move forward in this battle against the evil of pornography, let us remember that we engage in this fight for the well-being of our culture and of all humanity, and for the souls of pornography's countless victims today and in the future.

Mark Houck is the co-founder and president of a lay apostolate called The King's Men (*www.thekingsmen.us*).

Just Cause and
Natural Family Planning

E. Christian Brugger, D.Phil., Senior Fellow in Ethics
June 17, 2010

WASHINGTON, D.C., JUNE 16, 2010 (Zenit.org).—Here is a question on bioethics asked by a ZENIT reader and answered by the fellows of the Culture of Life Foundation.

Q: Are there any conditions to follow Natural Family Planning (NFP) by a married couple, or is there blanket approval by Catholic Church? Wouldn't NFP be against life if the intention of the couple involved in sexual act is just pleasure and not life, provided they don't have any valid reason to postpone pregnancy? In this case, can NFP be also considered similar to using condoms? Thanks and Regards—D.R.P, Bangalore, India.

E. Christian Brugger offers the following response:
A: This is an excellent question, and one that I have been asked many times over the years by devout Catholic spouses. The answer is "no," NFP is not unqualifiedly good and can be used wrongly. The reason for this is subtle and needs to be stated carefully, because there is a popular, although erroneous, belief among some Catholic couples that NFP is "second best," and that if a couple is seriously Catholic, they will not self-consciously plan the children they conceive, but simply "let God send them." I do not mean to offend anyone's practices, but this "come what may" attitude is found nowhere in Catholic teaching on procreation in the last 150 years. There is no decision more serious to a Catholic couple than whether or not to participate with God in bringing a new human person into existence. The more serious a decision, the more it is due prayer, discussion and discernment. I teach my seminarians in Denver that God has a plan for every married couple; that the plan includes how many children they should have; and therefore if a couple is concerned about doing Jesus' will, they should try to discover whether Jesus wishes them to have more children. They should have all the children that Jesus wants them to have, no less, and no more. Therefore, whenever they are conscious that they might become pregnant, they should discuss and pray over the question: "Does Jesus want us to have another child?" The idea that this question is intrinsically tainted with selfish motives is rigoristic and should be rejected. Every potentially fertile couple, as well as infertile couples capable of adopting, has the responsibility to ask it.

At the same time, NFP can be chosen wrongly. Pope John Paul II summarized the Church's teaching in this regard during an audience at Castel Gondolfo in 1994; (note the seriousness with which he says couples should take the decision to have a child); he writes: "In deciding whether or not to have a child, [spouses] must not be motivated by selfishness or carelessness, but by a prudent, conscious generosity that weighs the possibilities and circumstances, and especially gives priority to the welfare of the unborn child. Therefore, when there is a reason not to procreate, this choice is permissible and may even be necessary. However, there remains the duty of carrying it out with criteria and methods that respect the total truth of the marital act in its unitive and procreative dimension, as wisely regulated by nature itself in its biological rhythms. One can comply with them and use them to advantage, but they cannot be 'violated' by artificial interference."[1]

Principle of "*iustæ causæ*"

John Paul II says the choice whether or not to have more children "must not be motivated by selfishness or carelessness;" and then states: "When there is a reason not to procreate, this choice is permissible and may even be necessary." What kind of "reason" renders permissible the choice not to procreate and hence to use NFP to avoid pregnancy? Pope Paul VI helps us answer this question. In "*Humanæ Vitæ*" (No. 16) he teaches: "If therefore there are '*iustæ causæ*' for spacing births, arising from the physical or psychological condition of husband or wife, or from external circumstances, the Church teaches that married people may then take advantage of the natural cycles immanent in the reproductive system and engage in marital intercourse only during those times that are infertile."

The Latin term "*iustæ causæ*" is sometimes translated "well grounded reasons," sometimes "serious motives", and sometimes "grave reasons." But the term is simply the plural of "*iustæ causæ*," which literally translates "just cause." According to the encyclical, a couple may space births, and do so through a deliberate recourse to the woman's natural fertility cycle [i.e., they may choose a form of NFP], if there are "just causes." This implies that if there are not just causes, then spacing births, and spacing them in this way, is not legitimate; in other words, that a couple ought not to space births, even through recourse to natural fertility cycles.

The Catholic Church first taught on intentional recourse to a woman's cycle in 1853. The Roman Sacred Penitentiary was replying to a request for an official clarification (a "dubium") submitted by the Bishop of Amiens in France, which asked: "Should those spouses be reprehended who make use of marriage only on those days when (in the opinion of some doctors) conception is impossible?" Rome replied: "After mature examination, we have decided that such spouses should not be disturbed [or disquieted], provided they do nothing that impedes generation." The quote implies that choosing intercourse to avoid procreation can be different morally from choices to "impede procreation"; the latter are never legitimate; the former are (at least sometimes) legitimate. One hundred years later Pope Pius XII spoke at length on periodic abstinence for purposes of spacing births in his well-known "Address to Midwives" (1951). He uses several terms as synonyms for Paul VI's "*iustæ causæ*": "serious reasons," "serious motives" and "grave reasons." The Pope says that such reasons "can exempt for a long time, perhaps even the whole duration of the marriage, from the positive and obligatory carrying out" of the marital duty to procreate.

The Catechism of the Catholic Church summarizes the teaching when it says: "For just reasons (de iustis causis), spouses may wish to space the births of their children. It is their duty to make certain that their desire is not motivated by selfishness but is in conformity with the generosity appropriate to responsible parenthood. Moreover, they should conform their behavior to the objective criteria of morality" (No. 2368). That objective criterion excludes as legitimate the alternative to impede procreation through choosing to contracept. What constitutes a just cause?

Neither the Sacred Penitentiary, Pius XII, Paul VI, nor John Paul II specify concretely what constitutes a "*iustæ causæ*." "*Humanæ Vitæ*" gets nearest. It teaches that "with regard to physical, economic, psychological and social conditions, responsible parenthood is exercised by those who prudently and generously decide to have more children, and by those who, for serious reasons and with due respect to moral precepts, decide not to have additional children for either a certain or an indefinite period of time" (No. 10; see also No. 16).

The text itemizes four areas of life from which such reasons might arise: physical and mental health, and economic and social conditions. This is still very general, but together with the prior statements, it provides us with enough information to formulate the following moral norm (note: this is my formulation): "If a couple has serious reasons, arising from the physical or mental condition of themselves, their children, or another for whom they have responsibility, or from the family's economic or wider social situation, they may defer having children temporarily, or, if the situation is serious enough, indefinitely, providing they use morally legitimate means. Recourse to natural fertility cycles to space births (NFP) under such circumstances is an example of a morally legitimate means. Contraception is not." If there is any further interest, I would be happy in a future piece to discuss concrete situations that might rightly be judged to be "serious reasons."

One final important point to note. If NFP is chosen wrongly, the wrongness lies in the fact that it is chosen without "good reason" and therefore usually selfishly. The sin here (presuming a person knows what he is doing and freely does it) is the sin of selfishness. (For a Catholic, it can also be the sin of disobedience to authoritative Church teaching.) But choosing NFP selfishly is not the same as contracepting. Strictly speaking, persons can only contracept if they also choose intercourse: a contraceptive act renders sterile an act of intercourse (recall the famous definition from "*Humanæ Vitæ*," No. 14: "Any action which either before, at the moment of, or after sexual intercourse, is specifically intended to prevent procreation—whether as an end or as a means."); a contraceptive act always relates to some act of sexual intercourse; it is an act contrary to conception (literally contra-conception). If there is no act of intercourse between a potentially fertile heterosexual couple, there is no potential conception to act contrary toward. Those who choose not to have intercourse, that is, choose abstinence (as NFP practitioners do when they want to avoid pregnancy), cannot act contrary to any conceptive-type of act, since they are specifically avoiding such acts. Therefore, those who choose NFP wrongly, although they do wrong, they do not do the same thing as those who contracept. Strictly speaking, they do not, indeed cannot, have a "contraceptive intention," although their frame of mind might be characterized by what John Paul II called a "contraceptive mentality" (by which I take him to mean, a mentality that sees the coming to be of new life as a threat, something rightly to take measures against).

[Note: some moral theologians would disagree with me here; they believe that NFP can be chosen with a "contraceptive intention" and therefore constitute for some couples a form of contraception.]

E. Christian Brugger is a Senior Fellow of Ethics at the Culture of Life Foundation and is an associate professor of moral theology at St. John Vianney Theological Seminary in Denver, Colorado. He received his Doctorate in Philosophy from Oxford in 2000.

[Readers may send questions regarding bioethics to *bioethics@zenit.org*. The text should include your initials, your city and your state, province or country. The fellows at the Culture of Life Foundation will answer a select number of the questions that arrive.]

Just Cause and
Natural Family Planning 2

E. Christian Brugger, D.Phil., Senior Fellow in Ethics
July 1, 2010

WASHINGTON, D.C., JUNE 30, 2010 (Zenit.org).—Here are two questions on bioethics asked by ZENIT readers and answered by the fellows of the Culture of Life Foundation.

Q: Thank you for responding to the question regarding when natural family planning (NFP) is appropriate to use. […] I can understand why the Church has never formally identified "just causes," but nevertheless, in our world today, I believe we thrive on tangible examples and responses to help us make good decisions rather than simply on abstract concepts. In your article, you suggested that you could further provide specific examples of what is meant by "just causes" to postpone children. While I know that no list will be complete and it really depends on each couple's situation, […] I would appreciate the further explanation. Sincerely—K.M., Lake Worth, U.S.

E. Christian Brugger offers the following response.

A: I am happy to speak further on the question of "just causes" for spacing births. Some may believe that only extraordinary situations can constitute legitimate reasons for practicing NFP to defer pregnancy (e.g., severe illness of a spouse; extreme financial difficulties; mental breakdown, etc.). In my opinion, this extreme interpretation is incorrect and can result in avoidable harms. Recall the moral norm I formulated in my last piece on NFP, in which I drew on the reasoning taught in "*Humanæ Vitæ*," No. 10:

> If a couple have serious reasons [i.e., just causes—"*iustæ causæ*"], arising from the physical or mental condition of themselves, their children, or another for whom they have responsibility, or from the family's economic or wider social situation, they may defer having children temporarily, or, if the situation is serious enough, indefinitely, providing they use morally legitimate means. Recourse to natural fertility cycles to space births (NFP) under such circumstances is an example of a morally legitimate means. Contraception is not. (This wording is mine, not that of "*Humanæ Vitæ*")

In order to translate the generality of this norm into more concrete terms, we need to attend to the pivotal concept "iusta" (i.e., the adjective "just") in the long-standing Catholic teaching. The correlative noun is "justice". In order to rightly apply the Catholic teaching on "*iustæ causæ*" I suggest that we attend to the concept of justice as an interpretive lens (a "hermeneutical principle") through which to assess whether in any concrete situation a serious (iusta) reason (causa) to space births is present.

All people have duties arising from their morally significant relationships: spouses to each other; parents to children; children to parents; employees to employers; employers to employees. Generally speaking, the closer the relationship, the more serious the duty. The fulfillment of these duties is the domain of justice. So, for example, a man who neglects his family in favor of unreasonable participation in a leisure sport such as golf or fishing commits an injustice toward his family. The classical definition of justice is "rendering to each person what is due to him based upon the relationship that we have to (or with) him." This sounds very general, but applying it in most situations is quite straightforward. An employee who has committed himself to eight hours of work per day should work for eight hours per day (if he is able); and his boss should pay him the agreed upon wage for working eight hours.

Now husbands/fathers and wives/mothers have very serious obligations in justice to the members of their families, chiefly to their dependent children, especially those who are most vulnerable to harm (e.g., infants, small children, and infirmed and disabled children). Perhaps it need not be said, but parents' duties to their existing children are prior to children they have not yet procreated. When discerning another child, couples therefore should ask: Can I fulfill well my existing duties while bringing another child into the world and fulfilling well my duties to that child? Absolute certainty, of course, is not required. But I think reasonable certainty based upon objective criteria is required (e.g., family relationships are in order; mother and father's mental and physical health are stable; finances are in order; etc.). If one has reason to believe that a relationship for which one has some duty will unfairly (and hence wrongly) suffer if another child is brought into the world, then, as an issue of justice, one ought to abstain from bringing another child into the world.

God has a personal and unrepeatable plan for every Christian's life. This is his or her "personal vocation." Husbands and wives too have personal vocations. At the center are the overarching commitments of marriage and parenthood. But their personal vocations might include other commitments as well, commitments that must be compatible with the fulfilling of their marital and parental duties. God may give to one woman an ability to organize people, to another the capacity to sing opera, and to another the personality to make friends easily. Because a woman believes God has called her to be married and to become a mother, does this mean she must set aside founding an organization for the defense of the unborn, or being a part-time opera singer, or a university professor? If God has given her special aptitudes, desires and opportunities, this is an indication that he may be calling her to use them in specified ways.

But one thing parents know with certitude is that if they already have committed themselves to being spouses and parents, then their personal vocation right now (immediately, presently) includes fulfilling well those responsibilities. They know that they have a moral duty to ensure (as best they can) that new commitments they assume are compatible with being a spouse and parent. If they judge that their existing children will be unfairly harmed by mommy choosing to sing opera professionally, or found a pro-life organization, or daddy taking a new job that will keep him away from the home, then they ought to set aside those alternatives as incompatible (at least for the time being) with their personal vocation. My purpose here is not to criticize generous couples for welcoming many new children into their families. Such couples are a salutary expression of respect for a culture of life. And they should be encouraged and supported by their brothers and sisters in the Christian community.

But couples who for good reasons refrain from having more children (which for them can be painful) should not be considered less generous. Our generosity is first and foremost assessed relative to Jesus' will. We want to "do whatever he tells us" (cf. John 2:5). Both excesses and deficiencies in this regard are moral problems. So Christian family planning means assessing prudently and prayerfully the family size God wants us to have, which means the size that is as compatible as possible with our resources (spiritual, emotional, physical, material and relational). A few concrete examples of "*iustæ causæ*" for deferring pregnancy might include:

1) Physical or mental illness of one of the spouses;

2) Serious financial instability (e.g., during a period of unemployment);

3) Needs arising from caring for "high-needs" children;

4) The instability of transitional periods such as spouses in graduate school;

5) Debilitating stress that can arise from having a large family in societies where large families are no longer valued (see "Gaudium et Spes," No. 50).

Husbands need to be especially attentive to the welfare of their wives when assessing whether or not to have more children. Since wives will bear the exclusive burden of gestating their children, and the disproportionate burdens associated with nurture and education in the early years, husbands should listen very carefully to their wives' input. Most happily married pro-life wives find it difficult to resist their husband's solicitations for more children. But if as a result of caring for one or more small children, one's wife is experiencing long-term exhaustion or depression, or if she has fallen into the habit of chronically doubting her worth as a wife and mother, and she has doubts as to whether she can fulfill peacefully the duties associated with caring for another infant, then a husband should assist her in expressing those doubts, and avoid manipulating her in accordance with his own will. Doubts, of course, can be unreasonable, based on non-rational diffidence or immoderate caution. And spouses should assist one another in judging whether such doubts are expressive of or temptations away from Jesus' will. But if in the face of just reasons a husband disregards the clear doubts of his wife (even if communicated non-verbally), he may commit an injustice toward his wife. The same can be said of wives toward their husbands.

Although serious reasons ("*iustæ causæ*") ordinarily pertain to the welfare of the members of the family, they also can arise from a commitment to apostolic works. A pro-life Ob-Gyn might be called to open an NFP-only practice, or a parent caring for a child with Down's Syndrome a Catholic daycare for disabled children, or an attorney a pro-bono practice for Christians being denied their civil rights. They might reasonably judge that a period of disproportionate investment of time is necessary to set the new initiative on a stable foundation. If they discern that Jesus wants them to do this; and they also believe that doing it is morally inconsistent with having another baby; then they can confidently conclude that Jesus wants them to postpone having another baby until the practical conditions change.

Q: One final question. Acknowledging that good reasons justify periodic abstinence, do they morally oblige a couple to abstain?

A: I would say that if either spouse has reasonable doubts that he or she can fulfill well present responsibilities and, in addition, the duties of care to a new child, then the couple should not pursue another child (at least until the conditions giving rise to the doubts are overcome). It would be unfair to those for whom we have responsibility to freely pursue a state of affairs in which we are unable to render what we owe to others in justice. Having said that, individual spouses, who have reasons based upon their own welfare—and not the welfare of another for whom they are responsible—are free to adopt personal sacrifices that exceed what the moral law requires. So, for example, a mother with chronically severe headaches or a father with non-incapacitating M.S. may choose—in consultation with his or her spouse—to pursue more children knowing that the "cost" to him or herself likely will be considerable, presuming they have good reasons to believe they still will be able to meet their duties. But although one is free to exceed the demands of the moral law in one's own life, one is never free to make that choice for another.

$\mathcal{E}$NDNOTES

From the Pastoral Letter

1. United States Conference of Catholic Bishops, *Marriage: Love and Life in the Divine Plan* (November 17, 2009), 3; hereinafter cited as *Marriage: Love and Life.*
2. *Marriage: Love and Life*, p. 3.
3. *Familiaris Consortio*, 1.
4. *Familiaris Consortio*, 1; cf. *Gaudium et spes*, 52.
5. *Marriage: Love and Life*, p. 6.
6. Gn 1:26–27.
7. Address of His Holiness Benedict XVI to the Participants in the Ecclesial Diocesan Convention of Rome, June 6, 2005.
8. Hans Urs von Balthasar, *Love Alone: The Way of Revelation* (London: Sheed & Ward, 1970).
9. Edward T. Oakes, SJ, and David Moss, eds. *The Cambridge Companion to Hans Urs von Balthasar* (Cambridge University Press, 2004), 270.
10. Pope John Paul II, *Gratissimam Sane*, (Year of the Family, *Letter to Families*, 1994), 6.
11. Dr. William White, *A Catholic Physician Talks To Engaged Couples* (San Francisco: Ignatius Press, printed in Homiletic & Pastoral Review, March 2008), 10.
12. Gn 2:23.
13. White, *A Catholic Physician Talks To Engaged Couples*, 10.
14. *FC*, 18.
15. CCC 1702.
16. Dorothy Day, *The Long Loneliness* (New York, NY: HarperCollins Publishing Inc, 1952), 138–39.
17. *Deus Caritas Est*, 18.
18. *Mulieris Dignitatem*, 7.
19. Ibid.
20. Columbia Magazine, November 2009, Vol. 89, No. 11, p. 7.
21. Pope Benedict XVI, excerpt from homily, May 31, 2009.
22. Merton, Thomas, *Seeds of Contemplation*.
23. *Deus Caritas Est*, 18.
24. St. Catherine of Siena.
25. Gn 2:17.
26. Gn. 3:1.
27. Rev 12:17.
28. Kevin Burke and Dr. Theresa Burke, *A Study Guide to Humanæ Vitæ of Human Life* (Staten Island, NY: Clergy and Pastoral Associates of Priests for Life, 2008), 24.
29. Gn 3:1.
30. Gn 3:5.
31. CCC 405.
32. Concupiscence is defined as an ardent, usually sensuous, longing; a strong sexual desire; lust. In Christian theology, concupiscence is selfish human desire for an object, person, or experience.
33. Cf. CCC 400.
34. Cf. Gn 3:12.
35. Cf. Gn 2:22; 3:16b.
36. Cf. Gn 1:28; 3:16–19.
37. Gn 3:12–13.

38. Pope Benedict XVI, excerpt from a homily, April 24, 2005.
39. Pope Benedict XVI, excerpt from a speech, March 7, 2010.
40. St. Josemaria Escriva de Balaguer, as found in *Conversation with God*, by Francis Fernandez (Scepter Press).
41. USCCB, United States Catholic Catechism for Adults (Washington, DC: USCCB, 2006), 287.
42. St. Josemaria Escriva.
43. Cf. Gn 3:9,15.
44. Gn 3:15.
45. Cf. *Lumen Gentium*, 63–65.
46. Hans Urs von Balthasar, *Theo-Drama IV: The Action* (San Francisco: Ignatius Press, 1994), 471–476.
47. Pope Benedict XVI, excerpt from homily, April 24, 2005.
48. Rom 5:20.
49. Eph 4:1.
50. Cf. *GS*, 48.
51. Joseph Bolin, *Paths of Love: The Discernment of Vocation According to Aquinas, Ignatius, and Pope John Paul II* (2008), Chapter 4, Part II: Pope Benedict XVI.
52. Jn 15:12–13.
53. Mt 18:35.
54. Mt 18 21–22.
55. Mt 20:28.
56. CCC 1534.
57. Eph 5:21–33.
58. Christopher West, *Good News about Sex and Marriage* (Ann Arbor, MI: Servant Publications, 2000), 62–63.
59. *Casti Connubii*, 27.
60. *Familiaris Consortio*, 22.
61. *GS*, 48.
62. Joseph Bolin, *Paths of Love: The Discernment of Vocation,* Chapter 4, Part II: Pope Benedict XVI.
63. Tertullian, *Ad uxorem.* 2, 8, 6–7: PL 1, 1412–1413; cf. FC 13.
64. *GS*, 48.
65. CIC, cc. 1056, 1141; CCEO, cc. 776 §3, 853.
66. CCC 1662.
67. *The Rite of Marriage* (New York, NY: Catholic Book Publishing Co., 1970), 43.
68. Jason Adams, *Called to Give Life: A Sourcebook on the Blessings of Children and the Harm of Contraception* (Dayton OH: One More Soul, 2003), 53.
69. St. Josemaria Escriva de Balaguer, *Conversations*, 91.
70. Quoted in *www.marriagemissions.com/quotes-on-childrens-effect-on-marriage*, © Marriage Missions International, (2009). Reprinted with permission of Marriage Missions International. All rights reserved.
71. Quoted in *www.marriagemissions.com/quotes-on-childrens-effect-on-marriage*, © Marriage Missions International, (2009). Reprinted with permission of Marriage Missions International. All rights reserved.
72. William C. Creasy, *The Imitation of Christ: Thomas À Kempis* (Notre Dame, IN: Ave Maria Press, 1989), 44.
73. St. Catherine of Siena.
74. *www.savior.org/saints/corsini.htm*.
75. Clive Staples Lewis (29 November 1898—22 November 1963), commonly referred to as C. S. Lewis was an Irish-born British novelist, academic, medievalist, literary critic, essayist, lay theologian, and Christian apologist. He is also known for his fiction, especially *The Screwtape Letters*, *The Chronicles of Narnia*, and *The Space Trilogy*. Lewis's works have been translated into more than 30 languages and have sold millions of copies over the years.
76. The Christian concept of the *Logos* is derived from the first chapter of the Gospel of John. The *Logos* (often translated as "Word") is explicitly identified with Jesus, the Son of God. Christians often consider John 1:1 to be a central text in their belief that Jesus is God, in connection with the doctrine of the Trinity: one God in three Divine Persons.
77. Jn 1:1–5; 14.
78. This means that the visible sign of a Sacrament effects what it signifies. For example, the water used in the Sacrament of Baptism not only signifies a cleansing, it also actually effects a washing away of Original Sin. "The sacraments are efficacious because in them Christ Himself is at work: it is He who acts in His Sacraments in order to communicate the grace that each Sacrament signifies" (Catechism, no. 1127).

79. CCC 1131; Efficacious means that the visible sign of a Sacrament effects what it signifies. For example, the water used in the Sacrament of Baptism not only signifies a cleansing but it also actually effects a washing away of Original Sin. The Sacraments "are *efficacious* because in them Christ himself is at work: it is he who acts in his sacraments in order to communicate the grace that each sacrament signifies" (CCC 1127).

80. Tim Gray, *Sacraments in Scripture*, 12.

81. David Lang, *Why Matter Matters: Philosophical and Scriptural Reflections on the Sacraments* (Huntington, IN: Our Sunday Visitor, 2002), 19.

82. See CIC, c. 849; CCEO, c. 675 §1.

83. See CIC, c. 1055 §1; CCEO, c. 776 §2. A valid marriage between any two validly baptized Christians, whether Catholic or not, is a Sacrament. This includes marriages between a Catholic and a non-Catholic Christian, whether Orthodox or Protestant, although certain canonical requirements must be fulfilled for these marriages to be valid. A marriage between a Christian and an unbaptized person is still valid as a natural marriage, but is not a Sacrament. Here, too, for a Catholic to enter such a marriage validly, certain canonical requirements must be fulfilled.

84. An excerpt taken from Pope Benedict XVI's homily at the 2010 Chrism Mass; Saint Peter's Basilica Holy Thursday, April 1, 2010.

85. Ibid.

86. Gn 2:24.

87. *SC*, 59.

88. Cf. Lk 5:17; 6:19; 8:46.

89. Although in an emergency, for example, fear of death, anyone may baptize. The person baptizing should have the right intention and use the Trinitarian formula of Baptism.

90. If the Catholic party is marrying a non-Catholic, he or she may obtain a canonical dispensation to be married in another church, such as an Orthodox or Protestant church.

91. New Advent on Marriage: *www.newadvent.org/cathen/09707a.htm*.

92. Mt 19:6.

93. *Humanæ Vitæ, 8.*

94. Gn 2:23.

95. Lang, *Why Matter Matters*, 172.

96. Ibid., 172.

97. Mt 7:7.

98. CCC 1642; Eph 5:21; cf. Gal 6:2.

99. CCC 1534.

100. Luigi Santucci, *Wrestling with Christ* (London: Collins, 1972), 155–157.

101. Jn 13:1.

102. Cf. Gal 2:20.

103. CCC 1380.

104. Dorothy Day, *The Long Loneliness*, 138–41.

105. *FC*, no. 57.

106. *DCE*, 13.

107. *DCE*, 14.

108. CCC 1396.

109. *FC*, 56.

110. Blessed Columba Marmion, *Christ, the Life of the Soul*, (Herefordshire, England: Gracewing Publishing, 2005), 329–330.

111. Rev. James Socias, *Introduction to Catholicism: A Complete Course* (Woodridge, IL: Midwest Theological Forum, 2003), 176.

112. Ibid., 176.

113. *FC*, 13.

114. 1 Cor 13:4–8.

115. Text taken from *www.michaeljournal.org*.

116. Mt 19:17.

117. Address of Pope Benedict XVI, Meeting with the Youth, Apostolic Visit to Brazil, May 10, 2007.

118. White, *A Catholic Physician Talks To Engaged Couples*.

119. Pope Benedict XVI, excerpt from homily, April 24, 2005.

120. Pope Benedict XVI, excerpt from homily, April 24, 2010.

121. See CIC, cc. 226 §2, 774 §2, 793, 867 §1, 1125 1°; CCEO, cc. 618, 627, 686 §1, 814 1°.

122. 2 Tm 2:11–12.

123. Jn 8:7.

124. Jn 8:10–11.

125. See *GS*, 48.

126. Karol Wojtyla, (Pope John Paul II), *Love and Responsibility* (San Francisco: Ignatius Press, Translated by H.T. Willetts 1981, reprinted by Ignatius Press, 1993), 272–275.

127. CCC 2363.

128. *GS*, 48; see CCC 1652.

129. Mt 19:5–6.

130. Dietrich von Hildebrand, *The Encyclical Humanæ Vitæ, A Sign of Contradiction: An Essay on Birth Control and Catholic Conscience,* trans. Damian Fedorvka and John Crosby (Chicago: Franciscan Herald Press, 1969), 36.

131. St. John Chrysostom, *On Marriage and Family Life*, trans. Catharine P. Roth and David Anderson (Crestwood: St. Vladimir's Seminary Press, 1997), 44.

132. Article reprinted from: *http://www.conversiondiary.com/2007/06/contraception-and-womans-self-image.html.*

133. *One More Soul.* Reprinted by permission of the publisher: *www.omsoul.com.*

134. *GS*, 48; see CCC 1652.

135. This article was published in the summer 2008 issue of Mosaic, a publication of Sacred Heart Major Seminary, Detroit, Michigan, *www.shms.edu* and reprinted by permission of the publisher Sacred Heart Major Seminary. All rights reserved.

136. *Homiletic & Pastoral Review*, June 1991. Reprinted by permission of the publisher. All rights reserved. © Ignatius Press (*www.ignatius.com* or *www.hprweb.com*).

137. Charles D. Provan, *The Bible and Birth Control* (Monongahela, PA: Zimmer Printing, 1989).

138. Walter J. Schu, LC, *The Splendor of Love* (New Hope Publications: 2003 Circle Media), 20.

139. *The Sacramento Bee*, June 19, 2003.

140. *San Francisco Chronicle*, September 19, 2003.

141. "An Open Letter from the Parents of Holly Patterson," November 6, 2003.

142. John C. Ford, SJ, and Gerald Kelly, SJ, *Contemporary Moral Theology*, Vol. 11: Marriage Questions (Westminster, MD: Newman Press, 1964), 245–255.

143. *Casti Connubii*, 56.

144. "Divorce statistics collection: Summary of findings so far," Americans for Divorce Reform, *www.divorcereform.org.*

145. *Humanæ Vitæ*, 23.

146. CCC 2370.

147. CCC 2371; *GS*. 51, 4

148. Reprinted from *www.conversiondiary.com/2007/06/contraception-and-womans-self-image.html.*

149. Laura R. Nelson, Certified NFP Educator, Chicago, IL.

150. Saint Augustine; Philip Schaff (Editor) (1887). *A Select Library of the Nicene and Post-Nicene Fathers of the Christian Church, Volume IV* (Grand Rapids, MI: WM. B. Eerdmans Publishing Co.), *On the Morals of the Manichæans*, Chapter 18.

151. Marilyn Yalom, *A History of the Wife* (New York, NY: HarperCollins, First ed., 2001), 297–8, 307.

152. Mark A Pivarunas, *On the Question of Natural Family Planning, cmri.org. Congregatio Mariæ Reginæ Immaculatæ,* February 18, 2002. *http://www.cmri.org/03–nfp.html.*

153. "A Brief History of Fertility Charting." *FertilityFriend.com. http://www.fertilityfriend.com/Faqs/A_brief_history_of_fertility_charting.html.*

154. Katie Singer, *The Garden of Fertility* (New York, NY: Avery, a member of Penguin Group, 2004), 226–7.

155. Brian W. Harrison, "Is Natural Family Planning a 'Heresy'?" *Living Tradition* (Roman Theological Forum: January 2003), *http://www.rtforum.org/lt/lt103.html.*

156. Sheila and John Kippley, *The Art of Natural Family Planning* (Cincinnati, OH: Fourth ed., 1996).

157. John Billings, (March 2002), "THE QUEST—leading to the discovery of the Billings Ovulation Method". *Bulletin of Ovulation Method Research and Reference Centre of Australia* 29 (1): 18–28. *http://www.woomb.org/omrrca/bulletin/vol29/no1/thequest.shtml.*

158. Laura R. Nelson, Certified NFP Educator, Chicago, IL.

159. CCC 2363.

160. Pope Pius XI, *Casti Connubii* (United States Catholic Conference: 1930), Section 59. *http://www.vatican.va/holy_father/pius_xi/encyclicals/documents/hf_p-xi_enc_31121930_casti-connubii_en.html.*

161. CCC 2370.

162. CCC 2368.

163. *Humanæ Vitæ*, Section I.10.

164. Laura R. Nelson, Certified NFP Educator, Chicago, IL.

165. Ibid.

166. Ibid.

167. See *FC*, 32; see also CCC 2370.

168. *Humanæ Vitæ*, 13.

169. *Humanæ Vitæ*, 14.

170. CCC 2297.

171. James Socias, *Marriage is Love Forever* (Princeton, NJ: Scepter Publishers, 1994), 59.

172. Printed in the November 2005 issue of *First Things*. (*www.firstthings.com*).

173. Ibid., 3.

174. *Raison d'être* is a phrase borrowed from French where it means "reason for being"; in English use, it also comes to suggest a degree of rationalization, as "The claimed reason for the existence of something or someone."

175. Von Hildebrand, *The Encyclical Humanæ Vitæ: A Sign of Contradiction*, 31; 37–38.

176. *Donum Vitæ* II, 8.

177. *Donum Vitæ,* intro., 2.

178. CCC 2366.

179. *Donum Vitæ* II, 1.

180. *Donum Vitæ* II, 5.

181. *Donum Vitæ,* II, 4.

182. Helen Hull Hitchcock, "Saint Gianna—A Model for Mothers," *http://www.wf-f.org/StGianna.html#Anchor-Introduction-49575.*

183. *FC*, 17.

184. *FC*, 17.

185. "The Ten Commandments of Communication" is reprinted by permission of the publisher and taken from: Frederick W. Marks, Ph.D., *A Catholic Handbook for Engaged and Married Couples* (Steubenville, OH: Emmaus Road Publishing, 2001), 32–35. *www.emmausroad.org.*

186. Eph 4:26–27.

187. Gary Chapman, *Five Love Languages* (Chicago, IL: Northfield Publishing, 1992).

188. Marks, *A Catholic Handbook for Engaged and Married Couples*, 54.

189. Austin Flemming, *Prayer Book for Engaged Couples* (Chicago, IL: Liturgy Training Publications, 2004), 59.

190. Plato, *Apology of Socrates*, 38a.

191. St. Catherine of Siena (1347–1380): *The Dialogue.*

192. St. Gianna Bretta Molla: (1922–1962) Quote taken from the Movie: *Love is a Choice: The Life of St. Gianna Beretta Molla,* Salt + Light Catholic Media Foundation. Fr. Thomas Rosica, a priest of the Congregation of St. Basil (C.S.B.), is Chief Executive Officer of Salt+Light Catholic Media Foundation.

193. The following section has been reprinted by permission of the publisher and taken from *www.Catholicpages.com http://www.aquinasandmore.com/index.cfm/title/The-Seven-Capital-Virtues/FuseAction/store.displayArticle/article/247/ http://www.aquinasandmore.com/index.cfm/title/The-Seven-Capital-Sins/FuseAction/store.displayArticle/article/252/.*

194. St. Alphonsus Liguori, *The True Spouse of Jesus Christ*, translated from Italian (published 1835), 282.

195. Pseude-Macarius, quote taken from Donald DeMarco, *The Many Faces of Virtue* (Steubenville, OH: Emmaus Road Publishing, 2000).

196. Joseph N. Perry, Auxiliary Bishop, Archdiocese of Chicago—address to Men's Prayer Breakfast, St. Victor Parish, Calumet City, IL. (January 9, 2010); reprinted by permission of the author.

197. Written by Coleen Kelly Mast, Catholic Radio Show Host and author of *Love & Life* and *Sex Respect*. *www.sexrespect.com.*

198. Austin Flemming, *Prayer Book for Engaged Couples* (Chicago, IL: Liturgy Training Publications, 2004), 23.

199. CCC 1656.

200. See CIC, cc. 226 §2, 774 §2, 793, 867 §1, 1125 1°; CCEO, cc. 618, 627, 686 §1, 814 1°.

201. USCCB, *United States Catholic Catechism for Adults* (Washington, DC: USCCB, 2006), 287.
202. St. Therese of Liseux, *Manuscrits autobiographiques*, C 25r.
203. St. John Damascene, *De fide orth.* 3, 24: PG 94, 1089C.
204. Ps 130:1.
205. Cf. Lk 18:9–14.
206. Rom 8:26.
207. St. Augustine, *Sermo* 56, 6, 9: PL 38, 381.
208. St. Gregory of Nazianzus, *Orat. theo.*, 27, 1, 4: PG 36, 16.
209. St. John Chrysostom, *Ecloga de Oratione*, 2: PG 63, 585.
210. Cf. Mk 4:4–7, 15–19.
211. St. Teresa of Jesus, *The Book of Her Life*, 8, 5 (quoted in *The Collected Works of St. Teresa of Avila*, tr. K. Kavanaugh, OCD, and O. Rodriguez, OCD [Washington DC: Institute of Carmelite Studies, 1976], I, 67).
212. Sg 1:7; cf. 3:1–4.
213. Cf. Lk 7:36–50; 19:1–10.
214. Cf. Jer 31:33.
215. Mother Teresa. Edited and with Commentary by Brian Kolodiejchuk, MC, Doubleday, *Come Be My Light—The Private Writings of the Saint of Calcutta.* (New York: Random House, 2007).

APPENDIX: The Sanctity of Marriage and the Family

1. *GS*, 48.

APPENDIX: Married Couples Who Intentionally Chose Sterilization for Contraceptive Purposes and Lasting Repentance

1. Germain G. Grisez, *The Way of the Lord Jesus: Living a Christian Life Volume II* (Quincy, Illinois: Franciscan Press, 1993), 544.
2. John F. Kippley, *Sex and the Marriage Covenant: A Basis for Morality* (Cincinnati, Ohio: The Couple to Couple League International, 1991), 208–209.
3. Grisez, 544–545.
4. Kippley, 209–210.
5. Grisez, 545.
6. Kippley, 210.
7. Grisez, 545.
8. Ibid.
9. Kippley, 211.
10. Ibid.
11. Kippley, 211–212.
12. Kippley, 212.

APPENDIX: *Humanæ Vitæ* and Human Happiness

1. The following two articles were published in the summer 2008 issue of Mosaic, a publication of Sacred Heart Major Seminary, Detroit, Michigan, *www.shms.edu* and reprinted by permission of the publisher Sacred Heart Major Seminary. All rights reserved.

APPENDIX: Marital and Family Commitment: A Personalist View

1. *AAS* 76 (1984) 644.
2. *Gaudium et Spes*, nos. 48; 50.
3. Cf. my essay: "Marriage: a personalist or an institutional understanding?" in *Communio* 1992–III, pp. 301–303.
4. Ibid. pp. 285ss.
5. Cf. *Catechism of the Catholic Church*, nos. 293ss.
6. *AAS* 22 (1930), 547–548.
7. *GS* 48.
8. *Lumen Gentium*, no. 11.
9. *Apostolicam Actuositatem*, no. 11.
10. *GS* 48.
11. *Ordo Celebrandi Matrimonium*, no. 25; cf. *GS* 48.
12. 1987 Address to the Roman Rota: *AAS* 79, 1456.

13. *Covenanted Happiness*, Ignatius Press, 1990, pp. 42ss.
14. Isa 43:1.
15. *Casti connubii*, AAS 1930, 553.
16. *Insegnamenti di Giovanni Paolo II*, V, I (1982), p. 1344.
17. *GS* 48; cf. *Casti connubii*, AAS 22 (1930), 553.
18. No. 20; cf. *Catechism of the Catholic Church*, no. 1648.
19. See *Humanæ Vitæ*, no. 12
20. Cf. *Covenanted Happiness*, pp. 37–38; 41; 51–52.
21. Cf. HV, no. 9.
22. *Insegnamenti di Giovanni Paolo* II, II, 2 (1979), p. 702.
23. *GS* 50.

APPENDIX: Pornography: What's the Problem?

1. • D. Zillman and J. Bryant, "Pornography's Impact on Sexual Satisfaction," *Journal of Applied Social Psychology* 18: 5 (1988) 438–453; and D. Zillman and J. Bryant, "Effects of Prolonged Consumption of Pornography on Family Values," *Journal of Family Issues* 9: 4 (Dec. 1988) 518–544.
   • M. Allen, T. Emmers, L. Gebhardt and M. A. Giery, "Exposure to Pornography and Acceptance of Rape Myths," *Journal of Communication* 45: 1 (1995) 5–26; R. M. Saunders and P. J. Naus, "The Impact of Social Content and Audience Factors on Responses to Sexually Explicit Videos," *Journal of Sex Education and Therapy* 19: 2 (1993) 117–131.
   • Neil M. Malamuth and James V. P. Check, "The Effects of Aggressive Pornography on Beliefs in Rape Myths: Individual Differences," *Journal of Research in Personality* 19 (1985) 299–320.
   • Neil M. Malamuth and Edward Donnerstein (eds.), *Pornography and Sexual Aggression* (New York: Academic Press, 1984). Linda Marchiano, *Final Report of the Attorney General's Commission on Pornography* (Nashville, TN.: Rutledge Hill Press, 1986), 232–236, and Ordeal (Seacaucus, NJ: Citadel Press, 1980).
   • Gary R. Brooks, *The Centerfold Syndrome: How Men Can Overcome Objectification and Achieve Intimacy with Women* (San Francisco: Jossey-Bass Publishers, 1995).
   • Neil Malamuth, "Rape Fantasies as a Function of Repeated Exposure to Sexual Violence," *Archives of Sexual Behavior* 10 (1981) 33–47.
   • Dolf Zillman and Jennings Bryant, "Pornography, Sexual Callousness, and the Trivialization of Rape," *Journal of Communication* 32 (1982) 10–21.
   • Jmi Dyar, "Cyber-porn held responsible for increase in sex addiction," *Washington Times* (Jan. 26, 2000), quoting Dr. Robert Weiss (Sexual Recovery Institute); available at *www.freerepublic.com/forum/a388eaebe7770.htm*.
2. *internet-filter-review. toptenreviews.com/internet-pornography-statistics.htm*.
3. *www.nationalcoalition.org/resourceservice/stat.html*.
4. *www.reuters.com/. /technologyNews/idUSN3030000720080130feedType=nl&feedName=ustechnolo gy&sp=true*.
5. *The Call to Biblical Manhood*. Man in the Mirror. July 6, 2004; cited at *www.nationalcoalition.org/statisticspronography. asp*.
6. Kiram Amin, et al., "Internet Pornography and Loneliness: An Association," *Sexual Addiction and Compulsivity* 12: 1 (2005).
7. Of 81 pastors of various denominations surveyed (74 males, 7 female), 98% were exposed to porn; 43% intentionally accessed a sexually explicit website; see *www.nationalcoalition.org/resourceservice/stat.html*; 47% of Christians said pornography is a major problem in their home; see *internet-filterreview. toptenreviews.com/internet-pornography-statistics.htm*.
8. Most Rev. Robert W. Finn, *Blessed Are the Pure in Heart* (Feb. 21, 2007); available at *www.diocese-kcsj.org/content/diocese/bishop/homilies_and_statements*.
9. Most Rev. Paul S. Loverde, "Bought with a Price: Pornography and the Attack on the Living Temple of God"; available at *www.arlingtondiocese.org/familylife/about_boughtprice.php*.
10. Ibid.
11. The Centers for Disease Contol estimates that in the United States there are 19 million new cases of STDs annually, and almost half of those occur among young people ages 15 to 24. Available at *www.cdc.gov/STDS/STATS/trends2006.htm*.
12. *en.wikipedia.org/wiki/pornography_addiction*.

13. Dr. Patrick Carnes, a leading researcher on sex addiction estimates that 3 to 6% of Americans are sexually addicted. [That could amount to more than 18 million people.] Cited by R. Borys, *Love, Marriage & ... Pornography, How the Forbidden Fruit of the Modern-Day Tree of Knowledge is Destroying our Relationships* (A Concerned Cyber Age Parents Publication, October 2006).

14. See footnote 12.

15. Dr. Mark Laaser, *Healing the Wounds of Sexual Addiction* (Grand Rapids, MI: Zondervan, 2004). Dr. Laaser founded Faithful and True Ministries (*www.faithfulandtrueministries.com*), lectures nationally and is a consultant to hospitals and treatment centers around the country.

16. For more information on professional counseling, visit *www.catholictherapists.com*.

17. See CCC, n. 1804–1829; see also Tim Gray and Curtis Martin, Boys to Men: *The Transforming Power of Virtue* (Steubenville, OH: Emmaus Road Publishing, 2001).

18. Quoted in *Magnificat*. 8: 12 (January 2008).

19. Most Rev. Paul S. Loverde "Bought with a Price: Pornography and the Attack on the Living Temple of God"; available at *www.arlingtondiocese.org/familylife/about_boughtprice.php*. Most Rev. Robert W. Finn, *Blessed Are the Pure in Heart* (Feb. 21, 2007); available at *www.diocese kcsj.org/content/diocese/bishop/homilies_and_statements*. Also recommend is Ralph H. Earle, Jr. and Mark R. Laaser, *The Pornography Trap* (Kansas City, MO: Beacon Hill Press, 2002).

20. The following organizations and men's groups are great resources for parishes and men:
    - e5 MEN, *www.e5men.org*
    - National Fellowship of Catholic Men, *www.nrccm.org*
    - St. Joseph's Covenant Keepers, *www.dads.org*
    - That Man is You, *www.paradisusdei.org*
    - The King's Men, *www.thekingsmen.us*
    - True Knights, *www.trueknights.org*
    - The Serenellians, *www.pornnomore.com*

21. The following filter programs are recommended: *www.netnanny.com, www.cybersitter.com, www.bsafehome. com*, and *www.cyperpatrol.com*. Some recommended home accountability programs are *www.xxxchurch.com, www.covenanteyes.com*, and *www.internetsafety.com*. Parents also are encouraged to obtain spy software, such as SpectorSoft; see *www.SpectorSoft.com*.

APPENDIX: Pornography: What's the Problem? (ADDITIONAL RESOURCES)

Teaching Documents
- Pontifical Council for the Family. *The Truth and Meaning of Human Sexuality*, 1995.
  Available at *www.vatican.va/roman_curia/pontifical_councils/family*.
- Pontifical Council for Social Communications. *The Church and Internet* (Feb. 28, 2002).
  Available at *www.vatican.va/roman_curia/pontifical_councils/pccs*.
- Pontifical Council for Social Communications. *Ethics and Internet* (Feb. 28, 2002).
  Available at *www.vatican.va/roman_curia/pontifical_councils/pccs*.
- Pontifical Council for Social Communications. *Pornography and violence in the communications media: a pastoral response* (May 7, 1989).
  Available at *www.vatican.va/roman_curia/pontifical_councils/pccs*.
- United States Conference of Catholic Bishops. *Married Love and the Gift of Life*, 2006.
  Available at *www.usccb.org/laity/marriage/MarriedLove.pdf*.
- United States Conference of Catholic Bishops. *Your Family and Cyberspace*, 2000.
  Available at *www.usccb.org/comm/cyberspace.shtml*.
- United States Conference of Catholic Bishops. *Renewing the Mind of the Media*,1998.
  Available at *www.usccb.org/comm/renewingeng.shtml*.

Print
- Evert, Jason et al. *Theology of the Body for Teens*. (West Chester, PA: Ascension Press, 2006).
- West, Christopher, *Theology of the Body for Beginners*. (West Chester, PA: Ascension Press, 2004).
- West, Christopher, *Theology of the Body Explained*. (West Chester, PA: Ascension Press, 2007). Visit *www.christopherwest.com* for more resources, including audio and DVD on this topic.

- Wood, Stephen. *Breaking Free: 12 Steps to Sexual Purity for Men.* (Greenville, SC: Family Life Center); *www.familylifecenter.net.*
- Healy, Mary. *Men and Women are From Eden.* (Cincinnati, OH: Servant Books, 2005).

DVD
- "As for Me and My House" video for parishes with manual and a wealth of resources, links, and programs for education and recovery. Visit *www.myhouse.archkck.org*
- Recommended movie: *Fireproof: Never Leave Your Partner Behind* by Kirk Cameron and Erin Bethea.

Internet
- *www.myhouse.archkck.org* Archdiocese of Kansas City (KS) multifaceted "Peace Through Purity" Initiative.
- *www.unityrestored.com* Catholic website on pornography addiction. Resources for researchers, those with a pornography addiction, and their family members, Church teaching explained, and where to find help.

APPENDIX: Just Cause and Natural Family Planning
1. Available at *http://ccli.org/oldnfp/b2010morality/churchteaching.php.*